I Was There

An Autobiography

Joshua Sieger CBE

(with Conclusion by Rosemary Sieger)

POOLE HISTORICAL TRUST - 2003

This volume is published by the Poole Historical Trust whose primary aims are the promotion of research into and the publication of works on the history and life of Poole and the surrounding area.

Previous Publications
The Pride of Poole, 1688-1851
An Album of Old Poole
Mansions and Merchants of Poole and Dorset
Brownsea Islander
Poole and World War II
A Portfolio of Old Poole
Ebb-Tide at Poole
History of the Town of Poole, 1839 (reprint)
The Sydenhams of Poole (booklet)
Art in Poole and Dorset
Victorian Poole
Poole after World War II 1945-1953
D-Day Poole (booklet)
The Spirit of Poole 1953-1963
Lifeboatmen Never Turn Back
Schools of Old Poole
Poole's Pride Regained 1964-1974
Poole Was My Oyster
For Nature, Not Humans

Copyright © Joshua Sieger 2003
Conclusion © Rosemary Sieger
First Published 2003
ISBN 1 873535 50 3

Prepared for publication by Ian Andrews.
Designed by Andrew S Arnold. Production by Graphic Editions, Poole.
Printed and bound in Great Britain by Biddles Limited,
Guildford and King's Lynn.

CONTENTS

ILLUSTRATIONS

Family group: Ettie, Mother, Freda,
Father and myself.

Celia, my youngest sister.

CHAPTER 1

EARLY DAYS

I have been persuaded to write an autobiography after just completing, for limited private circulation, a book on the history of my pioneering gas detection company. As an engineer my writings have always been based on facts, and this started when I joined the Technical Press in London at the age of seventeen.

The incentive in writing a book was to record the actions and thoughts of an individual who was involved in the earliest days of wireless and television. First, I suppose, it is important to mention the facts about myself.

My father was the son of a farmer in Austria during the days of the Austro-Hungarian Empire - he did not like farming and wanted to be a costumier and dressmaker, so left his home and came to London at the age of fifteen. My mother was born in Amsterdam, the daughter of a diamond cutter who was also a professional double bass player. She had three brothers and a sister. Her sister married a schoolmaster and went to India and the three brothers were professional musicians. One was a cellist, one a violinist and one a cornet player who was in the Royal Scots Guards Band. The cellist went to Australia in 1914 just before the war and was part of a famous Quartet and a member of the Sydney Conservatoire of Music. When my mother was ten or twelve the family moved to Glasgow where her father became first double bass player for the Scottish Symphony Orchestra. They moved to London and it was there that my parents met, my father having a job as a cutter and fitter in the well-known store in Kensington, John Barker & Co. My mother worked in the same store; they married in 1881.

I was born in their first house in Shepherd's Bush on January 5th 1907. My elder sister Ettie was eighteen months old when I was born, my second sister Freda was born eighteen months after myself, followed by the third sister Celia sixteen years after me.

I remember my father had a white bull terrier, this breed being fashionable in those days. He also had a gramophone, His Master's Voice, with a large brass trumpet and he would love playing a record of Caruso, which the dog seemed to like as well!

He always had a canary to which he would talk, and the bird would sing beautifully, particularly when the cover was taken off its cage.

In 1912 we moved to a house in Bedford Park, West London, where my father by that time had a partnership business in Queensway, Bayswater. There was apparently some disagreement between the partners and it was decided that they could not keep the house and the shop going, so in 1914 they moved to Kensington High Street where the upper four storeys of the building were given over to our accommodation and a showroom and workrooms for my father.

When we lived in Bedford Park we had electric light for the first time in the house; this to me was fascinating and I would enjoy turning the lights on and off as it happened so quickly compared to the old gas mantle that had to be re-lit with a match. Our next-door neighbour was an electrical engineer and he said to me "If you continue to do that it will cost you a lot more money to pay for your electricity". Being a child I had to question the statement and he explained to me carefully that when the wire inside that lamp was cold the electricity would rush in to heat the wire, and when it produced light it meant it was very hot and less electricity was used, therefore by my turning the light on and off I was using considerably more electricity than was necessary. I still believe that this is how I started to think electrically.

The move to Kensington was quite successful for my father, in that we had a very good primary school across the road where the three R's education was so sound that it is stored in my mind even today and I can repeat the tables up to 15 times 15. In 1914 when the First World War was declared I was seven and I always remember the front page of the 'Daily Mirror' showing soldiers with rifles on horses and with gun carriages. Within a year my father was called up into the Army Service Corps, and his knowledge of horses, gained in his early youth on his parents' farm, gave him a niche when transport was by mule and horse for gun carriages and ammunition carriers. My mother had to carry on the business which she did by selling womens' underclothing, and in the meantime I was accepted to go to the Latymer Foundation School in Hammersmith, cycling there every day.

This school was founded by Edward Latymer in the 14th Century and it was of interest that my basic education at the Council Primary School in Kensington gave me the advantage of being probably the youngest boy in any particular class. When I reached the Sixth Form I was fortunate in having two friends called Keene and Snow. Keene, on leaving school, was going to be a Wireless Telegraphist and was studying for his examination, and Snow had ambitions to become an Electrical Engineer following in the footsteps of his father who was carefully educating him on the basic principles of that science.

Living in Kensington was a great advantage in that a short distance away was the Kensington Public Library, which I note today houses an Arab Bank. Each Saturday I would walk round to the library and collect every possible book available on wireless. One of these was by a man called Hugo Gernsback who, incidentally, was also Editor in America of the 'Radio News'. The Americans called it 'radio' in the earliest days, whereas we still used the terminology of 'wireless'. The description in the book of various wireless receivers, mainly crystal, prompted me to build a crystal detector set.

Across the road from our home was a shop called Lorbergs which sold everything from toys to model steam engines, in fact it was a Model Engineer's shop. Obviously it was impossible for me to buy wire as the war was now in its worst phase as far as our country was concerned, and my mother had great difficulty in meeting the school fees and providing us with food and clothing. I had a hobby which was making miniature Transatlantic Liners out of wood, never more than 3 ins. long, and these were carefully painted; by arrangement with Lorbergs I could exchange these models, which they sold, for copper wire and other parts I needed.

I managed to obtain a copy of the 'Wireless World' and an advertisement in there was by a company in Euston Road, London, who sold germanium and silicon crystals, iron filings and glass tubes, so that it was possible to make a coherer. For those who do not know of a coherer, this was a device that would be sensitive to high frequency currents and consisted of a glass tube filled with minute iron filings with a contact at each end of the tube. High frequency currents would make these filings adhere and therefore conduct electricity. It was essential to have a small battery in series with the coherer and a suitable detecting device such as a telephone earpiece or a buzzer. By making more models for Lorbergs than were needed for barter I continued to get enough money to buy these pieces for my first wireless sets.

In 1917 I put up an aerial on the roof of the house in full view of everybody, who obviously did not know what it was, and wound my first tuning coil to pick up (I hoped) the high power spark transmissions from Gibraltar. With great difficulty I scraped enough money together to buy a pair of headphones made by S.G. Brown and I proceeded then, having assembled a complete unit with a galena crystal, to wait up night after night hoping to get a spark transmission - one night I finally received some morse signals, the call sign from Gibraltar, and that converted me to concentrate on a profession which has proved to be so interesting over these many years.

I got to know two brothers, the Deadmans, who operated a pleating company in Kensington where these machines would pleat various materials for the womens' clothing of those days. These brothers were qualified engineers who had complete Machine Shop facilities for making pleating machines, and they were interested in my simple crystal detector and coherer (which I could never make work!). I spent many years helping them to build equipment and, of course, utilising the facilities of their excellent Machine Shop which allowed me to make components and parts not possible without such a Machine Shop at my disposal. My years with them on a part-time basis gave me an engineering apprenticeship so that I could operate milling machines, lathes, drill presses, etc. I learnt as much from them as I did from my later years at the Polytechnic, and the combination was one of extreme value to my general education.

My reading of every possible technical book on electrics and wireless at the library made me familiar with linear motors, with an experimental railway of that time, and with the inventor Nipkov who was anxious to have a device to send pictures over wire so he invented a spiral disc to divide the picture into a number of horizontal lines which could be transmitted and reformed at the receiving end. This was a brilliant invention in that all television today is based on scanning lines.

I managed to obtain publications such as 'QST' (an American radio amateur journal) and became a member of the ARRL (The American Radio Relay League) and, much later, the RSGB (The Radio Society of Great Britain).

It was interesting that in 1917, on one of my early visits to the library, I was prevented from leaving because we had the first Air Raid by German Taubes aircraft which dropped hand grenades or small bombs on various parts of London. These Air Raids carried on for quite a time and at the end of 1917 I saw the first of the Zeppelins, L.21, flying not more than 1,000 feet above the house fully illuminated by searchlights, and one fighter bi-plane flying all round it trying to shoot it down. He finally did, and it landed in the Thames - I won a school prize for drawing a picture of this incident. In writing about this I am reminded that when I was at Primary School I read about the great British invention to win the war called the tank, and I made a model of this out of cardboard with an old alarm clock movement fitted to the base so that when wound up the main gear would propel this tank. I took it to school where we had the usual morning chanting of the arithmetic tables followed by prayers, and then placed it on the desk of the headmaster, who wrote to my father saying that I had a great future if I could do that at the age of eight!

By 1918 when the war ended I had designed a number of crystal sets, all of which were capable of receiving morse signals, and I had tried a number of crystal detectors such as galena, silicon, carborundum (which required a biasing voltage) and two crystal combinations such as zinc and iron pyrites. The latter was extremely sensitive and would hold its position - a certain amount of pressure was required to get the two crystals together as against the cat's whisker which, having found a sensitive spot, could soon move out of position if one even coughed at it.

It seems to me that the end of the First World War was markedly different from the end of the Second World War, in that things appeared to return to normal much faster. By 1920 it was possible to buy a valve, and my first valve was made by Edison Swan, which I used as an amplifier in a reflex circuit picking up music from Radio Paris at the Eiffel Tower and from Phillips Station at Hilversum. A number of amateur transmitters using audio rather than morse were coming on the air, and the transition seemed very fast from a morse code signal originating in Gibraltar to music and speech within a very few years.

Through my association with the two friends at the Latymer School they informed me of the necessity of obtaining a broadcasting licence and one was duly applied for from the General Post Office and received in May 1921, giving me permission to use a crystal set with an aerial of fixed dimensions of 100 ft. including download. As I was allowed to use an aerial 100 ft. long my father arranged to get a flagpole situated in the garden at the back of the house, with a flat top aerial using stranded enamel wire (which was then obtainable) into my bedroom on the third floor of the house.

More valves were coming on the market - Cossor made a Green Spot and Red Spot, the Green Spot having low internal capacity as a radio-frequency amplifier and the Red Spot as an audio amplifier. In addition there were various Mullard valves, all of them having either 2V or 4V filaments which had to be heated by battery. The indirectly heated mains valve had not yet been devised, although I gathered from reading the American journals that these valves were obtainable over there with a 6.3V directly heated cathode; the reason for the 6.3V being that it was the normal charge condition of a 6V battery as fitted to all

American cars at that time.

So much was published on the development of the valve in those early days by researchers, mainly in America, England, France and Germany, that I feel a brief résúme of the development is important for this book.

The work on the thermionic vacuum valve was probably based on the work performed in 1873 by F. Guthrie. Further work was done by two German scientists - Elster and Geitel - between 1880 and 1900; they noted the unilateral conductivity of a 2-electrode device which they had built without apparently realising the advantage of this device as a rectifier of alternating currents. As so often happens, many people do parallel work thousands of miles apart; Thomas Edison in 1883, without knowledge of the earlier workers, noted the blackening of the envelope of a lamp when he was playing with his carbon filaments. He then made a new lamp with a metal plate adjacent to the filament and noted, using a galvanometer connected between the plate and the negative end of the filament, that no current flowed but when connected to the positive side of the filament he could obtain a reading; this was known as the Edison Effect. Preece in England recorded in the Proceedings of the Royal Society that variations in the distance of the plate placed adjacent to the filament greatly influenced the current as did the temperature of the filament and the potential difference supplied between the plate and the filament.

Many others were involved in individual work and J.A. Fleming of the University of London carried out work on the Edison effect at the end of the century and realised the ability to rectify low-frequency alternating currents, although he did suggest (again in the Proceedings of the Royal Society) that it would be possible to detect high frequency oscillations by converting them into direct current through the rectifying action of the valve; this was known as the Fleming valve. At the same time work was being done by Professor J.J. Thompson when he wrote books on conduction of electricity through gases, which he called electrons. Early in the century Fleming continued the work on using the valve as a diode, improving methods of detection; and then a considerable amount of research and development went on producing vacuum pumps to reduce the air in the glass tube. The air was sometimes replaced with Argon gas and later on of course it used mercury vapour as a rectifier for high current alternating voltages.

It was in 1907 that Lee de Forest filed a patent in the United States and in 1909 one in Britain, when he put a third electrode in between the filament and the plate to control the flow of electrons. This then changed the device from a rectifier to an amplifier, and a three-electrode valve was used to improve the telephone system throughout the United States by amplifying the speech over long distance cables. One should not forget the work done by H.J. Round of the Marconi Company, where it was discovered that a triode valve could be made to produce oscillations, and considerable work was published by Round in Britain and Armstrong in the United States.

Within the year, in March 1922, I received a licence from the GPO to use valves in any circuit I desired, provided I did not cause interference. The industry was growing very quickly and audio transformers, tuning coils and tuning condensers were appearing in a very few wireless shops. The biggest centre was in Soho where the Government surplus equipment was being sold - an excellent source of components.

In February that year the first regular broadcasting started from the Marconi Station at Writtle near Chelmsford, with the call sign 2MT. Most of the music was recorded and I had the idea that if residents of the houses alongside ours in Kensington, covering a whole block, would agree to my wiring up these houses, I would provide them with headphones and they could rent from me the ability to listen to music. My attempt to be the first person to provide a wire service to other houses failed as I could not get anybody to take this proposed system!

Three doors away from our house, which was the second in the row, an electrical contractor named Cunningham had his shop and I designed and built for him crystal sets which he sold, giving me a very small income which helped pay for all sorts of things I needed. The crystal set had a very simple design and the tuning was by variometer, invented I believe by two Italians named Belini and

My bedroom, June 1924. Two pleated paper loudspeakers are shown, and also the violin type on the chair in the foreground.

Tosi. It consisted of two cardboard discs which had radial slots cut into the rim and a wire was threaded in and out of each tongue like a basket, in the form of a 'D'. By keeping these two flat coils close together it would cover a wide tuning range by rotating one coil which changed the inductance and therefore the frequency. With my income from selling crystal sets I was able to purchase more valves and transformers and I got to know a local wireless ham - a watchmaker in Bayswater who, before the war, had a spark transmitter and after the war had a valve transmitter and was just changing over to voice from Morse. His call sign was 2PY and I spent many evenings with him after school helping him set up his audio amplifiers and testing various types of carbon microphones.

At the end of 1921 I left the Latymer School, having reached the Sixth Form, and went to the Regent Street Polytechnic School of Engineering. The education at the Polytechnic was 80 per cent practical and 20 per cent theory, an excellent balance. Their well-equipped machine shops and very practical instruction appealed to me; a lot of time was spent using hand tools. As we lived in Kensington High Street the No: 73 'bus took me to Regent Street, for which the fare was four pence. The school was extremely well equipped with an indoor swimming pool (and swimming was part of the curriculum), a billiard hall where I learned to play billiards and snooker, and excellent canteen facilities which gave a good lunch for eight pence.

Every spare moment was spent in my bedroom, which was converted to a form of laboratory; my bed was dispensed with and in its place I had a large folding-up armchair which converted into a bed by pulling off the back cover, immediately releasing the folded up portion, and no doubt was quite comfortable. A large bench in the room soon got filled up with various components, amplifiers, receivers, etc., using valves. So-called bright emitter valves were the only types available with filaments rated at 4V which was obtained from an accumulator with two 2V cells. The high-tension battery as such was usually designed with a tapping, the maximum voltage between 90-100V and the tapping between 5-10V biasing the amplifier valves.

Many radio amateurs were appearing on the air - including W.W. Burnham who was transmitting music from records using a modified pick-up. He later formed a company called Burndept, one of the early manufacturers, the name being his own and Deptford - the London district where the firm was based.

I was interested in the modified gramophone pick-up which Burnham described and I made one based on a Brown telephone earpiece. S.G. Brown manufactured most of the telephone headsets used during the First World War and the earpiece consisted of a moving iron reed coupled to an aluminium-spun cone. These were extremely sensitive and were relatively simple to modify by putting the essentials of the Brown earpiece inside a standard acoustic gramophone pick-up, coupling inside to the vibrating reed. Naturally it was very heavy and the shellac discs did not last very long, so I finally changed to the fibre needle which I believe was a natural material and gave longer life to my records. A company called Broadcast were manufacturing records which played longer than the standard, they ran at 33 r.p.m. and they were the first company to make a relatively long-playing record - this type of record did not come into use until many years later 'invented' by Dr Peter Goldmark of Columbia Records. I cannot remember what happened to Broadcast Records but they were certainly, in my opinion, first with the long-playing record.

The Notting Hill Electric Light Company, one of the many hundreds of private electricity supply companies in the country, provided DC for the whole of the Kensington area; a central cable was neutral or negative and earthed, and each side of the road would have a positive cable which balanced the load on the power station. The fact that the DC - Direct Current - supply was available allowed me to dispense with the use of the high-tension battery and gave unusual quality and sound from the output amplifiers due to the perfect regulation.

At the Polytechnic there was a science master by the name of Flanders who taught physics and mechanical engineering; these included the well-known physics at that time - heat, light and sound, and mechanical engineering covered draughting, mechanics, hydraulics and two sessions a week in chemistry. Flanders was very interested in wireless and I designed and told him how to build equipment. We became very close, he teaching me and, believe it or not, me teaching him. The Principal of the school was a man named Hobart Pritchard. My father was always interested in my career and Flanders persuaded him to switch me from the Engineering School to the Matriculation School because he maintained that unless I got a degree in Engineering I would never be successful and the important examination to pass would be Matriculation. After two years in the Engineering School I transferred to the Matriculation School; I did not like it, I had to learn a language called French, and at the end of the year I took the examination, which was held in the University of London. Just before the examination Pritchard wrote a letter to me saying that he felt I did not like the ordinary subjects of study and he feared I would not pass the Matric, however I was undoubtedly a genius at wireless work - a real genius, and that it was in the direction of practical work - experimenting and designing that my future lay - and he believed and sincerely hoped it would be a great future for me.

He was quite right - I failed, obviously in French but not so obviously in mechanical draughting, because by being over-precise in my design I did not complete the whole of the exercises in the time given.

During my year in that department I formed the PARC - The Polytechnic Amateur Radio Club - and found myself busy with all the students who were becoming interested. There is no doubt that my concentration on that which should have mattered was watered down in favour of my main interest.

CHAPTER 2

FIRST EMPLOYMENT

I left the Polytechnic in September 1923 with the idea of getting a job. My father had many titled women as customers, and asking around resulted in my having one or two interviews with their husbands. One of these was the Managing Director of Cromptons and I gave him a list of all the things on which I had worked and which I thoroughly understood and could design. He was very impressed and said to me: "Go back to school and get a degree and I can employ you".

I was building up a considerable amount of equipment, making high-powered valve amplifiers and of course using the DC mains as my power supply. Large output signals were not followed by the power supply due to the fact that many kilowatts of storage existed, therefore regulation was perfect. It was apparent in many so-called Hi-Fi systems in later years, where a poorly regulated power supply was used, distortion occurring on loud bass frequencies.

A company in Liverpool, the Automatic Telephone Manufacturing Company (ATM), made a very good loudspeaker which consisted of a large iron diaphragm and an exponential horn. This could be loaded to quite a high level without distortion, but of course all music sounded like a brass band.

Early in 1922 the Marconi Company transmitted from Writtle regular music, broadcasting from records, and later that year the British Broadcasting Company started broadcasting from 2LO - the aerial situated on top of Marconi House in the Strand. On November 11th of that year they broadcast a trumpet solo of the Last Post and Reveille at the end of the two minutes silence when the whole of Great Britain came to a halt in remembrance of the Great War. Living in Kensington High Street with the heavy traffic of those days, I put the loudspeaker out through the third floor window and broadcast the transmission. It was most interesting to watch all the buses, taxis, commercial vehicles including horses and carts, and people, standing still for the two minutes silence until the Reveille sounded, and I continued that broadcast every year until 1927 when I found it difficult to get back to the house from work.

I got to know W.G. Parr, a design engineer at Ediswan, and Stanley Mullard who had a small company and from whom I managed to obtain valves for 'test'. They were both very helpful to me. A number of companies now manufactured valves - Marconi, GEC, Osram, Ediswan, Cossor as well as Mullard.

The indirectly-heated filament valve was becoming available in this country, first from Metropolitan Vickers followed by other valve companies, including a new company called Six Sixty. The original indirectly heated filaments ran from 4V but not from the typical American 6.3V valves which were becoming quite prolific in the USA. As mentioned before, I subscribed to most of the American Journals - 'Radio News' edited by Hugo Gernsbach, 'QST', 'ARRL' and, of course, 'Wireless World'. I happened to see a copy of 'Amateur Wireless' on a bookstall, bought it, and wrote a letter to the editor asking for a job, giving a comprehensive list of all the things I knew about wireless for his information. I was asked to go for an interview to the offices of the publishers, Cassell & Co. Ltd., who were responsible for a number of magazines. Their offices were in Ludgate Hill down a cul-de-sac called La Belle Sauvage, just after the bridge across the bottom of the hill, and in view of St Paul's. The editor was Bernard E. Jones who handled 'Amateur Wireless', 'Amateur Mechanic', 'Model Engineer' and a series of 'Work' handbooks. All the printing presses and editorial staff were situated in these buildings and next door was a firm manufacturing Phospherene, a tonic for the elderly. I got the job immediately and started within a week at a salary of £4.10.0. a week.

The No. 9 'bus which went past our house in the High Street took me all the way to Ludgate Hill for fourpence. I was to work with the Technical Editor called Rogerson, and my job was - under his direction - to design and build two wireless sets a week, to photograph them and work in conjunction with a draughtsman who would make all the drawings. Short-wave transmissions from KDKA, the Westinghouse Station in Pittsburgh and WGY from General Electric Co. in Schenectedy, both in the 100 metre band (30 mHz), were being received well in this country and Bernard Jones wanted a receiver designing to pick up these stations. I had already made one or two of these receivers and had a fair experience in the super heterodyne type of circuit. I collected the components together, sat, down, produced an ebonite panel and baseboard, and assembled the parts to begin wiring. Bernard Jones came to me and asked "Where's your circuit diagram?"; I replied "I do not need a circuit diagram", and he was very impressed - the set, nevertheless, was a great success.

I joined 'Amateur Wireless' in February 1924 just after I had reached the age of seventeen. A month or so later the Editor came to me and said that he had just taken on a young man who was very interested in wireless and had built his own equipment but also had great journalistic abilities. His father was Editor of the 'Financial Times' and his older and younger brothers were later to occupy the same position; his name was Alan S. Hunter. We were introduced and that was the start of a lifelong friendship which exists today. Alan and I worked together for six years, when I left to become Chief Radio Designer in a wireless company in Liverpool.

During our holidays we travelled all over Europe and to the United States, and I learned so much from him and, I believe, he from me. Alan had a way of expressing himself clearly and he wrote a book entitled 'The How and Why of Radio' which was a best seller at that time.

The first visit we made together was going into the Bernese Oberland, staying at Interlaken and Grindelwald. We naturally went by train, sitting up all night to be quite sure we missed nothing! I always remember having breakfast when the train stopped at Basle on the borders of France, Germany and Switzerland, and the excitement of seeing the mountains for the first time.

Our next visit was to an hotel by Lake Lugano, where we could take a rowing boat across and have a meal in Italy. I remember going to Juan-les-Pins in the South of France for the first time with Alan in 1929.

I was working on various designs in my home with the idea that portable radios would one day be as popular as fixed systems, and naturally with the very small selection of valves to choose from and the fact that they were battery-operated, a portable would have to be very light in weight and could not have more than a single valve. Reflex circuits were being talked about and written about in various journals and it seemed to me that it would be possible to use a crystal of iron pyrites and zinc as a detector (no diodes in those days) - a stable crystal detector not as sensitive as a cat's whisker and galena but nevertheless of a rigid construction which could be used in conjunction with a single valve.

Myself with Alan Hunter

I developed a circuit at the end of 1923 with a single triode valve which acted as a radio-frequency amplifier and a low-frequency amplifier. It worked so well that I decided to apply for a patent. The patent was in the name of myself and a Mr Joseph Cornrich who lived in Mayfair. I built a 3-valve radio set for him and he was so impressed that when I said I wanted to apply for a patent he suggested he would pay for the patent provided he could have his name on the application, and he would finance me to go into business manufacturing these units.

A complete patent specification was applied for in June 1925. The portable was arranged in a mahogany box with carrying handle and a place for headphones, as well of course as the 2V accumulator and high tension battery. It worked very well and a company was formed called 'Portadyne Radio', while the set was called 'The Olympus'.

As a manufacturer it was a requirement to become a member of the British Broadcasting Company, and a sticker had to be provided (each costing one shilling) on every unit made, which was a tariff or licence fee. I became a member on the 23rd June 1924, an arrangement which was cancelled on the 5th March

In the research laboratory at "Amateur Wireless" November 1925.

Looking at a rdaio set designed at "Amateur Wireless".

1925. A year and a half later, in December 1926, the British Broadcasting Company was dissolved and the British Broadcasting Corporation took its place on 1st January 1927.

Incidentally, no further finance came from Joseph Cornrich. Although I was working for 'Amateur Wireless' I managed to borrow £100 from Barclays Bank to set up manufacture, which I did in my bedroom. I made approximately 20 units but found that my work at 'Amateur Wireless' was so time consuming that I gave up the idea of being a manufacturer, although it is possible that this could have been one of the very first portable sets in the world.

The first year at 'Amateur Wireless' seemed to pass extremely quickly as the wireless industry was expanding. Many loudspeakers appeared on the market, so many in fact (from horns to cones etc.) it was decided to do a test on all the makes available at that time. A complete laboratory bench was set up and the first job was to built a good oscillator which would cover frequencies from approximately 100 Hz. to 10,000 Hz. Microphones were basically of the carbon granule type which seemed to perform alright, but finally one was made from an American Magnavox loudspeaker which had a mica diaphragm and a coil that moved inside a magnet. By removing the horn, the unit was very sensitive and coupled to a resistor-type amplifier readings were obtained on a wattmeter. Each loudspeaker was tested in this way, the oscillator driving a resistor amplifier and transformer coupled to the loudspeaker. It was interesting that the loudspeakers which gave what appeared to be a flat response did not sound at all good when driven by music or speech.

It was during this time that I met Captain H.J. Round, who was Chief Engineer of the Marconi Company, and went to his laboratories in Marconi House on the Strand. He was interested in the microphone I had made from the Magnavox loudspeaker and suggested that the idea could be usefully re-designed with a large paper cone attached to the coil which would give a more even frequency response than the various devices which made use of standard telephone technique.

Naturally, in my position at 'Amateur Wireless' I met the majority of pioneers in wireless. One of these was Ted Newland and his company was called Goodmans - today, sixty years later, one of the major manufacturers of loudspeakers in the world. At that time he was engaged in reconditioning military headphones and selling them, and he showed great interest in the idea of a moving coil loudspeaker.

Because permanent magnets then were few and far between of the size needed, we decided to make one of steel and wind an energising coil which we would feed from the mains off a suitable AC rectifier. Within two years he had made the first model with aluminium castings to support the cone at the edges and a moving coil wound to an impedance of about 10-15 ohms. To obtain the full bass response from the cone, which was 12″ in diameter, it was necessary to have a large baffle so that the front and back waves generated were not cancelled out for the low frequencies.

As wireless sets were becoming mains operated the high tension battery disappeared and the high voltage was provided by a transformer from the AC mains and a rectifier. It was essential to have adequate smoothing and the winding inside the magnet of the loudspeaker acted as an ideal choke with a large capacitor to smooth out the ripple so that adequate magnetism was obtained for the loudspeaker without having a separate supply.

The excellent quality of the transmitted music from the British Broadcasting Company, Phillips in Holland, Radio Paris and, of course, the transmissions on short wave from WGY and KDKA, demanded more attention to loudspeaker design. The firm of Lumiere in France described a loudspeaker with a flat diaphragm using pleated paper. This was interesting in that if a sheet of paper about 8 ins. wide was pleated, then opened up into a circular fan with the ends joined, you could get a circular diaphragm of extreme strength in the centre where there was a full pleat, and this reduced as it got to the edge where it was flat. The idea appealed to me and I set to work on designing loudspeakers of that type. My friends the Deadman brothers never realised how important pleating would be in the manufacture of loudspeakers.

We experimented with various materials and found lightweight craft paper was the best. A miniature cotton reel was used in the centre and the paper was pulled round and joined at the edges, the result was a 360° fan. The miniature cotton reel was secured with sealing wax (before the days of Araldite) and the whole was assembled in a frame with the edge of the diaphragm fixed between two pieces of plywood suitably cut out and clamped together. The driving unit was made by Blaupunkt in Germany and was a moving-iron device; the quality was truly unbelievable.

About the same time I met Guy Fountain who had a company called Tantalum Alloy Products making accumulators - this title was condensed to the one word 'Tannoy' which has become a household term to describe any public address system in the world. He was very interested in the moving-coil loudspeaker, and the kit of parts at that time could be obtained from Goodmans, a number of articles appearing in 'Amateur Wireless' for the home constructor to make his own unit.

In order to obtain flat frequency response several methods were used before the moving coil became universal. One of these was interesting, a circular wooden unit built as a violin. A moving iron unit drove the top plywood diaphragm with the usual violin slots cut in it and all violin music - in fact most strings - gave an uncanny reproduction, but of course it was impossible to reproduce speech which sounded like someone speaking inside a large wooden rainbarrel. Another one used a cone of paper about 16 ins. diameter, driven again by a moving iron unit, the whole being assembled in a box, and inside were a number of helical steel springs to resonate and compensate for the flat spots of the cone.

Horn speakers were plentiful, one of the most sensitive being by S.G. Brown with their moving iron driving an aluminium cone diaphragm. Many paper-cone speakers were produced, such as Western Electric, and the unusual Celestion which had a thin paper diaphragm strengthened by fine bamboo fibres glued to the paper radially and concentrically.

Whilst on the subject of loudspeakers, I saw a description of a loudspeaker in 'Radio News of America'. This consisted of a square frame over which was stretched a sheet of linen fastened at the edges. It was then treated with collodion

- the centre was pulled out and there was a second frame, which had a wire stretched across it connected to the centre of the linen diaphragm. A moving-iron loudspeaker unit was connected to this and the article said that the reproduction was of a very high order.

My work on loudspeakers and my strong interest in general set my imagination going. The trouble with most loudspeakers was to obtain an even frequency response from the low frequencies to the high. I constructed a unit identical to the American model and noticed that the bass was very poor and there was quite a resonance from the stretched wire at the back. It occurred to me that instead of the stretched wire a smaller diaphragm made of a stretched linen and adjustable for tension, with the centre of each diaphragm joined together, would give a more even frequency response; and by adjusting the distance between the two frames containing the diaphragms it was possible to adjust the loudspeaker to an optimum flat response. The linen-diaphragm loudspeaker was a very popular device for the home constructor and certainly increased the popularity and sales of 'Amateur Wireless' as against its competitor 'Popular Wireless', then being published by Amalgamated Press.

A number of the linen-diaphragm loudspeakers were described in various issues of 'Amateur Wireless' and 'Wireless Magazine' (I will refer to this latter journal later on). Various methods of construction were used, briefly as follows:

Two wooden frames were prepared, square in shape, one larger than the other, and of course variations in the many loudspeakers were due to the difference in the size of these two frames. The linen was stretched across each frame and nailed in position; the two frames were mounted parallel, with a means of adjusting the space between the two. The exact centres were fastened together and each diaphragm was treated with collodion meth applied by brush, then the two frames were slowly drawn apart until an exponential cone appeared - in this position it was left to dry. It was noted, however, that on certain high frequencies where the linen was in contact with the wooden frame a rattling noise appeared, and it was decided to use a common material at that time (and of course today) - rubber draught stopper. This was fixed round the whole periphery of the frames so that the linen was not in contact with the wood from its active surface.

It made a major improvement to the quality and I remember successfully demonstrating the loudspeaker at one of the Radio Exhibitions where we had a stand, in those days held at the White City in Shepherds Bush.

The popularity of this loudspeaker was quite incredible and we had a visit by two very well dressed gentlemen whom Bernard Jones brought to see me. Apparently they were manufacturers of draught stopper and they could not believe their luck when thousands of yards of draught stopper were being sold, and had great difficulty in finding out why their sales had increased to such an extent when draughts had not got any worse!

The home constructor was our main source of readership and, incidentally, the main source of production in the country, and with the majority of issues of the journal blueprints were given free for all sets and loudspeakers, and where they were not free a nominal charge of l/- was made; sales of these blueprints was always a good indication of our readership.

I mentioned 'Wireless Magazine' before - Bernard Jones, the Editor, decided that he would like to own 'Amateur Wireless' which was a weekly and also produce 'Wireless Magazine' as a monthly so managed to purchase the rights from Cassells and formed a company called Bernard Jones Publications Ltd. We moved from La Belle Sauvage to a set of offices in Fetter Lane. This street was well known in that the Patent Office was situated there and many patent attorneys as well. Fetter Lane ran between Fleet Street and High Holborn and was an ideal centre for such an enterprise. We naturally had a lot more room and the Set Design Construction Department could be properly equipped with test equipment of various types. It was here that 'Wireless Magazine' started publication and various loudspeakers, including the linen-diaphragm model, were described in that journal. One of these speakers did not have a square frame but a hexagonal one and this showed a great advantage over the square frame due to the diaphragm being of a more circular shape.

Designing, making and writing about two different wireless sets a week with Press Day each Thursday when everything had to be complete by that deadline or else, plus continuing to work in my room on reaching home in the evenings until the early hours was becoming too much, and Bernard Jones decided we needed an assistant to do some of the construction work. A young man from Pontefract in Yorkshire by the name of Croft was hired. He had recently won a prize in a competition for the assembly and wiring of a wireless set. The wiring between each component was done in a square section tinned-copper wire, and the art was to bend the wires in right-angled bends where possible, which had to look symmetrical from all views, particularly when the photographs were taken. Most components had screw terminals and Croft was a master at doing a perfectly good job of wiring using this technique.

Our new premises brought a number of visitors. Most of them would arrive, as they did at the various wireless exhibitions, with a brown paper parcel of a set which they had built to our specification but it did not work. Quite a time was spent with these people in testing and showing them where they had gone wrong. It was a useful service in that it was a perfect example of market research. We learnt a lot from these home constructors in finding out where the weakness was in our description, and the quality of our designs improved.

One visitor was the Duchess of Bedford who came with her chauffeur, and not long afterwards she was unfortunately missing on a solo flight to America. The most important visitors, however, were two equerries to the Duke of York. Due to the slight impediment in his speech the Duke was a very quiet individual who built wireless sets, presumably as a therapy; on the other hand he thoroughly enjoyed building them. These representatives of the Duke brought in two wireless sets which he had built but had problems, and we successfully put them right, showing them where the mistakes had occurred, again learning that a description in the accompanying article was not sufficiently clear. I have not seen any reference to the Duke of York's interest in this field, and I do not know whether he found time to pursue this hobby after he became King.

Again a most important visitor to the company was Alfred Blackmore. He had made a number of wireless sets and we became very close friends for many years until I left for the United States after the war. He was in the cinema and theatre business and occasionally I received invitations to go to First Nights at London theatres.

Early in 1927 he came to me and asked if I could give him a hand as an entirely new talking-picture system was coming into England and he was to be responsible for the installation and running of the theatre. It turned out to be Western Electric equipment sponsored by Warner Brothers, the film was 'The Jazz Singer' with Al Jolson, and the Piccadilly Theatre in London was going to be converted to take moving pictures with sound. It was to be the very first talking picture in England.

I spent many evenings with 'Blackie' as he was called, and learned a lot from the Western Electric engineers who installed the enormous exponential-horn loudspeakers and three projectors with synchronised turntables taking 16" records. The average film time per reel was about 9 or 10 minutes and the 16" disc, which started from the middle and worked out towards the ends, ran at 33 1/3rd revolutions per minute. Synchronisation was achieved by putting the pickup at the start of the groove and running the film until a sign appeared, and then the turntable turned and that was perfect synchronisation. 'The Jazz Singer' was extremely popular and ran for a considerable time at the theatre.

Some time later a British movie called 'Old English' with a star by the name of George Arliss had been recorded on the Western Electric system and was to be shown at the New Victoria Theatre, London. Blackie told me that it was an important opening night in that Royalty would be present. There would be a show on the stage, organised by Albert de Courville, and the première of this movie was of very great importance. In order to be sure that nothing would go wrong he obtained the services of the Chief Projectionist from the Empire Theatre, Leicester Square, and other projectionists, and rehearsals were held to everyone's satisfaction.

On the opening night the programme started with the stage show; on the set was a large head and shoulders and a long arm which stretched across the stage. The arm was raised, the orchestra played and dancers came in from the side and danced the usual high-kicking routine for about five minutes. Then they were supposed to dance backwards towards the exit side but when the arm dropped down it blocked the exit; the first girl fell over, followed by two or three others, and there was real consternation, however stage hands came in quickly, moved the arm over and the girls made a proper exit. The film then started, after much applause.

During the second reel suddenly George Arliss's voice changed to that of a girl, from a girl it went to another man, and then back to a girl. After three or four attempts it returned to George but not quite in synchronisation with his lips! Blackie rushed into the projection box to find out what happened and apparently the Chief Projectionist, deciding to work in the dark, used a torch, however the torch suddenly went out and he unscrewed the cap, a spring inside the torch shot the cap across the room and hit the pickup of the turntable, and that was the problem. Being skilled, in a few seconds he found the right groove and the sound returned to normal.

From then on the film went fine until the end of the programme. It was customary in those days to throw a picture of the King onto the screen, the orchestra would play the National Anthem and everybody would stand until the end. However, not at the New Victoria. The picture of the King went on the screen but the orchestra did not play, so the picture came off the screen and the curtains were drawn. The orchestra then played the National Anthem and the picture came on, on the curtains. The curtains then opened, the orchestra played only one verse, the curtains closed, the picture came off, and that was how the programme finished - a disaster, but we understood that the Royalty who were present were thoroughly amused and had a most interesting evening.

The experience I had in dispensing with the high-tension battery and using a choke-filter system from the DC mains prompted a number of designs for those home constructors who had the DC supply in their areas. Southend-on-Sea was such an area and Eric Cole, an engineer, teamed up with a business man, Bill Verralls, and manufactured these battery eliminators. Fortunately for them Southend changed over to Alternating Current and that immediately created a demand for a transformer rectifier filter system - and they had so many orders that they formed a company called E.K. Cole, known as EKCO Radio. This was the start of a company which was well-known for many years in the radio field.

Alan Hunter designed a wireless set which he called the Ether Searcher Three, consisting of three valves, the first a high-frequency amplifier, the second a detector and the third a low- frequency amplifier. This became very popular and we agreed that the next Ether Searcher would be a joint venture. Alan, being more editorial, concentrated on his journalistic ability. A third Ether Searcher was entirely under my name.

The medium waveband was becoming very crowded, high powered stations all over Europe trying to outdo each other, and it was essential to have selectivity. The band pass circuit was becoming popular and so this 1931 Ether Searcher, as it was called, was designed to use a band-pass circuit and a three-gang variable capacitor (in those days called a condenser). One of the best examples of this capacitor was made by A.B. Cardwell in America, using logarithmic-shaped plates. A firm called Jackson Brothers in England also made similar units, and I was about to recommend either the Cardwell or the Jackson Brothers unit when a Mr Sydney S. Bird came to me with what appeared to be a Cardwell condenser. Sydney Bird was a toolmaker at Johnson Phillips and he was also a home constructor who, being a toolmaker and having seen the American condenser, decided he could do better. Apparently he and his wife, Mary, set up a flypress in their kitchen and he made the dies and manufactured a beautiful example of precision engineering. He wanted to know if we would be prepared to recommend it and gave me two models. Both of them performed excellently with no noise, but in this case I recommended the Jackson as they were already in production; however his condenser was recommended in the test report.

Sydney Bird was so successful that his condensers started being used in a number of designs and he naturally had problems in manufacturing enough on the kitchen table, so he got a factory at Enfield and started manufacture. He named the company after his two sons, Cyril and Donald, and the company was called Cyldon.

The selectivity of the 1931 Ether Searcher was extremely good and the coils made by the Collinson Precision Screw Company (Colvern) were so precise that it was possible to publish, in that January 31st 1931 issue, a tuning scale which could be stuck to the drum dial of the condenser with all the stations marked - approximately 50 stations all told. The preponderance of radio sets used 2 volt or 4 volt valves - directly heated filaments by an accumulator, with dry batteries for high-tension supply and a small battery for biasing the output valve.

Without realising it, of course, designing sets for the home constructor was an excellent exercise in production engineering, because it so often happened, in later years, that when the Development Department designed a unit, made one and it went into the factory for production, then all the changes had to be made to make it work in quantity. In 1926 there was a General Strike and in theory the whole country should have come to a standstill. It did not, because everybody was anxious to work to keep their jobs and all sorts of transport - open lorries, charabancs etc. - were used to carry people to work. I travelled to work on the back of a lorry. Cassells had just produced a new magazine but due to the Strike had no means of distribution. I offered to drive a van, with one of their publishing people, and we delivered this magazine to various wholesalers and newsagents throughout the London area. The little van became very useful, as I took it home in the evenings and drove to work the following morning. However I found it more interesting to assist by driving a solid-tyred B- Type 'bus on Route 1A for a few hours one afternoon, until I was required to design more wireless sets and devices as a sort of stockpile for future issues.

About 50% of the pages in 'Amateur Wireless' were given over to the technical side, usually one or two radio sets were described with full constructional details, various news items by technical contributors like J.H. Rayner and W. James and, in addition, we had a review of the past week's programmes; I cannot remember by whom it was contributed but it was either Sidney Moseley or one other person. A real problem occurred, which Bernard Jones found very difficult to explain, when this contributor made a comment about the singing of a particular artist, a soprano, who was appearing with the BBC Orchestra. The comment apparently was not too favourable and unfortunately he wrote his report based on the information in the Radio Times and rushed it through to be in time for Press Day, which was Thursday, not realising that due to illness that particular soprano did not sing!

Mentioning the Radio Times brings me back to where most Saturdays the BBC broadcast a football game. In order to make it easy for the commentators a plan of the pitch was printed on a page of the Radio Times and divided into a number of squares, from one to six if I remember rightly. The commentator then could always describe the play and in which square it was taking place, and so often you would hear 'Now they are back to Square One', and I believe that is the origin of the statement so much in use today.

The rapid increase in broadcasting world-wide and particularly in the United Kingdom was supplemented by other types of transmission. For a short time in July 1926, when Baird had his Nipkow disc with 30 lines, the BBC ran experimental pictures, although I am not sure whether any components were on the market for home constructors; however, due to the short duration of the transmissions it was unlikely.

Late in 1927 I was invited to Marconi House to meet a Captain Otto Fulton.

He had on demonstration a facsimile unit which consisted of a transmitter and receiver. I witnessed the demonstration of a photograph being placed on the drum of the transmitter and a photo-electric cell mounted on a lead screw moved across the picture drum. The variations in contrast, picked up by the photocell, were sent by wire to the receiver, which consisted of a similar drum with a similar lead screw on which was mounted a thin wire pen. Synchronisation of the two drums was obtained by a pulse transmitted on each rotation of the transmitter drum, and this pulse activated a solenoid which controlled the receiver drum at each revolution. The receiver utilised a filter paper immersed in a solution of potassium iodide, and the variations in contrast picked up from the photo-cell of the transmitter changed the electric potential of the wire in contact with the paper on the receiver, producing stains of various intensities of brown.

I was very enthusiastic at the demonstration and remember signing the visitors' book, and in October 1928 the BBC broadcast in the afternoons for about half an hour various press pictures, weather charts, and so on until the end of October 1929. I immediately decided, with the approval of the Editor, to construct a Fultograph, as it was then called, and enlisted the assistance of Frank Collinson of the Collinson Precision Screw Company who made most of my coils for the radio sets. The device was described in detail in 'Amateur Wireless' and 'Wireless Magazine', and Collinson would provide most of the equipment in parts for the home constructor.

The picture quality of this unit was extremely good, in clear detail, and when the transmissions ceased at the end of October 1929 they started again in April 1930, and continued until June 1932. This gave an opportunity of designing a number of wireless sets having the output in the form of a variable direct current voltage which could be connected directly to the recording pen on the Fultograph receiver.

A company interested in the Fultograph were Wireless Pictures Ltd. Unfortunately the stain on the paper did not last very long and most of my records, although they were carefully kept, lost the picture after two or three years. I should mention that the BBC London 2LO transmitter, which was on top of Marconi House in the Strand for some time, was transferred to the roof of the Selfridges building in Oxford Street.

In August 1929 the BBC, from their new Oxford Street transmitter on medium wave, sent pictures from Baird's 30-line Nipkow disc transmitter, and a number of home constructors became enthusiastic. Kits of parts were available and various sets were described with some constructional details on making these units. I did not have a lot of enthusiasm because I could not see the future. Having seen the good definition obtainable with the Fultograph, I felt that television would have to be quite different in order to get a picture of any quality. The Fultograph picture, if I remember rightly, was approximately 225 vertical lines which took about five minutes to record on the paper, which was about 4 ins. wide. The Baird transmission was only 30 lines vertically scanned at about 12 pictures a second. This was the maximum which could be transmitted at that time over the medium-wave transmitter.

In 1928 I again became involved in portable radios and designed quite a number, in some cases using reflex circuits and other using conventional circuits.

A number of smaller loudspeakers were coming on the market, cones driven by moving-iron units, and it was possible to make loudspeaker portables. One of my early cars was a Standard 14, a convertible (or drophead as we called them in those days), and I made a large frame aerial and installed a receiver using three valves with 2V filaments connected in series off the 6V battery of the car. This worked exceedingly well until the engine started up and the ignition interference was very severe until the frame aerial was turned to the minimum signal-strength direction.

One of these portables was built into an attaché case, a small case approximately 12 ins. x 9 ins. and 3 ins. deep. In here it was possible to install a 2V accumulator and filaments, and high-tension battery for the anode supply. The frame aerial was built into the lid and arranged with two bands, medium wave and long wave, which would give a good signal from Daventry, Eindhoven and Radio Paris - the last was a transmitter from the Eiffel Tower. This unit could use headphones and we took it to various parts of London, to the amazement of onlookers.

Bernard Jones took space at all the Radio Exhibitions, which were held usually at the end of August/early September in London. For many years the White City in Shepherds Bush was the main venue. I would be on the stand every day and all day as I found it most interesting talking to all the various people who had constructed the sets and their comments and requests for what they would like to see in the design of the future. I remember very well the linen diaphragm loudspeaker which we had working on the stand and that created tremendous interest. Another time we had a pleated paper loudspeaker on demonstration. At times there would be a queue of people with brown paper parcels under their arms waiting for advice. Naturally inside the parcels would be one of the many sets shown in the journals.

I believe by about 1935 the venue changed to Olympia because whereas in the early 20's the industry was relatively small in complete sets but fairly large in components, by the time the home constructor slowly died away and people bought branded sets from manufacturers, the exhibition became too large for the small hall of the White City. The exhibitions were held at Olympia until September 1939, when at short notice it closed because of the declaration of war.

CHAPTER 3

VISITING AMERICA

Alan Hunter and I had a meeting with Bernard Jones and said that we would like to have a holiday in the USA so that we could become fully informed on progress in that country, and he agreed to let us go. Early in 1929 we set sail for the USA on board the Cunard liner 'Majestic', and we took with us a portable wireless utilising a small loudspeaker.

The visit to America was probably one of the most important interludes in our lives. The 'Majestic' was the largest ship afloat at that time, having been called 'The Fatherland' when it was owned by the Germans before the First World War. We travelled Tourist Class and had good company with a number of American students who had been studying at a Scottish University; they were returning home, hoping to be intern doctors.

We used the portable from time to time and found that we could receive the long-wave station at Daventry almost two days out in the Atlantic. It then began to fade and nothing was received until we were one day out of New York City, when a number of medium-wave stations were receivable, and as we got nearer there seemed to be so many and so different from the number in Europe at that time.

When we landed in New York I was carrying among other possessions the little portable wireless in its case, which the Customs official eyed with great suspicion. "Say bud, what have you got in that case - open it up". I explained it was simply a wireless but Customs didn't believe me until I turned the switch and out came the sound of one of the local stations. "Well, what d'y know!" exclaimed Customs. "Give you fifty dollars for it". But we hung onto the portable and were frequently asked to sell it in our travels by amazed Americans - apparently they had never come across a portable, much less having heard one in action.

Our first visit was to the Bell Telephone Laboratories at Murray Hill, New Jersey, where we were shown various examples of some of the development going on, including a colour television demonstration. It was a low-definition picture, I believe about 45 lines, scanning by means of a mirror drum and a colour disk rotating in the light beam giving the three primary colours. The picture was of remarkable clarity, being a closed-circuit system, certainly enhanced by the colour.

We visited the Radio Stations in the city and shortly afterwards went to Campden, New Jersey, to visit the Radio Corporation of America, and saw the assembly of their radio sets. We travelled on to Philadelphia and met the

President of the Dupont Chemical Co.; he was very interested in who we were and why we were in the United States, and he said to us "If you go into business manufacture something which is expendable that costs a dollar and you sell for ten dollars". Alan and I discussed this conversation afterwards and realised that we were more interested in creating something which could be wealth in the long run.

Our next visit was to Pittsburgh to see the Westinghouse Station KDKA. We went out into the country and saw the transmitter and aerials and were taken by the Chief Engineer back into the city to look at the studios and medium-wave transmitter. The aerial for the medium-wave system was on top of a 20-storey building in the centre of Pittsburgh. In order to gain adequate length with a flat top aerial, two towers were built on the roof leaning outwards. We went onto the roof with the engineer, who stated that on one of the towers halfway up was a platform where they kept their meteorological equipment, which they used for giving weather information over the radio regularly during their newscasts. He asked "Would you like to have a look?" and we said "Yes, we would". He then went up the iron-runged ladder towards that platform, followed by Alan Hunter, followed closely by me. When he reached the top he looked down and saw Alan "frozen" halfway up. He froze because he looked down and saw this narrow street with tiny little objects moving around, presumably the cars, and realised the height. I did not look down because I saw what he did and he told me he could not move up or down. I remember holding each ankle and telling him to put one foot down at a time, and slowly we both progressed to terra firma or, I should say, roof top. This was an experience we did not want to repeat.

Whilst in Pittsburgh we were interviewed on radio and left soon after by train for Cleveland, Ohio. We took the ferry to Detroit across Lake Erie. It was an overnight trip and a storm blew up; it is amazing how rough the water can be on a lake in the middle of America, almost as bad as our English Channel. On the ferry we had our portable with us. A large crowd gathered around us when our little portable was 'doing its stuff' (picking up the commentary of a big fight that was being broadcast at the time). Again, gasps of amazement! A certain individual came up to us and said he was most impressed by what we had got there, he had not seen one before. We told him it was a British design which we had made. He suggested, as he was a representative of the Philco Corporation, he would like us to stay in America and join the company. We thought seriously about this for a while, but when you are young and very patriotic you do not like to leave the country where you were born, so we declined the offer.

Whilst in Detroit we went up to Dearborn and the Ford Motor Company and flew in a three-engined monoplane, the fuselage being of corrugated aluminium. From there we took the train to Buffalo to see Niagara Falls and The General Electric Company at Schenectady, then returned to England on the Cunard liner "Homeric" full of enthusiasm and raring to go. That visit to America stayed with me for many years, and my ambition was to go there permanently at the right opportunity.

Early in 1931 the 'Sunday Express' approached me to design a receiver which would pick up short wave stations throughout the world. Those who can remember the newspapers of that day would know they were promoting continually 'Empire Free Trade' and the small knight in armour with shield depicting, presumably, St George, still appears on the top of every 'Express' newspaper.

I had done a considerable amount of work on the design of super-heterodyne receivers and proposed to the 'Sunday Express' that I would produce an Empire 5 wireless. The receiver was arranged for either mains or battery operation, used five valves and was of a novel design. A book with complete constructional details was published by printers Hanbury Tomsett & Co., with a front cover showing a background of a Union Jack in red, white and blue. The booklet, which was sold at one shilling, contained all the necessary information for the home constructor and the wiring diagrams were full size, which left no questions unanswered. Every wire and component was shown clearly and no soldering was necessary as all components were fitted with screw terminals. The receiver covered long, medium and short wavebands, and was highly successful.

In trying to obtain confirmation of the exact date of publication I wrote, whilst compiling this book, to the 'Sunday Express' and Hanbury Thomsett, but their records did not go back to the publication date of January 1932; fortunately I still have one of the original copies of the booklet showing the designs. My work was also mentioned in a book entitled 'Audio Biographies' by Gerald Briggs.

The whole unit was put inside an excellent cabinet of Regency design, standing on four legs, with the possibility of using a gramophone turntable and pick-up. A moving coil loudspeaker was used - two of these were recommended, either a Celestion PPM.9 which was 9 ins. diameter, or PPM.29 which was 12 ins. diameter. Looking at the prices today, the 9 ins. speaker was thirty-five shillings and the 12 ins. £3 17s 6d. How times have changed!

With Croft as Assistant Wireman I found that we were designing and publishing the details of approximately four wireless sets a week for both 'Amateur Wireless' and 'Wireless Magazine'. We had a draughtsman who did all the wiring diagrams and circuit diagrams, a photographer using a Sanderson plate camera to take over the photography which I was doing, and Alan Hunter did all the writing and descriptions. 'Wireless Magazine', being a monthly, was run almost entirely by a man called Relph, who was also a very good technical journalist. An ex-wireless operator named Chapman was responsible for answering all the queries from readers, and as a result the whole organisation was a team. There was one exception with F.J. Camm, who was responsible at Cassells for the Work Handbooks and 'Amateur Mechanic'; he seemed to take a dislike to me because of the considerable publicity I was receiving in the twoadvertising journals, my photograph appearing in most of the advertisers announcements. He seemed intent on making life difficult for me and when I had an offer from a company in Liverpool, Garnett Whiteley & Co. (Lotus Radio) one of our main advertisers who made a range of components and crystal sets, to join them as Chief Radio Designer, I accepted the offer.

Bernard Jones was very upset when I gave my month's notice, but the interesting part of the offer was the fact that from receiving £4.10.0 a week with Bernard Jones, my salary would rise to £12.10.0 a week at Garnett Whiteley. The manufacturing experience was gained in the Technical Press by designing equipment which could be made by many thousands of different people, and a sign of a good design was when Chapman had little work to do in answering queries.

I remember driving up to Liverpool in a Chrysler and booking in at the Adelphi Hotel until I found suitable accommodation. With my very high salary I was naturally wealthy, and could afford the very low cost of full board at this expensive hotel.

The owner of Garnett Whiteley was a Mr Bulley and he had a company in the garden seed business called Bee's Seeds. The Managing Director was a Mr Mills, and my reputation was such that I was welcomed with open arms. An increased salary for a young man does a lot for the ego but, on the other hand, it makes one somewhat pompous!

I decided that my first priority would be to design a set of components which could be finally used in a complete wireless set. First was a switch which required simple tooling and was in production within two weeks. Second was a set of tuning coils where two windings for the medium wave and long wave were wound on the same former and to change wavebands the medium wave coil was shunted across the long wave.

Advertisement whilst designing radio sets for Lotus.

I made the first receiver based on the successful Ether Searcher, and to be AC mains powered. To be sure of high quality a moving coil loudspeaker was used with an electro- magnet, the winding of which acted as a choke for the rectified AC supply. A special wooden cabinet was designed and made by an outside cabinet maker. The design of this unit and trial models took approximately eight months to set up into production. The first sample models were then distributed to various people for testing and comment, and one went to Mr Bulley. I had my sample working in the laboratory and the quality was excellent with good selectivity.

I was busy designing the next unit which would be one with a shortwave band as the two American stations WGY from Schenectady of the General Electric Company and KDKA from Pittsburgh of the Westinghouse Company, were received regularly in England. Mr Mills called me in to have a word; he said "I have had an instruction from Mr Bulley to terminate your agreement with the company as the AC hum on your receiver is so bad you cannot leave it on for more than a few minutes". I was staggered and found that in manufacturing the models the Works had left off the smoothing capacitor and therefore an unsmoothed DC supply made as much noise as the music. I was about to investigate to find out how this occurred when Mr Bulley suggested that if I let that go past I would let other things go by, and I should leave as soon as possible. In a very righteous frame of mind I got into the car and drove home!

Whilst in Liverpool I made a number of friends and Claude Lyons (who handled the American General Radio equipment) and his family allowed me to stay in the house when I had a quinsy throat. My brother-in-law's brother also lived in Liverpool and at his instigation I took flying lessons at the local aerodrome. The cost was approximately just over £1 per hour, which naturally I could afford. The aircraft was a DH Moth biplane and the wings would fold back to go into the hanger. It was necessary, therefore, always to open up the wings and lock them into position. Starting the engine was by rotating the propeller, a thing I would not do today but thought nothing of it then. I did about eight hours flying and was ready to take a certificate for solo when I found I was not living in Liverpool any more! I enjoyed flying and was doing spiral dives and loops without any fear or concern about possible consequences of making a mistake.

When I arrived home we were then living in Barnes by the river, where the family had moved in 1930, and during the time here I had a mongrel dog called Bill who lived until 1939. I saw an advertisement for a radio engineer with a firm called Thorn Electrics in Shaftesbury Avenue, London. I went along there and met Mr J. Thorn who wanted somebody to design a loudspeaker portable for him to go into manufacture. I worked in the basement of the shop and designed a unit in an attaché case and he offered to give me a contract at £450 a year. I designed a receiver using two valves and a crystal detector in a reflex circuit with a four inch loudspeaker which had an aluminium diaphragm. When I completed this he felt that going into production would be too complex and could see no point in our carrying on. It is interesting that in later years, when I had a history of successful management and was lecturing students and those attempting to start their own businesses, I had the following philosophy. I would tell them that you do not learn management from a book, you have to learn real management the hard way, and the hard way is to be hired and fired more than once. The firing can be because you were right and the management wrong, or vice-versa.

CHAPTER 4

CARS

My interest in things mechanical was helped considerably by living in Kensington High Street from the age of seven, looking out of the window and seeing every form of transport proceeding along the main road. There were taxis called Charron, Napier, Renault and Unic, most with a single cylinder and steel studded tyres; to slow down or stop they had to put the gear into reverse, sparks would fly from the rear tyres on the wood-paved road, and they would sort of slow down. Intermingling with all kinds of horse-drawn traffic the exciting thing was the fire escape, which had four grey horses galloping down the road; I never saw them stop but presumably four horses had sixteen frictional contacts and brakes applied to the wheels must have assisted.

There were various buses, the LGOC (London General Omnibus Company) and the White Company which used Stanley Steamers - they were painted white as against the red of the LGOC. Then there were the limousines, the big Daimlers, Napiers, Rolls-Royces, Lanchesters, Delauny Bellvilles, Panhard Levaseurs and Minervas; the last used a sleeve valve engine similar to the Daimler. Also there were many motor-cycles and pedal-bikes. It was possible to know a vehicle by its noise, I became quite expert at this.

Across the road from our house was a Mews called 'Adam and Eve Mews', the reason for the name being that the public house on the corner had the same name. The Mews were all over London because they were the only space you could keep your carriage and horses and/or cars. Kensington, being a Royal Borough, was the home of many titled families and my sisters and I would enjoy walking on the streets behind our house, looking down into the kitchens and seeing the staff at work, a real 'Upstairs-Downstairs'.

In the Mews opposite us were a number of cars and one in particular was a French Voison. The chauffeur of this car lived above in the Mews and, typical of those days, the car was used in the summer only and in the winter, from September onwards, it was carefully dismantled and stored. I got to know the chauffeur very well indeed and finally was allowed to assist in the renovating work necessary.

The engine was first of all removed and dismantled on a bench. All valves were ground in, new bearings on the crankshaft fitted and the whole thing then covered in grease, wrapped in paper and stored until the Spring, when everything was then put together again. The car was an open one, as most were in those days, but did have a windscreen, which was only fitted to the most expensive cars.

In the same Mews was another car, a very early Studebaker, which really was a fixed head tourer, as the Americans would say. It had six cylinders and I remember driving this car, reaching an incredible speed of 58 m.p.h. The owner, a Mr Densham, allowed me to use this car for a time until I went into partnership with the chauffeur of the Voison and we bought between us for £10 a Morris Cowley Bullnose with Hotchkiss engine.

I received my first licence to drive in 1923, which cost five shillings. There were no tests in those days and I learned to drive with a school-friend of mine from the Polytechnic whose father had a French Darracq. I obviously knew all the controls before I attempted to drive a car, having dissembled and assembled the Voison. In addition, when going to school on the No. 73 'bus which went from our door to the door of the Polytechnic in Regent Street, by sitting in the front I could observe the driver.

The little two-seater Morris Cowley was a very soundly designed car, it required the minimum of maintenance but, naturally, aspirations for a bigger and better car had to be satisfied. I bought a Standard Fourteen two-door convertible, and painted this in two colours - pale yellow and green. This car performed perfectly, provided it was not driven at over 40 m.p.h. The reason for this was that the propeller shaft was connected to the gearbox and the differential by two Hardy Spicer flexible couplings. At speeds over 40 m.p.h. the out of balance was so severe that one or other of these couplings would break; I always carried spares in the boot and thought nothing of putting a new one in, lying on my back in the road.

The thirst for bigger and better naturally continued and I changed this car for a Palladium with an all-aluminium body which was polished, again an open tourer, four cylinder engine, and looked very pretty. It was, however, a source of trouble, particularly in the gearbox and differential. After a year of this car I got a French car called a Ballot. It gave a very rough ride, being very difficult to steer, but it had a delightful engine, slow revving with lots of power.

An American manufacturer, the Hudson Essex Car Co., were assembling cars in their factory on the Great West Road, and I bought an Essex, which was a saloon with wire wheels and six cylinder side valve engine, an incredibly silent car to drive. This company made two models, the Hudson had a straight eight cylinder side valve engine and the Essex a six cylinder side valve. They were extremely popular cars and the eight cylinder version was so successful that they manufactured a sports car called the Hudson Terraplane. I did not own one but a cousin of mine did, and it was unusual to drive a car at nearly 75 m.p.h. without the usual noise accompanying all the European cars which seemed to gain efficiency by an exhaust system that had minimum silencing.

When I took the job at Garnett Whiteley in Liverpool it was essential to have a more reliable car - the wire wheels on the Essex were continually producing punctures - so I bought a Chrysler Vauxhall which had the reputation of being the car with the fastest acceleration of any standard production car, 0-50 in ten seconds. It was called Chrysler Vauxhall because it had a fluted bonnet, a design feature of Vauxhalls at that time. I would do the journey from our house (by then in Barnes) to Liverpool in three and a half hours. The Chrysler was fitted with two RAG carburettors which is not the general American practice, and no intake filter, silencers or flashback arrestors were used in those days. I was driving the Chrysler, on a cold engine, to fill up with petrol (which was one shilling and two-pence a gallon) when I had one backfire which blew back into the carburettor, and immediately there were flames coming from the bonnet. Fortunately I was just approaching the garage and they came out with a fire extinguisher; I sold the car then and there.

I saw advertised the same day an Alfa Romeo with a 2.3 litre engine, two-seater with a boat-shaped body, the rear end being decked in with teak which came to a point, a very pretty car which would go really well but naturally had room for one passenger only.

During my time at 'Amateur Wireless' I naturally met a number of interesting people who would build the various wireless sets which were described, and if necessary come up with the unit which I was very happy to service and modify where they had obviously misread instructions. As most of these people were not engineers, if the set did not work first time a professional would have to look at it and put it right.

One of these people was a man called Basil Brooks, who was a solicitor. I never saw him have a meal at any time but always a large scotch. He said to me "You are wasting your time buying all these cars, there is only one good British car which combines all the features of a sports car with performance and, in addition, which has comfort". He said "I will take you out in my car and I will show you what I mean"; he had a Lagonda. These cars were manufactured at Staines and he was well-known at the factory and introduced me to the people there in the works. I bought a second-hand two litre Lagonda which had a fabric body, black, with the wings in glossy red. The car had a twin overhead cam shaft engine. The rating was 12 h.p. and in those days the tax was based on h.p., which was calculated from a steam engine formula which took into account only the area of the piston and not the stroke. Incidentally, that was the reason why so many cars had long stroke engines to avoid the high tax of £1 per h.p.

That car started me on Lagondas, which I kept until I sold my last car at the end of the Second World War. The performance of the car was extremely good but acceleration was poor and they made a supercharged version, which I had as my next car within the next two years. A Club was formed at that time for Lagonda owners, with the name 'Lagonda Car Club' but it was a haphazard sort of operation. Amongst the various members was Gordon Vokes. He also had a two litre Lagonda and between us we re-vitalised the Club and organised many events.

Vokes was an unusual engineer, he claimed (and I believe it was true) that he invented the windscreen wiper and he specialised in exhaust systems for which he had patents covering the silencer which had a number of radial fins allowing the exhaust gases to rotate and produce a vortex, thus reducing the sound quite considerably. He fitted these exhausts to various aircraft and demonstrated by flying these planes at low level, and there was no question a very great reduction in noise resulted, which was always quite considerable when added to the propeller noise.

Another one of his inventions was a honeycomb cell which was fitted between the carburettor and the intake manifold. This, he claimed, prevented the intake gases swirling into the cylinder and gave more even firing and better combustion. Following on that he then made gauze filters to fit over the carburettor so that the air was clean and the air filter acted as a flashback arrestor should there be a backfire which could ignite the mixture. He formed a company called Vokes Filters and came up with the idea that oil should be filtered, as the general method was to use a large sump with certainly two gallons plus of lubricating oil, which had to be changed quite often, and a good oil filter would give extended life. In order to get a large area of filtration he used a paper filter and these were pleated to give this greater area, and the first filters were fitted in the by-pass line on the engine. When, finally, he sold out to Streamline Filters they were sited in the main lubricating supply.

He had a farm at Alton and he bought a mansion at Guildford called Henley Park. At Henley Park he did his research, development and production, and in the Second World War his filters were used extensively on military vehicles and tanks in the desert, which overcame the problem of sand sucked in through the intake making the average life of an engine about 35 hours before complete failure.

The Lagonda Car Club was very active and we had hill climbs and competitions with competitors such as Bentley, Bugatti, Talbot and Alvis - the last made a wonderful front wheel drive sports car. I became a member of the BARC (British Automobile Racing Club) and the JCC (Junior Car Club). Many meetings were held at Brooklands and they were in the good old days before works entries which nowadays bear no relationship whatsoever to the standard model and seem to have taken the fun out of sporting events, particularly when the Mini-Metro with a standard engine developing 70 h.p. becomes 4-wheel drive with 300 h.p. out of the engine!One of the features of the Lagonda car engines was a combustion chamber fitted with two spark plugs, one set of plugs was driven from a magneto and the other from the normal coil distributor. It was possible to switch these two ignition systems in separately or together, and there was no question of the increased power when both systems were used together.

Racing cars seemed to be divided into three engine groups, the unlimited class such as the Napier Railton, the Bentleys and Mercedes Benz and others; the second was the 3 litre class such as Auto Union, BMW and Mercedes Benz. Included in that range were Alfa Romeo, Maserati and Talbot. The third class was the 1.5 litre size - this was extremely popular and included cars such as the Riley, BRM (British Racing Motors), Aston Martin, Fraser Nash, Bugatti, MG, and ERA (English Racing Automobiles). As this last class was so popular, Lagonda decided they would make the 1.5 litre car which would be suitable for racing and for family use. They decided it would be fitted with a Wilson gearbox, which was a semi-automatic pre-selector type where a lever on the steering column pre-selected a gear and this came into operation by depressing the clutch pedal. This type of gearbox was popular and was fitted to standard cars such as Talbot, Armstrong-Siddeley, Delahay and Delage. The Lagonda Rapier raced at Brooklands occasionally and did quite well, but as it was up against other vehicles driven with a lot of experience, particularly Freddie Dixon with his Riley, an ex-motorcycle man who tuned his own cars and would usually leave the field standing, the manufacture of the car was discontinued before the start of the Second World War.

Donnington Park race circuit was becoming popular because whereas Brooklands was a circular track, heavily banked and only just over two and a half miles in length, Donnington Park was basically a road circuit. I always remember a 4.5 litre Lagonda leading the field when, on one of the hairpin bends, the kingpin on the nearside wheel broke and, naturally, it was not possible to drive the car on three wheels. Car racing and trials were always very popular and had a large following of enthusiasts. Each car could be recognised without any trouble, so different from today when a computer designs the outline and therefore most cars look alike.

My association with Alfred Blackmore and the cinema industry in general brought me in touch with a different set of people. One of these was a famous Hungarian actress who was appearing in silent movies. Her manager took me to lunch in a restaurant on the Kingston By-Pass. On the way back to London and motoring relatively fast (one always used the gearbox more than the brakes so from 70 m.p.h. I would change down to third gear and then to second and apply the brakes for a roundabout or lights or any other obstruction) I was changing into second gear when an incredible noise came from the engine. I had to make a forced stop and lifted the bonnet to see if anything was apparent; it was not. Her manager wore a very nice light grey flannel suit. He said "The best way to find out what it is would be to take the oil filter cap off the engine and start it up to see if anything can be seen or heard". I proceeded immediately to do just that and the cause was very apparent because he was covered in hot black oil all over his suit, which meant that the top of a piston had disintegrated! Incidentally, I took her to tea! As a result I sold the 2 litre when I saw an advertisement for a three litre advertised at Askerswell, near Bridport. This car was built and belonged to Johnnie Hindmarsh, a well-known racing driver in those years. It had a fabric body and a wooden frame, and the engine was a six cylinder pushrod made by Crossley. The car had the achievement of winning the Double Twelve Race, which was similar to the Le Mans 24 Hour Race but was divided into two 12 hour days with no night driving.

When I got this car I painted it grey rather than the British racing green, changed the dashboard to an aluminium panel, and inserted a new speedometer, rev counter, pressure gauges, clock and a radio designed and built by myself. A very attractive car to look at with the usual Lucas P.100 headlights and foglights which I always mounted under the front bumper - the only way to navigate fog in London in those pea-soup days.

I saw advertised a four seater 3 litre sports Lagonda with cycle type wings which had a much lower mileage and did not require the complete engine overhaul of the present three litre. It was essential, therefore, to sell the three litre, and having heard of a buyer in Margate we were driving there at the usual rate when, again on a changedown through the gears, an entirely new and different noise came from the engine. It was impossible to do a mental costing so we had to be towed into the nearest garage and an examination showed that the crankshaft had completely broken in half. I had to sell the car where it was for fifteen pounds as its only real use was for spares. I got the 3 litre open tourer, which was a very good car indeed, and used it at many rallies of the Lagonda Car Club where we competed in various trials against Bugatti and Bentley.

In 1934 Lagonda advertised a new production car using a 4.5 litre six cylinder overhead valve engine made by Henry Meadows. The Press gave it a high commendation, particularly as it would go from 0-50 in under 10 seconds with a cruising speed of between 80 and 90 m.p.h. I waited a couple of years for the second-hand price to come within reach of my pocket and bought a tourer with aluminium panel body. This was painted in English racing green and my fiancé Sylvia and I toured most of the West Country with this car. We very seldom put up the hood and in rain, if one went quickly enough, the rain would go over the top of the windscreen and we would not get wet, but if it rained heavily we would find a bridge and get under it to wait until the rain stopped!

As we got married in 1935 it was essential to think of more comfortable motoring and when a 4.5 litre drophead Coupé with a magnificent Freestone & Webb body came along I bought it and that car took us on many journeys to the South of France.

A garage in Kingston, Fox & Nichols, who specialised in tuning the well-known Talbot car of that day which raced consistently at Brooklands, obtained a two seater Lagonda from the works, known as a Lagonda Rapide, and entered it in the 1935 Le Mans 24 Hour Race. It was the only Lagonda entered and it won the race outright at an average speed of 75 m.p.h. and, if I remember rightly, with one driver, again Johnnie Hindmarsh.

3 litre Lagonda sports tourer.

The most famous racing cars made in England in the 30's were designed by W.O. Bentley, and the Bentleys were all famous but unfortunately made little money. The last car designed by Bentley was a straight eight cylinder and it was reported that Forest Lycett drove this car, which looked like a locomotive and obtained a standing start to 100 m.p.h. in just over six seconds.

The Bentley Car Company failed and was purchased by Rolls-Royce. Lagonda immediately hired Bentley to design a new range of cars. I remember going to the works and seeing Bentley sitting on a high stool with a steering box in a vice, turning the wheel from side to side. This steering box used the re-circulating ball bearing drive, which was extremely light, and I found it possible, in my 4.5 litre Lagonda, to actually steer it with one knee. By 1939 he had developed a V12 engine installed in a chassis which had four torsion bar suspension, and would cruise at 100 m.p.h. I remember the first of these being driven on the German autobahn from Berlin to the French border and averaging just over 100 m.p.h.

There was a lot of competition between Lagonda and Bentleys manufactured by Rolls-Royce in various races at Ulster, Brooklands, Isle of Man, Donnington Park and other famous race tracks, and I suppose the result was even wins for both makes.

CHAPTER 5

JOINING SCOPHONY AND MARRIAGE

After leaving Liverpool so precipitately I naturally had time to think, and my laboratory at the house was well equipped so I could think and work. I came to the conclusion that I had spent quite a few years in pioneering radio, I had designed many hundreds of sets with some outstanding successes, and therefore I should think more into the future. An advertisement appeared in one of the national dailies for an engineer to join a company which had master patents in a high definition television system. My only experience in that field was reading. A book published by Jenkins in America in 1925 on his optical television system was one of my main sources of information, and my visit to Bell Laboratories when in America, showing the system proposed and demonstration and, of course, my knowledge of the Baird 30-line Nipkow disc device, which to my mind had no future.

I applied for the job advertised and got an appointment to visit a Mr George William Walton of a company called Scophony Ltd. in Dean Street, Soho, offices in the RKO building; at that time the area was the centre of the cinema industry. Walton interviewed me for a whole afternoon and made me very enthusiastic. I asked Walton why the company was named 'Scophony'; he said it was made up of two words Latin 'Scopus' meaning 'to view' and Greek 'phone' meaning 'Sound'. He introduced me to the Managing Director, Mr Solomon Sagall, who gave me a three year agreement as a technician at £450 a year, rising to £650 in three years.

Walton was a brilliant inventor and he started work on television problems as early as 1922 based on his considerable knowledge, particularly in the field of optics. Little was heard about Walton until late in 1931 when his inventions and patents were published. He did a considerable amount of work but naturally his financial resources were limited until he became associated with Solomon Sagall, when together they managed to get sufficient financial support and so a company called Scophony Ltd. was formed which, in effect, saved the Walton ideas for the benefit of the United Kingdom, whereas if the meeting with Sagall had not taken place he more than likely would have gone to the United States.

The German engineer, Nipkow, who designed and patented the Nipkow disc, was the first to realise that the only way to send a picture by telegraph or radio was to divide the picture into a number of horizontal lines and to put each of these lines end on so that, in effect, the picture (which had two dimensions) would be transmitted as one long line in a length dimension only. The thing that enthused me was the way Walton solved this problem by optics without a Nipkow disc, which could never go into high definition without a disc being of an enormous size. Walton's method was to have a wafer cylindrical lens for each line of the picture and these would be mounted in a frame in an echelon formation. A complete picture would be formed by a small oscillating mirror scanning from one side of the echelon to the other. The use of cylindrical lenses as against spherical was that a spherical lens would always focus to a point and cylindrical, being uni-directional, would allow a scan to take place.

I studied Walton's patents for some months, getting a fair understanding of the system, although my optical experience was naturally limited to that studied at school and the famous book of those days called 'Heat, Light and Sound'. Some months after joining Scophony a Hungarian called Gustav Wikkenhauser also joined. He had worked with Von Mihaly in Germany where development was going on with the mirror screw type of scanner. Soon afterwards an optical designer called J.H. Jefree joined the company and it was decided that the echelon system, which was then known as the Stixograph, had enormous possibilities to produce a continuously moving picture without the known system of the cinematograph where each picture is shown for a short period of time and then moved quickly to the next picture, so giving the eye the impression of a moving picture, the very system still in use today.

With Jefree's help I decided to make a combined camera/projector which would utilise the Stixograph and by calculation would show that a quarter plate could produce moving pictures for approximately five minutes. Jefree made a 60-line Stixograph and I built up a system using a clockwork drive with the quarter photographic plate held between two guides and driven by a rubber drive wheel, part of the mechanism of an ordinary alarm clock. When this was constructed it was put into a lightproof box and I photographed a rotating wheel to demonstrate that as the picture change was continuous there was no stroboscopic effect, which was always apparent with the intermittent cinematograph system. I processed the photographic plate and after obtaining the negative projected it onto a screen with an exciter lamp as light source and the Stixograph system was proved. Walton was horrified at my alarm clock drive, but the demonstration was sufficient for Sagall to obtain more finance to continue the basic work on television.

On the 8th March 1933 I sent a memorandum to Sagall entitled 'Report on the Cine Camera':

"The following is the exact position with regard to the stixograph cine camera:

The simple design in film guide and spools have shown that no more elaborate system than this is required at present. The device used relies on the edge of the film for location, the other edge being pressed by means of a light spring. The film used in tests was cut in the laboratory by means of a pen knife and straight edge, the original edge was used for location. Despite this rough method of cutting the film, the sprung surface was quite sufficient to hold the film constantly in position. Some of the original pictures were taken with ordinary roll film stock, where the detail is very large, and hence the pictures lacked definition. Some trouble was experienced in optical adjustments. A wire .002 inch thick was placed .8 m/m behind the echelon and adjustments were made so that this appeared completely in focus on the screen. The first adjustment was the field lens in front of the echelon. This was moved to its finest point, followed by the second and third cylindrical lenses. No tilting was done to the lens mounts, as with the coarse adjustments made, no difference could be noticed.

To summarise, the position appears as follows:

The mechanical side has proved to be satisfactory. The troubles seem to be definitely optical. The lines projected from the echelon are troublesome on the picture, and I think that some means should be found to eliminate these.

No really clear focus can be obtained at present, and this is the main reason why the pictures are out of focus.

Illumination is sufficient, but it could be improved with advantage.

I feel the time has come when, after Mr Jefree has made one or two optical adjustments to the present cine-camera, the optical system should be entirely re-designed, so that the apparatus is not so cumbersome and better detail could be obtained.

The final film taken on Kodak fine-grain stock has shown the apparatus to have enormous advantages."

In my first few months at Scophony I read all the Walton patents and he filled me in with great detail on all his plans for television of the future. The BBC was broadcasting Baird's 30 line picture and the Post Office put a tie line into our laboratories from the BBC which would cover the full frequency band. Walton said that one of the problems with high definition television would be being able to transmit the full frequency required, which would not be possible on a medium band, which was normally broadcast, and he said that the only way to approximate full definition would be to have a constant frequency and vary the voltage or amplitude of the fixed frequency, which would reduce the band width considerably; in other words he was forecasting a digital transmission. So many of his ideas were before their time that, looking back, the ideas of this brilliant inventor could not have been financially supported when everything ceased in September 1939.

With the addition of Wikkenhauser and Jeffree and the pressure by Sagall to show television pictures to satisfy the financial backers, it was important that we should utilise the best of the Walton ideas with a practical and quicker solution.

The 30 line transmissions from the BBC, because of the very nature of the Nipkow disc, were vertical and we made up a Stixograph using 30 cylindrical lenses and scanned this with a mirror which went from side to side. The light source was an exciter lamp and modulation of this light source was by means of a Kerr cell. The Kerr cell was a transparent glass container filled with nitro-benzene in which was situated a number of plates connected like a capacitor. Either side of the Kerr cell in the path of the light beam was a Nicol prism which had the ability to polarise the light in one direction. Applying voltage to the plates of the capacitor would change polarity and so variations in voltage on these plates would give a light-modulating device. The Kerr cell was highly inefficient but apart from the neon gas discharge tube was the only known method of modulating light suitable for still picture and television requirements. This set-up with the Stixograph and scanning mirror produced a very good picture onto the ground glass plate which acted as a screen in a rear projection arrangement. This was a very elegant way of demonstrating the BBC transmissions.

The oscillating mirror was not very successful and it was decided to use a mirror which would rotate continuously, driven by a synchronous motor. The success of that demonstration prompted us to build a 60 line unit which was duplicated, one acting as a camera, the image being a photographic slide, and a photoelectric cell to translate the variations of light into a voltage. Experiments were carried out using the Stixograph principle with lenses in the form of a screw rotating the whole Stixograph with a synchronous motor at the receiving end. As the resolution went up in lines so light losses occurred and Jeffree read of an interesting patent by Debye & Sears which formed in a liquid column the equivalent of a diffraction grating which, used in conjunction with the Schlieren dark field optical arrangement, would produce modulated light if the frequency operating the crystal in the liquid column varied its amplitude. In a matter of days we had constructed a system which, used in conjunction with the 60 line system, gave a picture which was visible in daylight; this was a tremendous step forward.

One of the claims of interest in the Walton patents was the use of a split focus optical system utilising two cylindrical lenses at right-angles to each other. In television the interest is in a single spot containing one picture element and a split focus system gave the advantage of focusing the spot in two planes so that where scanners were used it would be possible for a high speed scanner to be greatly reduced in size.

By 1932, with increased money coming into the company, Sagall and Walton, with the approval of the Board, decided to obtain larger premises as the one large area in Dean Street included four offices and was insufficient for additional staff and equipment, which was absolutely essential to progress. An old mansion called Thornwood Lodge was obtained, situated on the top of Campden Hill halfway between Kensington High Street and Notting Hill Gate. This was ideal in that it had very large rooms and a glass-covered conservatory approximately 60 ft. long x 30 ft. wide with a marble floor. In one of the ground floor rooms we could set up a proper workshop with precision equipment. A big dining room with a bay window onto a terrace was allocated to me and I employed two assistants, one was a Dane called Sven Doddington, and the other was R.E. Duggan. Doddington was a very good electronic engineer and Duggan was one of those typical British all-rounders who was a good mechanic, had served in various industries of precision engineering and had been a projectionist in a London cinema, so therefore it was a very good team operation.

There was competition throughout the world, Germany was transmitting 180 line pictures from Berlin, Phillips in Holland, the French from the Eiffel Tower and in the U.K. Baird was transmitting live pictures on 240 lines, using a very large Nipkow disc arranged as a spotlight scanner, and E.M.I. had experimental 405 line pictures.

We had decided that although the Stixograph system was a sound approach, it required a lot of experimental work and due to the fact of the split focus idea being so valuable, a system was built using two scanners, one high speed for line frequency and one low speed for frame frequency. The split focus system allowed us to use a small high speed scanner, the size of the low speed was much larger but as it ran slowly it was no problem. It was essential to have our own film transmitter and this was done with a combination of Duggan, who converted a film projector for continuously moving film, and Wikkenhauser and Jeffree with a spotlight scanner consisting of a large number of cylindrical lenses, wafer thin, with a 32W projector light as light source and a cylindrical lens at right-angles to the scanner, giving a perfectly square spot of light right on the film. The advantage of this projector was that we could run loops of film continuously and this gave us a chance of changing the speed of the high speed scanner for different numbers of lines on the picture. The light control we used was a liquid-filled cell based on the Debye & Sears invention with a Schlieren dark field optical system and a projector lamp as a light source. The liquid-filled cell had a quartz crystal mounted in the base and the ultrasonic waves produced the equivalent to a diffraction grating. Variations in amplitude of the crystal drive voltage produced more or less diffracted images to give us our variable light intensity.

The most incredible thing I remember about this system was when Jeffree came in one morning and said "I have a wonderful idea where, instead of putting one spot of light on the picture, it is possible to put a whole line of light on the picture simultaneously and this would give us many hundreds of times the light intensity". He explained the method in detail, in that as we had a high speed scanner it could be arranged that the distance between this scanner and the speed of the ultrasonic waves in the liquid column could be synchronised, because each face of the polygon of the scanner followed exactly the speed of the waves in the liquid column. This follow-up principle would allow a whole line to be projected on our screen simultaneously, containing all the picture elements because the movement in the cell would appear to be stationery on the screen. In my opinion this invention by Jeffree was one of the most valuable in the history of optical mechanical television projection.

Wikkenhauser and myself sent a memorandum to Sagall entitled 'Report on New Light Control':

'On Friday, the 2nd March 1934, in the afternoon, we obtained perfect light control by means of an entirely new device. This device consisted of a crystal oscillating at its natural frequency of about 40 metres in a small tube of chloroform. The high frequency oscillation was modulated at television frequencies and light passing through this glass tube was modulated sufficiently to see a picture on   the 30 line receiver.

A test was also made with modulations from a broadcast receiver, received from the light modulator by means of a photo cell and three-stage amplifier. Modulation was perfect, so much light being available that the amplifier was turned off.

The principle of the device is based on the traversing compression waves in the liquid excited by the crystal, these said traversing waves acting as a diffraction grating. A slit is put in the light path and adjusted so that by the interference pattern, the central image gets fully dark, which darkness according to modulation, changes to full brightness.

This device was developed by Mr J.H. Jefree and the first model was entirely constructed by him.

On Monday March the 5th the light control device was tested on our 120 line receiver and results showed its capabilities as the most efficient light device yet invented.

Signed: J. Sieger, G. Wikkenhauser.'

It was immediately decided that we would build a unit using a rear projection screen 5 ft. x 4 ft., having 240 line resolution 25 frames per second. The Jeffree design consisted of a small high speed scanner 2 ins. in diameter with 20 faces and a low speed scanner in the form of a mirror drum. The light cell was constructed using a 10 mHz quartz crystal, the system arranged with an optical bench so that sliding optical adjustments could be made using the picture signal from our film transmitter. Utilising a frequency multiplier generator, a standard 2-pole synchronous motor could be used for both transmitter and receiver scanners to get the necessary speed of 18,000 r.p.m. Our Machine Shop had a top man who came from Adam Hilger and we manufactured the high-speed scanners from stainless steel, using a Zeiss dividing head. After accurate milling they were optically polished, fifty polygons were mounted in a mandrel and the middle thirty were used, those at each end were not sufficiently accurate and were discarded.

Within two months of Jeffree's idea we had a 5 ft. picture which looked like a cinema projection, in fact the many visitors whom Sagall brought into the laboratory went behind the screen as they did not believe it was television!

There was a certain amount of pressure to produce a Home Receiver with what was considered to be an optimum size of 24 ins. Whereas the 5 ft. picture used a carbon arc light source, this was impossible for a Home Receiver. It was essential to develop a light source which would have the equivalent brightness of a carbon arc. Sagall hired an Austrian called Barasch who had done some work on super pressure Mercury lamps. A laboratory was set up with glass blowing facilities and some months after his arrival he was making experimental high pressure Mercury lamps in a quartz tube about 1cm. diameter and 10 cm. long. Immediately it was possible to think of the right design for the Home Receiver. It was obvious that the optical bench, which consisted of the high speed scanner, the light cell, lenses and a mirror drum would, apart from the mirror drum, be the same size for a large screen projection as well as a small screen.

Early television set.

45

Baird and EMI were transmitting experimentally and it was essential that we did the same thing. Permission was granted by the Post Office for us to set up a television radio transmitter and the two frequencies allotted to us were just above those of our competitors with 47mHz for sound and 49mHz for vision. Donnington and I built the transmitter using Raytheon RK20 valves with a 300 ohm feeder to a di-pole on the roof of Thornwood Lodge.

A generator to produce the synchronous pulses was part of the transmitter system, as with all laboratory work obviously a 50 cycle mains frequency was adequate for driving the synchronous motors, transmitters and receivers. The synchronising pulse generator was developed because of the problems we had in receiving the television transmissions from Alexandra Palace on the 405 line interlaced system. EMI derived their 10,125 synchronising signal by multiplying up the 50 cycle mains frequency. This meant that any transient in the mains supply was multiplied and it was impossible for our receiving scanners to follow due to their inertia. The synchronising generator was developed by Wikkenhauser and was installed at Alexandra Palace, which of course being a big inertia device allowed us to receive the pictures with our mechanical scanners and, incidentally, improve very considerably the pictures received on the small cathode ray tubes of those days.

In 1937 the Science Museum in Kensington intended to have a two months demonstration of television and asked us if we could demonstrate. We built two equipments, one a 5 ft. rear projection picture and an 18 ins. prototype Home Receiver. A di-pole on the roof of the Museum building picked up our signals and daily demonstrations were given for two months showing various films, mainly newsreels, from our own projectors. The transmission was on 240 lines 25 frames and was exceedingly successful. In all the history of television in those days there is no mention that I could find of the Scophony radio transmissions, it was all Baird and EMI.

The Baird and EMI systems were being run alternately until the Government Committee made a decision as to which system would be the final one for the BBC. EMI had the advantage in that Dr Zvorokin had developed the Iconoscope camera which was like a cathode ray tube and instead of scanning a phosphor it scanned a photo mosaic. Baird, on the other hand, had to use his Nipkow disc, which was alright for studio work but became very cumbersome for outside broadcasts. However it was announced that Baird would be showing the Derby from Epsom. A big store in Kensington called Derry & Toms had a roof garden and part of this area had an enclosed restaurant and a stage. Sagall wanted us to install a 5 ft. projector unit on the stage and show the Derby. By that time Wikkenhauser had developed a high speed synchronous motor which would synchronise easily with a Baird transmission of 240 lines because the inertia of the scanning disc could be synchronised without difficulty by our high speed scanners. The transmissions were well received with excellent publicity in the Press as we were the only company showing large screen television.

Demonstrations were also held at British Industries House in Marble Arch and I spoke to the audience describing the equipment and the system. These demonstrations, which were very valuable to us, were also valuable to Sagall because his job was to find the finance to keep the company going, and I remember so well in the early days not receiving any money in the way of salary for two or three months until another benefactor could be found to help us.

The success of our projected pictures, using the Jeffree ultrasonic light cell, was becoming well-known in the National Press as well as many technical journals, and the cinematograph and electronic industries were giving us favourable reports.

The first income the company had resulting from the sale of our equipment was in 1937 when an order was received from Russia for complete film transmitters and television projectors based on 405 line EMI transmissions with interlaced scanning. It was a major order for about £100,000 and consisted of two 5 x 4 ft. large screen theatre projectors, one film transmitter, one synchronising

Scophony equipment leaving Thornwood Lodge for shipment to Russia in 1937.

generator, and the complete amplifiers and video equipment including a 14 ins. monitor which used a filament lamp as light source. The equipment took six months to build and we had three Russian engineers for six months, who were replaced from time to time, until the equipment was finally packed and shipped. We never found out what happened to it, whether it was successful or not, and one can only feel that the day will come when that knowledge will be forthcoming because of the political and technical interchange between Russia and the Western world.

The equipment benefitted considerably from the high speed scanner motor developed by Wikkenhauser in his laboratory. This motor, which would go to 30,375 r.p.m. in 20 seconds and stayed absolutely synchronous, was a great achievement. I will always remember after the war, when I was for a short time Production Director of Hamworthy Engineering (engine, pump and compressor manufacturers in Poole), my discussions with the founder of that company, Sidney Hall. I mentioned that high speed and as a mechanical engineer of the old school he entirely disbelieved it, thinking nothing could ever run at that speed without flying to pieces!

Additional finance was coming into the company and the Board consisted of Arthur Levy an American who owned Monogramme Pictures, Oscar Deutsch responsible for the Odeon Group of cinemas, Eric Cole and Bill Verralls of Ekco Radio, and of course Sagall and Walton, with Sir Maurice Bonham Carter as Chairman. Albert Fletcher was the Company Secretary and lawyer. Board meetings were held regularly and of course demonstrations almost daily.

I remember so well some of the visitors; De Valera - Prime Minister of Eire, Sam Goldwyn - MGM, various Kennedys from America, and I suppose one interesting visitor was Bernard Jones, my boss of the days when I was with 'Amateur Wireless' and 'Wireless Magazine', who by that time had got another journal called 'Television'.

The staff were growing fairly rapidly, a Hungarian (an old associate of Wikkenhauser) called Okolicsanyi was responsible for the mirror screw, with von Mihaly in Germany. He was very enthusiastic over the Jeffree light cell because here was the perfect device which stored a whole picture line of television optically. Dr Dennis Robinson, the son of Captain Robinson whom I knew very well in the technical press days, assisted Okolicsanyi on his various ideas of utilising a second light cell to dispense with the high speed scanner, and early results in the laboratory showed great promise like so many of these ideas. The war which stopped all television in September 1939 certainly stopped development of an unusual system of television which could, I still believe, with the facilities obtainable today more than fifty years later, out-perform any of the proposed systems presently known on large screen projection television for the cinema.

The optical system which I used consisted of basic glass lenses without any correction for aberration. I felt that as one was interested in a line on the picture of a given width and length, the two cylindrical lenses in their split focus configuration could not be bettered. Despite this it was decided to employ one of the top optical designers in the country, Dr Lee, Chief Designer of Taylor, Taylor, Hobson. He had a comptometer which, if I remember rightly, would work to nine

Outside Monsiegneur News theatre, marble Arch for Boon v Danahar fight.

places of decimals, and he re-designed all the optics with corrected lenses for aberration and colours. We built the receiver and the measured light output was less than fifty percent of the light we were obtaining with the ordinary pieces of glass, with no better definition. In fact Lee told me one day that there was a requirement for a camera lens to have an aperture of I.4 and he passed his calculations into the lens grinding and polishing division. He told me, against himself, that when they saw what he wanted they put his calculations to one side and just polished the glass and sealed the multiple lenses without referring to his calculations whatsoever, and it was a very good lens!

A number of patents were being applied for and I had some, mainly in conjunction with Jeffree and Wikkenhauser, and others in my own name. The patents were intent on using more than one light cell to show more than one line simultaneously on the screen, and naturally this could be enlarged to have a multiple number of cells. Colour again was possible as three light cells could be used for the primary colours with either one or three light sources, but, as I have stated, the war stopped all this work.

One of the well-known theatre owners in London was Jack Davis who owned a number of News Theatres and one of these, the Monsiegneur in Marble Arch had an 8 ft. screen projector installed for a light heavyweight fight for the world title between Boon and Danahar. The Monsiegneur News Theatre was next door to the Marble Arch 'Pavilion' and Baird was showing their projected cathode ray tube unit at the same time. We found out from early tests in the building that considerable interference was obtained from various consultants in the offices above the theatre using diathermy for treatments; these diathermy machines caused considerable interference to the television reception. We had read about the work done by Yagi and our di-pole used a reflector and multipliers which gave us a very good signal from Alexandra Palace. No interference occurred from the diathermy machines however, because this had been discovered by Captain West of the Baird Company who arranged that these machines should be switched off for the night of the fight.

This was our first experience of a paying audience, what we did not expect was that the audience consisted entirely of fight enthusiasts. The queues outside the theatre were quite considerable and half an hour before the fight began a number of people broke down the doors, got into the theatre and sat down. Duggan, Doddington and I were very concerned because we had a ground glass screen for our projection, with suitable masking, and we did not know what sort of fight crowd there was going to be. We felt it possible that if individuals did not like the way the fight was going or the decision of the referee, they might start throwing things at the screen, and if that was broken in any way there would be no picture, certainly a catastrophe. As it was they were all very well behaved and applauded loud and long at the end of the transmission. The management did not know who they were, they had not got tickets, but nevertheless the show went on. I remember the 'Daily Sketch' had a full centre page in its picture paper showing photographs of the crowds outside the two theatres waiting to see the fight on television by two different systems. Jack Davis was so enthusiastic he sent a personal telegram to my home in Kensington inviting all members of the company responsible for the picture to have dinner with him.

The very great success at the News Theatre prompted Oscar Deutsch (who by that time had built a magnificent theatre in Leicester Square which he called the Odeon, like all the others he owned) to show a heavyweight fight which was due in the very near future. We went to the Odeon and looked at the stage, which had a 35 ft. wide cinema screen, and had to decide what size of picture we could comfortably use with adequate light, his requirement being that it would be expected to be smaller than the standard screen but nevertheless the brightness of the picture should be equivalent.

We built the whole of the projector with all its control equipment in a complete unit, the only external power being the AC mains to drive the equipment, which had 45 valves, and DC voltage for the arc lamp. The arc we used was a Hall & Connolly high intensity rotary carbon, similar to that used in most of the larger theatres and by calculation and measurement we felt that we could produce a picture of the same brightness as the cinema on a 15 ft. wide screen, rear projection.

We managed to obtain from Pilkington Brothers a piece of plate glass half an inch thick, 16 ft. wide and 14 ft. high, and this was suitably sand-blasted on one side to give a frosted appearance. The amount of sand-blasting was given to Pilkingtons on a sample we had made in the laboratory. This enormous piece of glass was delivered to Thornwood Lodge and was situated on the terrace outside the laboratory. In those days we seemed to have summer and we had sunshine for quite a time before the show. In conversations with the engineers at the Odeon we found it was impossible for their equipment to lift this heavy glass screen out of the way into the flies, which gave us a real problem. We realised the only way was to make a screen by spraying a suitable lacquer onto the glass.

After much searching we found that Courtaulds could supply such a lacquer, which would be air-drying and fairly tough. We then obtained some canvas with brass eyelets fitted and this was laid all around the glass screen to act as a frame so that when complete the screen could be suspended in a wooden frame. Duggan did the spraying and in two days we had sufficient thickness of approximately l/16 ins. The lacquer naturally bonded to the canvas surround and two days before the show we had a large 16 ft. rear projection screen. A big wooden frame was made with suitable supports as a stand, and the screen was tied with rope and fully tensioned; tests showed it would be easily lifted by the hoisting equipment at the theatre.

The fight, which was to be televised on 405 lines by the BBC, was between Armstrong and Roderick. Oscar Deutsch was naturally a good showman and on the night of the fight the theatre was converted into a 3,000 seat boxing hall. All the ushers and usherettes wore heavy white jerseys, presumably to represent Seconds, and the orchestra lift had a full sized ring installed. Before the fight started two boxers appeared in the ring and when the right signal was given the ring disappeared into the pit, the lights went out and the announcer came on the television screen. I had a position at the back of the theatre and Duggan and two assistants were on the stage. Telephone connection was provided so I could have conversations right through the fight. One important thing was that the carbons in the arc lamp would only last ten minutes, which was the normal time for a 900 ft. reel of film, and the carbons had to be changed after that period of time. Duggan was a past master at this, he managed to change these hot carbons and fire up new ones while the fighters were in the corners between each round. At first there was some consternation when the picture went black, but he ensured the audience did not miss any of the fight. They were aware that it was not a cinema picture and they marvelled that it was television with a picture quality equivalent to the cinema screen. This was proved, really, at the beginning and the end of the fight when a film was shown on the 35 ft. cinema screen. When this was lifted out of the way our screen was dropped down, half the size and a quarter of the area, but after the first few minutes it did not look small.

It was essential to have very good sound quality as we could not use the normal Western Electric loudspeakers. We made up two large baffle boards, each one with two 15 inch co-axial speakers made by Tannoy and from my position at the back of the theatre I could give instructions to Doddington to either raise or lower the gain.

Congratulations at the reception given after the show were unanimous. I shall never forget the evening, in that after only a few years from Jeffree coming up with his idea of using the light cell as a picture storage device, we had one of the major cinemas in London showing a large screen high definition television picture to a paying audience.

My social life was based round the Grasshopper Tennis Club in Cricklewood, London; with hard and grass courts I could play during the winter as well as the summer. Having three sisters we would hold a number of parties at our house in Kensington, using my father's showroom on the first floor and putting a drugget down for dancing. We danced either to American music through KDKA from Westinghouse on my short wave radio or BBC transmissions from the orchestras of Henry Hall, Jack Hilton, Billy Cotton or Joe Loss.

From time to time I would single out a particular girl and we would meet to go to a cinema in London, but these affairs never lasted more than two or three weeks. Either I fell out of love or was put off for various reasons. Once the father of one of these girls drew me to one side and suggested that we would make a good pair as he could finance me to have my own radio company. Another time I was going out on an all-night trial with the Lagonda Car Club and the particular girl at that time said she would love to come with me provided her father agreed. As I said it would be all-night driving he agreed; unfortunately by 2.00 in the morning of the trial the valve spring broke in the engine and the Lagonda would not go, so we had to stay in a lay-by on a main road and wait for daylight before we could get a tow. It was not particularly warm, and as the hood never went up on the car it was essential to make ourselves as comfortable as possible in the two bucket front seats. When I saw my female friend on waking up in the morning as soon as it was daylight, I decided yet again that marriage was not for me, because with little make-up and a nose that had turned blue with cold, the attraction had gone.

One of the parties we went to was in Ealing and I saw two sisters there, both of them had auburn hair and the younger one immediately attracted me. Their surname was Tabbernor, the elder one called Marjorie and the younger one Sylvia. Sylvia and I started to go out together and for the first time the association lasted longer than the usual few weeks as we seemed to have a lot in common and she took part in all the events of the Lagonda Car Club and other meetings we had at Brooklands, hill climbs and trials in general.

Sylvia had a very strong independence and despite wealthy parents she went out to work. After two years at a finishing school on the Rhine in Germany and subsequent secretarial education in London, she took a job in the East End of London with a shirt manufacturer. She assisted the owner of the factory, did all the bookwork, timesheets and payroll, a job she kept until a week before we were married. The work involved her rising at 6.00 in the morning and taking a train to Whitechapel, not returning home until after 6.00 every evening. Her experience with shirt production, sewing machines, etc. gave her a valuable insight in later years when I had my own business in the manufacture of gas detection equipment. Her ability to speak German was of great value to me when we visited the Radio Exhibition in Berlin.

After a year of association Sylvia and I had a good understanding and became engaged. On December 23rd 1935 we married at Caxton Hall, Westminster. The reception was held at the luxury apartment of Sylvia's mother and step-father in Alford House, Park Lane. My best man was Lew Dexter, the husband of my eldest sister, and I had arranged Daimler hire for my parents and family. We had decided to have our honeymoon at St Mawes in Cornwall but the

Wedding day, December 23rd 1935. Sylvia and I outside Caxton Hall, Westminster.

one thing we did not anticipate was a London fog, which appeared from nowhere. My parents could not find the Daimler cars and took a 'bus home, and we set off in the open three-litre Hindmarsh Lagonda and got as far as Reading, travelling at not more than 10 or 15 miles an hour. We stayed overnight at an hotel and the chambermaid came into the bedroom and said "Shall I lay your girlfriend's nightdress out on the bed?", and very proudly I replied "That girl is my wife!". By the morning the fog was not too bad and after six or seven hours driving we managed to reach the Ship and Castle Inn at St Mawes, right by the water's edge.

We had managed to obtain a ground floor flat in Kensington, in a new block of flats built on American lines with the advantage of day and night porters. We went to Heals in Tottenham Court Road and bought all the carpets, curtains and furniture in one morning's shopping; I remember the total cost was something like £260!.

Sylvia decided she would like a cat at the flat and somebody we knew quite well had a kitten. The father was known as Caruso because he made a very loud noise when he miaoued. The kitten we had was a tom and so we named him Bing after a different sort of singer called Bing Crosby. It was ideal at the flat because the cat could get out through a window and walk around in the Garden Square opposite and if it was late at night the night porter could let him in through the front door.

I have already mentioned my friend Alfred Blackmore and my connection in getting involved with the equipment for the first talkies. Alfred Blackmore had a friend, a Mrs Morgan, living with a Dr Mackenzie who was one of the doctors attending George V for, I believe, his chest complaints. Dr Mackenzie and I got quite friendly and he had a house in Hillhead, near Lee-on- Solent, and a 30 ft. diesel engine fishing boat. I spent many weekends at Hillhead and got to like the small village and its inhabitants. There was a small boatbuilder there called Robertson, and after we were married I took Sylvia down there and bought an 18 ft. Gunter Rigged sailing boat, which we re-named 'Sailor Whaler'. I remember we decided that a little pram dinghy would be worth having to tow behind the sailing boat, and Robertson made a clinker built dinghy for £4.10.0. This was named 'Itsy Bitsy'. Both these names were borrowed from a movie quite popular at that time, but I just don't remember the title.

Almost every weekend when work finished on Saturday morning at about 1.00, we would drive to Hillhead, stay at the local pub called 'The Osborne View' and take part in the various sailing races, which we never won, but nevertheless it was all very enjoyable. The boats were of many mixed origins and therefore handicapping was essential and whatever we did to the rigging the race was always won by the local milkman and his son, followed closely by the local postman! The inquest was usually held at 'The Osborne View' in the Mens' Bar, where the only woman present would be Sylvia, and we could discuss all manner of things in conjunction with various pink gins!

On some other weekends we visited Gordon Vokes on his farm at Henley Park and helped with the work, clearing the river or driving the tractor. During 1935, 1936 and 1937 we took winter holidays because we had the boat at Hillhead for the summers. We went to Devon and Cornwall, staying at Brixham or Fowey every Christmas.

In the summers of 1938 and 1939 we visited the South of France. We took the Lagonda and in those days there were no roll-on/roll-off ferries so the car was put aboard the cross-Channel steamer by being hoisted on a crane and dropped into a hold, to be pulled out the same way at Calais. We thoroughly enjoyed our visits to the South of France, particularly the journey down where the small towns on the now notorious RN7 would always find accommodation for us and excellent food. The journey usually took two days. It was in July 1939 that we were reading stories about the possibility of a war and we decided to drive back to Paris. A friend of ours had a front wheel drive Cord, a famous American car with outside exhausts, and the idea was to see who could get there firSt Well, we did, because unfortunately he took no notice of a road which had a sign saying 'Tres glissant!'. When we reached Paris there was definite depression, it looked as though the Army had decided to fit out their troops and here and there were soldiers with ill-fitting jackets (one I remember in a long coat which had been roughly cut short with scissors) guarding various roads and buildings. We spent one night in Paris and made for Boulogne as quickly as possible, despite the fact of the assurance given by the Prime Minister, Neville Chamberlain, that there would be no war.

There was no question that television had arrived in the United Kingdom. The Radio Exhibition which took place every year was now held at Olympia and Scophony exhibited in both the 1938 and 1939 Exhibitions. An aerial was erected by the BBC on the roof of Olympia and a distribution network was installed feeding the various stands which intended to show television pictures. In 1938 we showed a Home Receiver with a 24 ins. screen using a super-pressure Mercury lamp. The stand was very elaborate and very futuristic, Sagall employed a

Scophony stand at Radio Exhibition, Olympia 1938.

Hungarian designer and I suppose without any doubt it was one of the best looking stands in the whole of Radio Olympia.

It was interesting to read in the August 20th issue of 'The Daily Telegraph' in 1987, the usual column which they publish entitled '50 Years Ago...' when a man called L. Marsland Gander was their Radio Correspondent, and the heading was "Television to be Cheaper". He was writing about Home Receivers in particular and mentioned the projection cathode ray tube unit developed by Philips of Holland, which was advertised at a price of 165 guineas. He then says, and I quote, "Another important development yesterday bearing on big screen television was the announcement that changes to the BBC transmitter at Alexandra Palace are in progress which will make it possible to receive transmissions in the home by mechanical methods of Scophony. This firm has made some impressive progress with big screens, and states that it is producing a Home Receiver giving a picture 24 ins. x 22 ins. and a small public hall receiver with a screen measuring 5 ft. x 4 ft. But as the new equipment at Alexandra Palace will not be ready in time there will be no Scophony demonstration at Olympia".

As mentioned previously, the problem was the synchronising line pulse which was erratic, and with the almost zero inertia of the cathode ray tube the picture received apparently appeared to be completely steady. In 1939 however, at Radio Olympia, we had a number of Home Receiver models on the stand, and we were working in conjunction with E.K. Cole of Southend, who assisted in making up some of the multi-valve chassis and cabinets for the Home receiver. No big screen unit was being shown because anything over 4 ft. or 5 ft. required a carbon arc light source and this was not possible, particularly as the Exhibition was based on radio and home television; it was on that side we concentrated.

It was always somewhat doubtful, in my opinion, whether an optical/mechanical system would be suitable for the home, although the small picture of the cathode ray tube which at that time had a maximum size of about 9 ins. diameter, was too small for general viewing in a room. The cathode ray tube had been developed entirely for oscilloscope purposes and not a lot of work had been done on phosphors which would have a limited after-glow.

It is interesting to note that after the paper I read in November 1986 at a meeting of the Institution of Electrical Engineers on '50 Years of Television' on the Scophony television system, one or two of the audience made statements that the 24 ins. Home Receiver exhibited in 1939 at Radio Olympia had the brightest and best picture they had ever seen at that time, and asked why it was not developed.

In 1936 a Dr Adolph Rosenthal joined the company as he had done some work on cathode ray tubes where, instead of a phosphor, he proposed an internal screen made up of a crystal which, after impingement by a cathode ray beam, would discolour. He called the system 'Skiatron' but I cannot remember how he derived this title whereas, as mentioned before, the Scophony name was an obvious combination of two Latin and Greek words.

Rosenthal had patented his device, which in theory looked very interesting, because a crystal plate could be so arranged in the cathode ray tube that a light source would be projected through the plate and, with suitable lenses, projected onto a screen. A considerable amount of work was done in the laboratory as we had a glassblower and facilities for evacuating, but the real problem was with the dark area formed by the cathode ray beam deciding to stay there until it was dispersed by heating; unfortunately it took some seconds of heating to get rid of the stain.

All this work was going on in 1939 when the outbreak of war stopped television transmissions and there was a general search for applications such as secret signalling, using television methods, to assist in the war effort. It was interesting that on 25th October 1933 I produced a patent application using the ultrasonic light cell as a delay device. The fact that you could put a radio frequency into the quartz crystal and produce a train of waves in a liquid column and use another crystal for a pick-up at the end of the column would give a delay of the radio frequency in milliseconds, because effectively it converted the speed of the radio frequency from 167,000 miles per second (300,000,000 metres per second) into the speed in liquid of about l,000 metres per second. When I finally joined the Telecommunications Research Establishment on radar this particular invention was proposed, and I will say more about that in the next chapter.

The letter I received from Sagall on the 25th October 1933 stated:

'In reply to your letter of October 16th, in which you submit means for producing a time delay for multiple aperture television, we have decided to file a provisional patent application in connection with this idea, in the name of the Company and yourself. We will instruct Messrs. Reddie & Grose to prepare an application in conjunction with yourself. Please get in touch with them'.

During my period with Scophony I produced a number of patents in my name or in conjunction with one or other of my colleagues, and I still have a list of these patents, dates and titles. In later years we had a resident patent attorney called Tom Brown, whom I was to encounter again during the war years.

CHAPTER 6

OUTBREAK OF WAR - RADAR RESEARCH

All development of projection television systems ceased and everyone in the Scophony laboratories became involved in secret signalling systems based on television techniques. I developed a very small unit which consisted of a cylinder with 20 holes in the form of a helix. Inside was a neon lamp, and a typewriter keyboard would visually produce letters and numbers and other symbols.

About 1933 the ex-Chief Engineer of the BBC, Captain P.P. Eckersley, became involved in a company called Rediffusion. His main object was to transmit radio programmes over cable, certainly with television programmes in mind. One suggestion was to transmit radio over the electricity mains, feeding the signal between neutral and earth.

My real interest, however, was to transmit television over the mains based on Eckersley's ideas. We realised there was a very low impedance circuit between the neutral of the 3 phase distribution system and earth. Experiments conducted in the laboratory showed that a very low power radio transmitter of the order of a few milliwatts, when connected between neutral and earth, could be picked up without attenuation anywhere in the building.

This idea was not new to me. Some years before when I was with 'Amateur Wireless' and 'Wireless Magazine' I devised a system for inter-communication, utilising the electric mains wiring as the link. It consisted of two super-heterodyne receivers; the first unit housed the oscillator, which was modulated by a microphone and produced a beat frequency with the oscillator of the other unit, the intermediate frequency being the beat of the two oscillator frequencies. The second unit oscillator was also modulated by a microphone and the beat between that one and the oscillator of the first unit produced an I/F frequency where the detector and headphones or loudspeaker were connected. On the same tests I used an oscillator capacity coupled to the mains and found a good signal from any light socket in the house. These have been developed today, with transistors instead of valves, and are a very effective method of office communication.

By arrangement with the Notting Hill Electric Light Company we constructed a unit with a 10 mHz carrier with a low impedance radio frequency coupling, a sensitive valve voltmeter in conjunction with a tuned circuit which we carried around the area, and, authorised by the local authority, we measured the voltage at the terminals of the various street lighting connecting boxes. In some cases, within a mile, the signal had not been attenuated but the next test point was zero.

We found that various loops which connected to houses and to other street lamps formed adequate wave traps. Unfortunately we could not continue this work. As the future of the company was at stake it was essential to find some means of keeping this team of international engineers together to assist in the war effort.

The Government had set up a Television Advisory Committee through the Postmaster General. Before that time a number of meetings were held with the Selsdon Committee and various memoranda prepared by Sagall and Walton were submitted. However the war was now on and a new Post Office Television Committee was set up to investigate various ideas where television could assist in the war effort. As a result Sagall, Walton, Doddington and myself went to the GPO and met the Television Sub-Committee on Thursday, March 5th 1940. Sagall confirmed this in a letter of the 14th March, repeating his memo of February 14th, emphasising the three major points of his submission. They were as follows:-

(1) That the immediate reintroduction of television transmissions whether by radio or by wire is in the national interest.

(2) That television could be transmitted by wire and that for a variety of reasons a wired service would be preferable.

(3) That the new service should be operated by private enterprise.

How right we were, in that fifty years later cable television is here in the UK and in a big way in the USA.

Dr Robinson was the first to leave the company as he had been recruited by the Air Ministry Research Establishment to work on radar. Whether it was his suggestion or not, I received a letter from Sir Henry Tizzard, the Government scientist, inviting me to join the Air Ministry Research Establishment to work on secret radio direction finding at an Establishment which had been moved to Dundee. I went for an interview in Whitehall and was accepted as a Senior Technical Officer of the Air Ministry Research Establishment, Dept. RDF (Radio Direction Finding). This was in February of 1940 and I decided to accept, agreeing to commence the first week in March. I gave my resignation letter to Sagall and he replied on the 4th March as follows:-

'We beg to confirm receipt of your letter of the 20th ult. We fully appreciate the motives which prompted you to take an appointment with the Air Ministry Research Establishment.

We regret that we could not grant you in this connection 'leave of absence' as we have no precedent for such an arrangement.

Under your Service Contract you would have to give us normally six months' notice. We are, however, prepared in your case to waive this requirement without prejudice to all the other clauses of your Service Contract. Our waiver is conditional upon your signing the attached letter prepared by the Company's solicitors.

Needless to say we regret extremely that the cessation of television transmissions as a result of the war should have brought about a situation in which we are compelled, though reluctantly, to agree to release you after our association of several years in which you have given us such eminently satisfactory services.

We wish you the very best of luck in your new sphere and we hope that one day we may still be able to make use of your services in the field of television'.

It was necessary to make a number of plans and first, of course, was to give notice at the flat, which had to be one month to March Quarter Day. I sent a written notice at the end of February to terminate at the end of March, and because of this mistake I had the penalty of another quarter's rent or we could leave all the carpets and curtains, which we did. It had never struck me that Quarter Day was the 25th March and not the 31st!.

We had to find a home for the cat, fortunately a friend of Sylvia's, a Mrs Meyer whose husband was part of the Medana & Roamer Watch Company in Switzerland, was happy to have Bing. We had to store the Lagonda; the garage we used behind the flats in Kensington was fairly inexpensive for parking, so we put the Lagonda in their lock-up. The next thing, of course, was to store the furniture, pack two suitcases and proceed to Dundee by train. It was a tearful moment as we had only been married five years with a beautiful home, and to give it up so suddenly without knowing how long it would be before we could return and have a home again was rather traumatic.

We stayed the first week at the North British Hotel in Dundee. The mattresses were filled with straw or horsehair, very uncomfortable, and it was very difficult to get a meal. In Dundee I met the person for whom I would be working, a Mr Lutkin, and he and his wife showed us a suitable guest house where we could have a bedroom, with breakfast and an evening meal. It was extremely cold up there; we would sit in the Sitting Room of this house and at ten o'clock precisely the landlady would come in with a shovel and bucket, remove the coal from the fire and take it into the kitchen to go into the boiler there. As it got cold we had to go to bed. Some of the engineers were staying in the same guest house, an ex-science master Robert Cockburn, a mathematician G.G. Macfarlane, H. Priest, and Robert Hanbury Brown.

I was told that the move from the original site at Bawdsey Manor near Felixstowe was temporary as Bawdsey was considered too well-known and right on the East Coast. There were no facilities in Dundee to do much in the way of radar work, except by going off to one of the CH Stations (Chain Stations) which were by then in operation throughout the East Coast. The move by the most important research operation from Bawdsey Manor with its spacious buildings and grounds to the centre of the city in Dundee with two rooms, no open spaces, and most of the equipment dumped outside in the open, mainly in packing cases, was a bad decision by the Powers That Be and, as A.P. Rowe said in his book 'The Story of Radar', they learned a lesson that they should never forget.

A partial solution was found when Professor McLelland, Principal of Dundee Training College, cleared a floor and a half of his building, which gave us some opportunity to get work done. It was obviously impossible to do any real work in Dundee and discussions were taking place about moving the whole Establishment to the South Coast away from any possible German bombing, and a small area near Swanage in Dorset, known as Worth Matravers, was discussed amongst the senior people in the Establishment and my intimate knowledge of that area assisted with the decision to move. Those three months in Dundee were depressing, it was impossible to obtain any real food except fish and chips, we

T.R.E. site at Worth Matravers.

were living in a single room in a boarding house which, despite it being early Spring, was extremely cold, so we could not wait to move to Worth Matravers where Nissen type huts were being assembled. The advantage of moving there was the fact that the CH Stations, which were the early radar stations, covered right round the whole of the coast from South Wales, and two of these towers were at Worth Matravers.

I saw my first Aurora Borealis whilst in Dundee, but finally the decision was made that sufficient buildings were erected in Dorset and that we would move on May 5th 1940. As I had at that time not yet got much equipment in the laboratory I could move a day or so earlier, which I did. Sylvia and I took the train to London, retrieved the Lagonda, and motored to Swanage on May 4th, where we rented a furnished house at the top of the hill overlooking the bay. I remember it was a delightful drive down from London and the rhododendrons were in full bloom along the whole of the road to Wareham and beyond. There were a total of about 400 employees who would have to move to Swanage and we though it would be a good idea if we got in first!

On May 6th most of the equipment came down from Dundee and myself, J.C.C. Stewart and Freddie Lutkin helped to set it up in a hut; Freddie Lutkin was my Group Leader.

The war, which started on September 4th 1939, was known as 'The Phoney War' to start with, in that very little happened which affected our normal way of life, apart from blackouts and the possibility of rationing. We had only been in Swanage for two days when Rowe called me to spend two or three days in London at the offices of the Institution of Mechanical Engineers in Parliament Street to meet with Dr C.P. Snow and W.E. Barber, Chief Draughtsman at the Royal Aircraft Establishment, in order to interview and select RAF personnel who had been conscripted irrespective of their qualifications. Various sections of the RAF had been asked to do preliminary screening and we, as a committee of three, interviewed some hundreds of conscripted service personnel so that their professional backgrounds could be more usefully employed than putting them in the Front Line. I deemed it an honour to be asked to become one of the selectors, but I knew I had the ability, being young and enthusiastic with a certain amount of experience in industry, to make adequate contribution.

We stayed in Swanage for two years. In that time we made a number of moves as our rented accommodation leases expired from time to time. One was in a fisherman's cottage on the beach at Swanage with two rooms, one up and one down, and the toilet was situated in a terrace at the bottom of the garden where you had to walk up some steps and pick out the room with your house number on it. In that room was a bath and a geyser for hot water. The many disadvantages of that cottage were outweighed by the excellent lobsters which were brought up on the beach by the local fishermen. You could buy a lobster weighing one and a half pounds for two shillings (10p.)!

The rented accommodation we had in Swanage, which was still considered a holiday area, meant that we had to move to somewhere else when the accommodation was let to a holidaymaker. The famous hotel in Swanage called The Grosvenor was headquarters for the 'Sunday Soviet'. This was a meeting of Chiefs of Staff and other Ministry officials who would come down, usually on a Sunday, to discuss the work being carried out by the Establishment and the need by the Forces. Captain Balls was the proprietor of the hotel and we would eat there quite often.

Most visitors to the Establishment stayed at the Grosvenor and finally we decided the best thing we could do would be to take some rooms in the annexe of the hotel and have our evening meals, which were inexpensive, in the hotel. It had a very good tennis court. During my time with Scophony I became friendly with the Chief Patent Attorney and Licences Negotiator of the Radio Corporation of America, Herbert J.O. Barton. Herbie and I became very good friends, and as he had a house in Bournemouth he used to come down quite often and we would snatch an hour or two to play tennis, which kept us very fit.

We stayed at the Grosvenor some three or four months and our cat, Bing, came to us from London. He thought the move a considerable improvement on anything he had had in the past, as the kitchen had a number of rats who were obviously well fed on kitchen food, and by eating the rats he had twice the helpings! He became so much a part of that hotel that when we later moved to Parkstone Bing was perfectly happy to stay there. When we emigrated to America in later years we had a letter from Captain Balls, in about 1950, telling us that Bing was getting very old and would have to be put to sleep and he was asking permission, which of course we sadly gave. Bing had lived for fifteen years and certainly the Grosvenor Hotel and its beautiful grounds and perpetual food, as far as Bing was concerned, provided Heaven!

Part of a hut on the cliffs at Worth Matravers was allocated to me. The Establishment was called AMRE (Air Ministry Research Establishment) and the staff expanded very rapidly with a large contingent from the Radio Department of the Royal Aircraft Establishment at Farnborough, civil servants of long standing, and others recruited from industry and from universities. It has always been said in the history of British radar that the most valuable work was carried out during the two years spent at Worth Matravers.

I worked with Freddie Lutkin, our Group Leader, and I used my optical knowledge to design large screen displays of radar signals using the ultrasonic light cell and cylindrical lenses so arranged that one could produce a triangulation on the screen to pinpoint a target. Robert Cockburn, a science master recruited to the Establishment and responsible for radar countermeasures, was most interested in the ultrasonic cell in that it could produce a delay in time, the very device he was looking for to overcome the Lorenz guidance system used by the German bombers. This was a dot-dash system; provided the bomber could fly so that the dots and dashes produced a continual tone they were on course. Cockburn thought the device I had designed highly valuable. I made one for him and we were told that a German bombing raid intended for South-West England had been diverted to drop their bombs in Ireland.

After the war I applied to the Royal Commission on Awards to Inventors for some recompense for the ultrasonic light cell time delay device. As previously mentioned I had applied for a patent on this invention on 25th October 1933 through the patent attorneys Reddie & Grose whilst working at Scophony. The man who later became the resident patent attorney at Scophony, Tom Brown, transferred from the company to a Government Service and it was he who decided that my delay device was not new, he found a patent in 1928 which showed an acoustic delay using a loudspeaker and microphone. In correspondence I had with him I pointed out the ultrasonic delay cell delayed the radio frequencies three hundred million meters per second to a medium at the speed of one thousand meters per second. It was to no avail!

The engineering of the Establishment was run by a man called W.G.N. Chew, a Principal Scientific Officer, who I believe was an ex-Post Office engineer. The workshops were run by a man called J. Morley whom I got to know very well, he was a very practical all-round engineer. I was having discussions with A.P. Rowe, the Superintendent of the Establishment and a man for whom I had great respect, on the problems of getting the information into the workshops fast enough, and he suddenly said to me "You have given me an idea, you are wasted where you are, you will take over the workshops, drawing offices and all engineering facilities as Divisional Leader", and from that moment I felt I had got the right niche to give my best for the war effort.

The organisation I was handed was much bigger than I realised. I had the photographic department whose job was to make training films to train personnel in radar - run by a Mr Segaller, the experimental drawing offices, and the machine shops and mechanics at Christchurch aerodrome, which was twenty miles from

Swanage. The official library came under my jurisdiction, with the librarian, the Rev. H.A. Atkinson who was the vicar of the church at Langton Matravers. Mr Chew moved to Group I, together with Stewart and Segaller. With regard to the photographic section which I controlled for a short time, my knowledge of the cinema industry and my experience of eight years of optical/mechanical television as a member of the British Kinematograph Society, assisted Segaller, Fisher and I to produce cartoon training films for our operators who were manning the CH chain. I was given an assistant and deputy, Robert Munroe, a Scottish engineer with a tremendous imagination.

We were working a five and a half day week and I, with a group of others, went to see A.P. Rowe to suggest that it would be more efficient if we did a five-day week and cut out Saturday morning. Fortunately that coincided with the Germans over-running the Maginot Line and arriving at Cherbourg on the same day. We decided then and there to do a seven-day week with one day rest.

With the considerable influx of new people and new ideas, particularly the work on centimetre radar, Leeson House at Langton Matravers was requisitioned and centimetre radar was developed and became operational in a very short time. The expansion, however, was not enough and a school called Durnford House on the main road to Swanage outside Langton Matravers was also requisitioned and I had my office there with a personal secretary, a Miss Wareham. Not content with the three areas, Worth Matravers, Leeson House and Durnford, we requisitioned Forres School just outside Swanage and the whole Establishment was now called TRE (Telecommunications Research Establishment) and became a closely knit team.

Spread as we were over that area the first few months, most of us took sandwiches and ate at the Square & Compass, the famous pub at Worth Matravers, or we had sandwiches sitting in our cars or in the bright sunshine on the cliffs. Sylvia was not happy just looking after the dog, a golden retriever which we had acquired as a puppy after our move to Swanage from kennels in Buckinghamshire. He was a grandson of Crufts champion Bruce of Dewstraw but his kennel name was Rex. She proposed to Rowe that she would like to operate a canteen at Durnford House and could get voluntary help from other wives. This, of course, was immediately approved and sanctioned. She remembers on one important occasion when we had visitors from London that so many of our scientists apparently had not seen asparagus before, which she had obtained locally and cooked specially, and they did not know which end to eat!

I have found it difficult, in writing this book, to maintain a chronological sequel of events. This is due partly to the fact that there is the technical side and the domestic. The domestic side is important in that it needs a lot of co-operation and understanding so that the two people are united in their efforts. During the time of Sylvia's voluntary work in the canteen she became pregnant, and after six months she found the standing was too much and decided to hand the canteen over to a very excellent group of women who were happy to continue.

My daughter Jacqueline was born in the marvellous little Nursing Home in Swanage on January 8th 1942. It was interesting that around the same time the wife of one of the Project Leaders, Dr D. Taylor, Group 7, was in the only other private room also having a baby. The Matron was absolutely first-class as well as being a qualified midwife, and she took pity on me so that every night I visited a hot meal was ready! I cannot remember exactly the cost of the stay there but I think it was something between £4 and £5 a week. What a difference today! The trouble with Swanage is that it is very hilly in places and often I would have to help my wife push the pram up a steep hill to wherever we lived at that time, but the wonderful air which is so well-known in Swanage produced a very healthy baby who would be in her pram in the sun Winter and Summer with beautiful brown arms and legs. Her great companion was, of course, Rex, the large golden retriever.

Early in 1942 Rowe arranged for me to visit a panel at the Ministry of Aircraft Production as he had proposed that I be upgraded from Senior Technical Officer to Principal Technical Officer, and in July 1942 I received a letter from A.B. Jones, Civil Assistant and Accountant, as follows:-

'I have to inform you that authority has been given for your promotion in an acting capacity to the rank of Principal Technical Officer at a fixed salary of £850 a year, with effect from the 14th July 1942.'

Soon afterwards I was appointed Divisional Leader of Engineering which naturally brought me into close contact with all the scientists and all the projects in the Establishment. The major thing I learned was that there was a certain frustration by the Project Leaders in their liaison with commercial companies to develop and produce the various systems they had proposed. They would have liked me to extend the size of my workshop to carry out this original development work and produce prototypes which could be tested under service conditions. I had a meeting with Rowe and said to him that there was a great need for a Research Prototype Unit, completely independent of the Establishment but nevertheless under his control, to manufacture prototypes, the advantage being our having control of Christchurch Aerodrome and, later, Hurn, outside Bournemouth, which would mean that we could produce these prototypes and install them into various aircraft, so giving proper facilities to Project Leaders to see their ideas fulfilled. He suggested I should contact the Director of Communications Development, O.F. Brown, who introduced me to Sir Robert Renwick, who was Controller of Communications Development at the Air Ministry.

My assistant, Bob Munroe, and I looked around Bournemouth, having been to various estate agents, and found a large site north of the main London Road at the end of Wallisdown Road. It was about sixteen acres and we had been told that if we found something it could be requisitioned. We personally went to the Council at Bournemouth Town Hall and said what we wanted to do, and they said "Under no circumstances can you build a factory on that site, this is all zoned for residential development. Bournemouth is a residential area and we do not want any industrial development, it would ruin the town. An important individual came down from London, I remember his name was Green, and he had a word with the Council but got nowhere. His last meeting was on a Friday afternoon; the following Sunday a German ME.110 fighter bomber was returning from a raid and had a few bombs left. He saw a very nice town below him and dropped his bombs. One fell on the Metropole Hotel, one on Beales Department Stores and six were straddled through Westbourne; the war had come to Bournemouth. The

Council granted permission immediately for us to build on the site we had chosen!.

I at once contacted Sir Robert Renwick who, apart from his official position with the Ministry, was Chairman of the Central Electricity Company and also of Callender's Cables at Preston. He was very enthusiastic and told me to find a site and he would okay it through the D.C.D., O.F. Brown. We walked from building to building in Whitehall and finally arranged with the well-known government organisation called "Works and Bricks" to draw up plans for a building which would be situated on Francis Avenue in Wallisdown, north of Bournemouth, the very site we had chosen in the first place and had now been approved by the local Council. I was introduced to the Ministry of Labour officials and also the Machine Tool Directorate. Munroe and I drew a rough sketch of the type of building we wanted, with various areas given over to specialist test equipment, including environmental cabinets to provide conditions which would be experienced during flight. It was essential to have pretty well every type of machine tool because as a Research Prototype Unit we would be required to make as much as possible without calling in outside contractors who would normally be very busy on war contracts. I remember the beautiful Geneva jig borer arriving at the factory and Munroe, who was a Scot and a very good engineer, almost put his arms round it with enthusiasm.

The Works and Bricks people were incredible. In ten months, from an empty site, we had a building completely equipped, with the majority of people already employed and working. In later years this building became Edward Webster & Co. who manufactured all the lipstick cases, compact cases etc. for the cosmetic company Max Factor, who also built a factory adjacent. The big airfield at Hurn was operational, as well as the smaller one at Christchurch. We erected at Hurn Nissen huts for the use of installation mechanics and our design drawing offices. Some of those huts are still there, but I believe, with the improvements at Hurn, that one day they will be dismantled and a little bit of history will have disappeared.

In the middle of all this work, towards the middle of July, I had a 'phone call from Oscar Deutsch. He said "We need you desperately in the United States, we have shipped over all the Scophony television equipment and you are the only one capable of setting it all up and getting pictures". I explained that having left the company and joined the Air Ministry Research Establishment it would not be possible for me to leave as I had already reached a position in the organisation of some seniority and responsibility. He was extremely disappointed.

Bob Munroe, a great golfer, was responsible entirely for my never taking up golf! He said to me one day at Swanage "A game of golf would do you good, I'll lend you some clubs and we'll go round the golf course". He went round the course and I carried the clubs all the way behind him, because I am very good at a moving ball such as tennis, but very poor with a stationary ball such as golf, and I decided that walking with a heavy load was not for me!

Most of the work at Worth Matravers moved to the various requisitioned buildings we had in Swanage and the original site became more of an operational radar station manned by Service personnel. A number of WAAFs were employed and the Commanding Officer in charge told me he did have some problems with them. The majority of them were University trained and very quick on understanding and reading information on an oscilloscope, but he said that the difficulty was in talking to them and giving them instructions, knowing who they were. Apparently they were all daughters of well-known Air Commodores, Generals, Admirals, etc., and he said "I am an ordinary person talking to these WAAFs and giving them their instructions". I, personally, could not see the problem!

We moved to a house in Elms Avenue, Lilliput, called 'Far East' right on the shores of Poole Harbour because in my periodic visits to RPU where I had Bob Munroe in charge, and occasional visits to London, it was more convenient from the point of view of travel to live in the Poole area rather than the cottage at Swanage. Herbie Barton, on his various visits to his house in Bournemouth, called in to see us and told us that he was being moved back to RCA in New York and was selling the house, could we do something about his furniture? Sylvia suggested that if it was not too much we would have all his furniture moved into our garage, which was fairly big, and hold a Dutch Auction on his behalf. He was delighted and in due course the garage was filled. It was arranged that we would have one day for viewing at which time people could put in bids, and another day for acceptance, provided they would take whatever they had bought away with them. It worked extremely successfully, Sylvia doing a good organisation, and we collected a fair amount of money for Herbie which we deposited in his bank.

The only commission she took, obviously at his suggestion, was a very nice lady's Raleigh bicycle. She used this transport for shopping; it meant pushing the bike all the way up the road to Canford Cliffs Village and coming down the hill at high speed with a basket full of the very few items which one could buy but which nevertheless became a load. In those days Canford Cliffs Village was a real village and all the necessary shops were there; Harrison the fishmonger who, in addition to fish of all sorts including the best smoked salmon which he smoked himself at the back of the shop, stocked chickens and ducks, and there were also grocers, chemists, two butchers, a bakery and a greengrocer. Very different from today when most of the shops are either estate agents or building societies.

It was a Saturday morning when A.P. Rowe called us together and said that the invasion of France had happened so quickly that Swanage was an undesirable place to have a research organisation as the Germans would be just sixty-three miles away across a small part of the Channel. We would have to find accommodation more in the centre of the country and move everything out before the next full moon. The moon was an important part of life in those days as a full moon made bombing much easier.

He asked me to go with him and Professor P.I. Dee to find a suitable building which we could requisition for the whole Establishment. We set off in my Lagonda and went first to Marlborough College, which was one of the two places recommended by headquarters. It was not big enough and accommodation for some 1,000 people did not appear possible. We went on to Great Malvern and found Malvern College, set in beautiful grounds, absolutely ideal, with only one problem; it had been requisitioned by a Ministry and telephones were installed everywhere, but a week before we got there they had all been removed! However Malvern it was.

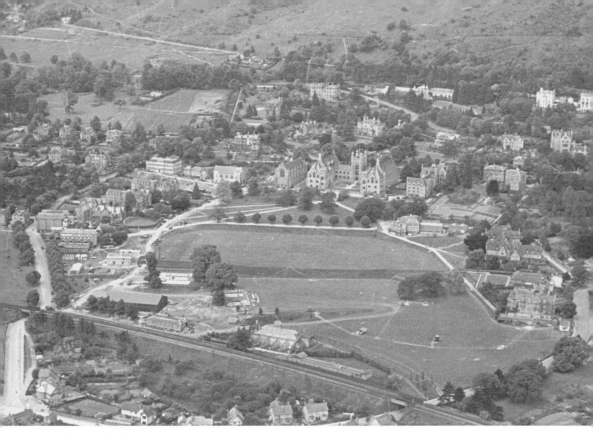

Malvern College.

I was then instructed to co-operate with Sir Alan Gordon-Smith, Chairman of S.S. Smith & Sons (now Smiths Industries), to organise the move from Swanage to Malvern immediately. With the benefit of Sir Alan, he obtained and requisitioned all the Pickford pantechnicons, I do not remember how many there were now but certainly one hundred or more, and I arranged with every laboratory and its Project Leader to load everything into one pantechnicon per laboratory, or two if necessary, drive straight to Malvern, then unload in various parts of the building as allocated. The whole move was organised and completed with a few days to spare before the full moon.

Munroe was down at RPU and I was at Malvern. I spent some days at RPU and some at Malvern and I managed to get a room in Malvern in a big house where two elderly spinsters lived who were very kind, but the residents of Malvern were not at all happy at having all these people suddenly coming into the town and requisitoning and requesting facilities to put people up temporarily until they could find proper accommodation. I did not like Malvern, something about the place depressed me, and I spent more time than I should at RPU. Rowe called me on the telephone and he said "The workshops here are inadequate, you must come up we have got to build one in the grounds and install it with all the necessary equipment, and that must be done as soon as possible". So back I went to Malvern complete with our dog Rex, who was a companion on the journey by car which, with the Lagonda, took approximately three hours. I stayed for a few weeks while the building went on and obtained the necessary machine tools. Morley was very effective, doing most of the hard work, but the priorities were such that, within reason, for anything I wanted I could call Sir Robert Renwick or O.F. Brown, the Director, and receive it within days.

I felt that I was not doing my best in the Malvern atmosphere, I was more interested in taking the experimental models from the various Project Leaders and turning them into reasonable production equipments which we could install on aircraft and fly. I noticed on one occasion the Mosquito aircraft, which was a cold-moulded wooden plane but very effective, was being used to install anti-submarine radar. The room inside the aircraft was so small that only one person could work at any one time. I managed to get a Douglas DC3, which was designed as a civilian aircraft, and any equipment we made for test could be put into this plane, where there was room for more than half a dozen engineers and, what is more, they could make coffee!

I was thinking very hard during my travels to and from Malvern, and I saw Rowe and said that I would like to be permanently installed at RPU as Superintendent and leave it to Morley and Munroe to run the workshops and engineering. He thought it was a very bad idea but he agreed to my request and I only paid occasional visits to Malvern; I could leave the house in Lilliput at 6.00 a.m. and be at Malvern before 9.00.

It was during one of these journeys, this particular time to London, that I was driving in the early hours of a bright Spring morning in my four and a half litre drophead Lagonda with the top down, on the road between Winchester and Basingstoke, which as no doubt many will remember, was an undulating road but very straight and seventeen miles long. I could normally cover that in thirteen minutes! I was going along at my usual speed, which would have been between 70 and 80 m.p.h. on that road, no traffic whatsoever, when I heard a noise from the engine. This noise got worse and worse and I started to brake, the more I braked the worse it got, and finally I skidded almost to a standstill and little pieces of road started coming up in front of me. I think it was an ME.109 German fighter aircraft which was machine-gunning me! There was nothing wrong with my car engine, it was the noise of the aircraft's engine!

America had not come into the war in those early days but an organisation called The Civilian Technical Corps. was formed, which comprised a number of American radio hams who banded together and decided to help Britain in its war. Through the Ministry of Labour we had some twenty or thirty of these individuals and we were starting to make a few ASV equipments (Air to Surface Vessel) - an airborne radar for detection of ships and surfaced submarines), providing them with pre-drilled chassis and components. We gave them a circuit diagram each and they wired and tested the equipment themselves, a most rapid pre-production operation.

An urgent requirement for 150 H^2S units was placed with RPU. Components, however, were in very short supply and working for me as a Component Procurer was a Mr Parkinson. He had red hair, knew all the backstreets in Soho where components were sold, and most of the radio shops in the country, as he had been a traveller in that field before the war. He guaranteed that if I could give him cash, like £5,000, he would buy all the components we needed from various radio shops. They would not be certified but there were very few component failures in those early days. I had a word with Rowe and then with the Director, O.F. Brown, and reluctantly the Treasury gave me the £5,000, known as "The bag of gold". Parkinson went out and within ten days was back with everything we needed, and some change.

With the enthusiastic labour force our productionising of laboratory equipment was quite rapid and the Project people found it was extremely valuable for them to be able to have working equipment in a relatively short time put onto an aircraft and flown.

The H^{2}S equipment we were building used a Magnetron, and a Project Leader familiar with this device was a Dr Priest. The Magnetron was an essential part of centimetre radar, developed by Oliphant and Randall of Birmingham University, E.G. Bowen, Bernard Lovell and Priest, who were part of the team on centimetre radar under the direction of Dr P.I. Dee, a nuclear physicist. The name given H^{2}S was suggested by Professor Lindemann - 'Home Sweet Home' and a bad smell.

I mention Priest because some time later we were given to understand by Intelligence that the Germans were operating a radar station in Normandy and it was essential that this should be investigated fully. It was decided that Priest, being a scientist, should go to Normandy (for which he would have to wear an officer's uniform) and bring back for interrogation one of the engineers operating the radar, complete with all the equipment. This required a Task Force and he, plus supporting soldiers and others, sailed in a destroyer one night from Portland. We saw Priest on his return and he said it was a frightening operation as a lot of firing took place and unfortunately some of the essential people operating the German radar were killed so there was nobody to interrogate, but the equipment was reasonably intact and was brought back and immediately analysed.

RPU had to run a separate Drawing Office from Malvern because aircraft layouts for equipment and so on and detailed modifications for designs had to be recorded. We were very short of draughtsmen so I had a word with the Minister of Labour, Ernest Bevin, through an intermediary, and he arranged to send down a large number of draughtsmen from the Post Office at Mill Hill. Unfortunately, although they were graded quite high in the Civil Service, they were not the draughtsmen we expected. They were very good at drawing pictures of telephone lines and switchboards but their expertise stopped at that point, and it was with great difficulty that we managed to send them back.

At Somerford, near Christchurch, was a very large Government operation, the Signals Research & Development Establishment (SRDE), not far away from the Military Experimental Establishment (MEXE) where the Director, Dr Bailey, had the famous bridge named after him. The officer in charge of SRDE was a Colonel Raby of the Royal Engineers. His Establishment was very much larger and more elaborate than the RPU, and capable of making anything from large gun turrets to radar equipment to be carried either by mule or man. He and I became very close friends, he being somewhat like me, only more so, in that when he wanted something he got it by going as near to the top as he dare without upsetting the Establishment!

There was a question by the Powers-That-Be as to whether the Magnetron should be used in the new centimetre radar when bombing over Germany. We were under the impression that the Germans had not developed the resonant Klystron which we called the Magnetron, and it was believed undesirable to have in a plane in case it was shot down and the radar equipment analysed.

At a meeting with Professor Lindemann, the Prime Minister's Scientific Adviser, he suggested that the equipment containing the Magnetron could be destroyed with an explosive charge which should be fitted to every equipment. It was pointed out that the Magnetron was designed in a large brass block and it would be impossible to destroy. He maintained very definitely that it could be. As a result an old Stirling bomber at RAE Farnborough had a radar equipment installed in the tail and a suitable charge was put in and fired. The equipment was removed and found to be in working order. A charge of double the weight was then installed and fired, and still the equipment was in order. Finally a large charge was put in, when unfortunately most of the tail of the bomber was blown away, but the Magnetron was still intact.

Having such an organisation as SRDE so close to RPU the co-operation between the Air Ministry and Military (which was completely de trop) was of great value. SRDE today has been taken over by the Plessey Group of Companies and, as I mentioned earlier, RPU became the manufacturing factory for Edward Webster, making the various cosmetic holders for Max Factor who also built on the same site. MEXE were still at Christchurch until recent years, presumably inventing more Bailey bridges, but the site is now closed.

Returning to our meetings at the Grosvenor Hotel, the various Chiefs of Staff were extremely friendly and helpful, and Sir Hugh Dowding, Head of Fighter Command, spent quite some time in talking to people in the laboratories, including myself. One of the problems was to see an aircraft at night, and I proposed that it would be possible to have a strong ultra-violet beam in the invisible part of the spectrum which would tend to fluoresce on the usual oil spattering outside the engine casing. Dowding was very enthusiastic about this idea and E.G. Bowen was a great supporter and did suggest that as he was going to America it would be a good idea if we carried on the work there. I decided that my place was still in the mother country and my abilities were not to do research on a single device but get involved in as much diversity as possible, which is natural in one who does not specialise in a particular branch of science.

RPU was successful and late in 1942 Sir Robert Renwick approached me and said that RPU could be much more successful if it were under private ownership without the restrictions of the Civil Service, labour relations, or pay scales without going through the Whitley Council, and what did I think of the idea if he arranged for Callenders Cables to take over RPU? I was somewhat horrified, as a temporary Civil Servant, at the idea of selling out to a private company, whoever they were, but he said it would be the best thing which could happen as the war would soon be over and I would have security. I could not believe him, one may be good at some things which were in three dimensions but not politics, which is one dimension. He was more sensible than I realised at that time, particularly as I read the following extract from E.G. Bowen's recent book 'Radar Days':-

'Sir Hugh Dowding was dismissed as soon as the battle was over, received a miserable pension and died in poverty. Sir Henry Tizzard, whose committee first inspired the development of radar, both airborne and ground, and led the Tizzard Commission to America, was dismissed as soon as he returned to this country, and to add to these seemingly ungrateful actions after the war, Churchill's Government was defeated in the General Election. He spoke for many when he remarked very severely that "ingratitude to their great men seemed to be common to democratic societies"'.

Not knowing these facts I telephoned Lord Llewellin, who at that time was Minister of Aircraft Production and spent his spare moments at his property, Upton House, Poole, in beautiful surroundings with grounds running down to the back of Poole Harbour. I made an appointment with him and when we met told him I thought it was very unpatriotic to think of Sir Robert Renwick wanting to take over RPU, a successful operation, and hand it over to a commercial company. He said "I will deal with this and let you know". All I remember was that Sir Stafford Cripps was appointed Minister of Aircraft Production, an employee of the Central Electricity Company was drafted into the Air Ministry and he came down to RPU to take over control, and I was relegated back to Malvern! That was my entry into politics, a very important lesson, but then in life one has to have every sort of experience, you cannot read about it, you have to do it.

The engineer who took over RPU, a Mr Ingles, who, incidentally, finally married my secretary at RPU, was quite sound and the takeover happened in one day; he was in and I was out. I was asked to report to Malvern. I went to Malvern, saw Rowe and said "It appears as though I have finished the work I have to do here, RPU is successful, the war in Europe is likely to finish within the next few months and I have an opportunity to stay in Poole and take over a senior position with an engineering company". He said "I fully agree there is nothing you can really do but resign from my Establishment with my very great regret, why didn't you talk to me first?". When you are thirty-five you are still a bit headstrong, by the time you go past forty you think before you act.

I should mention here that I was friendly with the Ministry of Labour representative in the Southern Area who became a friend due to our many meetings from starting the RPU operation with nobody, to finishing up with a strength of nearly four hundred in less than one year. He mentioned to me that Hamworthy Engineering, a very well-known company in Poole, had been bought by a financier called Ingram-Spencer who was looking for a deputy to act as Production Director, and suggested it would be a good idea if I arranged to meet him.

I told Ingram-Spencer of my background and the reason for suddenly resigning from the Air Ministry, which he very carefully checked and found that my statements were quite correct. He offered me the job at £2,000 a year but I would have to buy one third of the shareholding in the company, which consisted of 10,000 £1 shares and I could pay that by reductions of salary in the future. He did tell me that he would not be there as he had interests in Glasgow but I would have difficulty in dealing with a Mr Sidney Hall, the founder of the company, who was not happy at losing control, particularly when a young upstart was going to come in who knew nothing about his business.

Ingram-Spencer sent me a letter confirming my appointment and suggested I went to visit Sidney Hall at his home to also obtain his approval of my appointment. I had an interesting chat with Mr Hall and told him of my television experience and high speed scanner motor which ran at over 30,000 r.p.m. and the fact that aircraft were in an experimental stage of flying, with engines which worked on the jet principle as against a propeller. I pointed out to him that just before the war started Scophony were approached by the Air Ministry to assist a certain Group Captain Whittle who had devised a jet engine with a rotor running at very high speed, approximately 23,000 r.p.m. but they had difficulty in achieving a dynamic balance. Wikkenhauser had perfected a dynamic balancing system for our high speed scanner motor, and a system was designed for the Air Ministry which solved their problem. Sidney Hall wrote a report to Ingram-Spencer and a letter stating that the man he had appointed as Production Director was not an engineer and made statements which were physically impossible. He stated that an aircraft propelled by a jet would need a three stage compressor which would weigh about one and a half tons and it would never fly, and as for a motor running at over 30,000 r.p.m., this was impossible as whatever rotor it had it would fly to pieces. Fortunately Ingram-Spencer believed me and told me that the man I was dealing with would be a very difficult customer because he was a good old-fashioned marine engineer and thought anything that went faster than a steam engine would fly to pieces!

CHAPTER 7

HAMWORTHY ENGINEERING

I joined Hamworthy Engineering early in 1943. The company was situated on the West Quay at Poole, with J.R. Wood, the coal merchants, on one side where the coal was heaped in high mounds exposed to wind and rain. The Machine Shop, after my elaborate RPU operation, was appalling. The building was Queen Anne with various repairs carried out with corrugated iron covering holes in the wall, the machines were mounted on a dirt floor and the operators stood on wooden platforms. All machines were driven by overhead belts with the power coming from a large single cylinder gas engine designed by Sidney Hall, which also ran a DC generator and provided the lighting (50V DC) for the whole premises. Apparently Sidney Hall did not like paying for electricity supplied by the local authority and was happy to have his own power supply. Due to the fact that only 50V was used, most of the lighting was by ordinary vacuum bulbs suspended by flexible cords from the roof, with the advantage that a 50V lamp was no use to anybody who had 240V in their house! The offices had wooden floors covered in dust with a few windows overlooking the Quay.

The Foundry was a similar type of building, although built as a Foundry with space for all the castings, which were aged in the open air, and storage for all the coke which was delivered by train; a branch of the railway, incidentally, went down that side of the Quay.

I remember a large load of coke had arrived and Ingram Spencer came out, examined it and said "That is not twenty tons, there are two tons short". I was staggered, however it all had to be weighed and he was right! His company in the Docks at Glasgow employed a large number of stevedores and he had an uncanny skill in estimating weight by looking at the size of the pile of coke.

The Foundry also had a dirt floor and casting took place on Thursdays because that apparently was the day one could cast a cylinder without it being full of blowholes. I talked to the Foundry Manager quite often and he pointed out that there was nothing scientific about that casting except it had to be Thursday and it had to be the right sort of coke, and he did need certain steel bedsteads and other scrap iron to make sure that his castings had the minimum quantity of scrap.

The first thing I did, by agreement with Ingram Spencer who had to spend the money, was to put a building over the top of the Queen Anne building of the Machine Shop. This ensured that there would be no interruption in production, which was in two shifts of twelve hours each, starting at 7.30 in the morning and the second shift at 7.30 in the evening. This went on until 1.30 Saturday morning and started again at 7.30 on Sunday evening. The day shift and night shift personnel alternated every other week.

A small firm called James Bros. were specialists in steel work and they put the frame over the top of the Machine Shop building, roofed it in, the walls were built and the old building was removed, roof and all, between Saturday 1.00 p.m. and Sunday evening. Previously to this we had arranged to get the main electricity supply into the building and we motorised nearly all the machines and removed all the overhead shafting and belt drives. This was done every weekend until completed, with two very good millwrights. Sidney Hall had a brother called Percy whose son was an apprentice with us. Percy was responsible for the major building and the very fast re-construction of the Machine Shop.

Concrete bases were laid with the main lathes mounted on these blocks, which were placed in echelon formation. Every weekend the men would come in on night shift to find their position had been moved and they were standing on concrete rather than dirt. I must admit they did not like it, the lighting was too bright, there were draughts which were not there before, and as the lathes were then properly levelled they even complained they could not take a straight cut on a shaft!

However the total operation in the Machine Shop took four months. The biggest job was the Webster and Bennett boring mill which weighed many tons. The other was the horizontal planer, which was 30 ft. long. Ingram Spencer was delighted when he saw the Machine Shop looked like a Machine Shop for the first time, and there was not the noise of the belts slapping on all the machines or the overhead shafting vibrating; all that had gone and I believe, despite the Union unhappiness at the change, in their hearts they welcomed the improvement.

The next move was the Foundry. Ingram Spencer was the one who said something should be done because it was not good engineering to depend on the various mixtures of scrap iron which were used to produce our compressor castings. Some of these were very large and in some cases the bore was 15 ins., which was machined on the Webster and Bennett, and it was most disconcerting if, just before taking the final cut, one found a blowhole and the whole job had to be scrapped.

We decided to call in a firm of consultants on Foundry design and they came up with a scheme for a completely automated Foundry. We found the site in Mannings Heath Road, Poole, and the Foundry was built and working in less than one year.

The various pumps and compressors we made went into many different industries, and we made a special pump for lubricating oil for the Southern Railway. The machining of this was done on a small boring mill and I introduced a magnetic chuck to hold the casting. In order to allow it to sit squarely on the chuck table we added a small lug in the casting which would give it stability during the machining operation. We had an order for six of these and they were fitted to Southern Railway locomotives. They had, on the first turn, to lubricate all the necessary wheels and bearings of the engine. A letter came through from the Engineering Department of the Railway saying they would never give us another contract because we had modified the design. Apparently the addition of this extra lug meant that the unit would not fit in the place it had always fitted before, so we had to chop this lug off before delivery. You would think there would be enough room on a steam engine to put a small device of that sort without hitting anything else, but there was not!

We were making pumps for oil firing and Ingram Spencer decided we would enter that field, and bought a combustion engineering company who specialised in this type of pump providing fuel oil at high pressure through a nozzle. The pumps were gear type and it was possible to get rid of pulses in the oil spray by passing through a ballast tank. This, I was told, was not desirable and the other way would be to increase the number of teeth. I had another suggestion - with my electronic background I had bought a Strobotac which was a light source able to be switched on and off at pre-set speeds; illuminating the spray from the nozzle from this source it would be possible to see the pulse quite stationary. These pumps ran at a constant speed and because of that I could use the electronic analogy by feeding the nozzle from the pump with a by-pass pipe which would be out of phase by 180° so that when there was a gap in the spray it would be filled by the pulse, which was delayed by that amount. The engineers at Hamworthy had never seen this device used and my reputation was certainly improving!

The company was very much a family concern. There were a large number of apprentices, all of whom had to pay for their training. In one or two cases we had three generations - grandfather, father and son - all working in various areas of the company. The main lines of the company, when I joined, were gear pumps, centrifugal pumps (mainly for marine purposes), and compressors. These covered a big range from small units suitable for garage purposes to large 3-stage compressors for the Admiralty. These last units were used to supply compressed air to the air-driven torpedoes and were highly complex machines as the final pressure was 1500 lbs. per square inch, approximately 100 atmospheres.

Apart from the Foundry there were three main areas at the Quay - the Machine Shop, the Fitting and Assembly Shop and the Test Area. Anyone looking today would find no evidence of these buildings ever having been there. The present Hamworthy Engineering site at Fleets Bridge was not yet in existence.

During one of Ingram Spencer's absences I had discussions with the Foreman in the Fitting and Assembly Area and we decided it would be much more convenient to change the Fitting and Assembly and Test areas over, which gave a smoother flow and better facilities. This was welcomed by the employees and one Sunday we did the complete change. After this the two areas ran for two to three weeks extremely efficiently. When Ingram Spencer returned he was astounded that I should have made such a change without reference to him first of all, but I pointed out that as Production Director I should do everything to get a smoother production with the facilities and area which we had. He would not give in, so I had to get the two organisations together and tell them that the plan we had carefully carried out to improve production was not approved by the owner, and we had to return it back to what it was! This was my first major altercation.

With the acquisition of the combustion heating company and their Chief

Engineer and Managing Director, there was a gradual expansion in that part of the business, knowing full well that when the war was over central heating by oil would become more prevalent in the United Kingdom.

The war in Europe finished in May 1945 and the old urge came back to me to emigrate to the United States. With the defeat of Churchill in the General Election and a Labour Government firmly installed, that urge got much stronger. The policy of the new Government was to nationalise industry where possible, and one of the main items was iron and steel Foundries. As we had almost completed the building of our new Foundry at that time this, to me, was a blow, as we would find ourselves back again in the hands of a Civil Service not of the type we had during the war but one where the appointment of a Minister would be made to look after that branch of engineering, without the expertise or the experience to control a business of that sort.

I decided to talk to Ingram Spencer about it. I had the feeling that as the war was over Ingram Spencer would like to come back and run the company completely himself, so we mutually agreed that I could leave Hamworthy Engineering but retain a consultancy for six months at a consulting fee. I resigned finally on the 31st May 1945, transferred my shares back to the company, and received the magnificent sum of £200 as compensation for loss of office! I did not know at the time that Ingram Spencer was negotiating the sale of the company, and having sold back my shareholding, representing almost one third of the company's share issue, Hamworthy Engineering was, some time later, sold to Powell Duffryn for a considerable sum of money!

CHAPTER 8

EMIGRATION TO AMERICA

In view of the six months consultancy agreement with Hamworthy Engineering, Sylvia and I agreed that it would be a good idea to finally emigrate to the United States, and the first move was to obtain entry permits.

There was a long delay of some months before we could visit the US Embassy and in the meantime a large garage in Canford Cliffs near Poole, which was occupied by the American Forces during the war, became vacant. It had two petrol pumps on Haven Road and a fair-sized workshop at the back. The owners also had the whole corner site of Ravine Road and Haven Road, a wooded area. I thought that if, for some reason, the emigration to the USA was delayed, my interest in cars was such that I could run the garage as a stop-gap.

In conjunction with my solicitor, Harry Kirk who, incidentally, was Town Clerk of Wareham, we arranged to buy the garage and the site for £5,000 with a £500 deposit. Before I had time to really investigate the modifications necessary to bring the garage back to its former glory, Harry Kirk said he had an offer of £6,000 for the garage, would I take £1,000 profit? Naturally I did - £1,000 was a lot of money at that time, for which I did not have to work!

Early in 1946 we managed to get the appointment at the US Embassy and we went through the strict emigration procedure - full medical examinations for Sylvia, myself and Jacqueline (who was only four years old), background history of parentage, profession and so on. This required two separate visits to London and we finished up with all the necessary documents, British passports endorsed etc. We decided the best thing to do was to give up the house in Elms Avenue, Lilliput, put the furniture into store and move into a guesthouse in Bournemouth. In the meantime we employed a very nice Irish girl, Mary, who wanted to go to America, and she moved with us to the guesthouse, complete with Rex, the golden retriever.

However it was not to be so easy.

It was necessary to sort out all the papers which we did not require and I had two large tea chests, one contained all the necessary documents and other vital information, particularly a lot of Scophony information which I felt could be useful. I was in considerable correspondence with Herbie Barton of RCA, who was now back in America living in White Plains, New York, and he said there were considerable opportunities over there. I also corresponded with Arthur Levy of the Scophony Company who was persuading me as well to come over as soon as possible to carry on with the Scophony system where it ceased in 1939. In the meantime the equipment had been shipped over. It was that sort of security which decided us to make the move.

The garden at Elms Avenue went right down to the shore of the Blue Lagoon, part of Poole Harbour, and I took the tea-chest full of all the unnecessary documents down the garden and put a match to it. It burnt furiously for a bit and then for some reason I had to check the passports and US documents and the terrible thing was that I burnt the wrong box! We got the fire out as soon as possible and rescued anything we could but had to apply to the US Embassy all over again! We took the charred fragments of the documents and anything else we could save from the tea chest and when we arrived at the Embassy we were greeted with "Oh, you are the people who burnt up all the documents!". They were marvellous and repeated all the necessary documents including a second medical for all of us; they probably thought it was necessary! I did not realise how lucky we were really because the box had not burnt right through and the majority of the Scophony information was intact, which has been so necessary in later years when attempts to resuscitate the system in England appear to be possible.

We applied for transportation to Cunard to book the passage on any vessel that had accommodation. We were given two days notice that the 'Aquitania' was sailing from Southampton and we had to hurriedly pack and get to Southampton, only to find that the vessel was still fitted out as a troop carrier and the two sexes were in different parts of the ship! By this time Sylvia was five months pregnant and we sincerely hoped that no-one would notice.

We sailed on October 26th 1946 and arrived in New York City on November 2nd. Meanwhile Rex was sent to my sister Freda at Old Windsor and Mary temporarily returned home until we could send for them. The incredible thing about the 'Aquitania' was the very large Dining Room, somewhat like a warehouse, where we had our first lunch. We had white bread, real meat, real butter, real everything, and here we were still in the Dock at Southampton - all the food problems of the war changed immediately.

I was in a cabin with bunks, presumably a first-class cabin at one time, in company with a number of Russians who were on their way to America to take part in a United Nations meeting in San Francisco. Not one of them said a word to each other or to me, and this went on for seven days! We took it in turns to use the bathroom facilities and it was good to see Sylvia and Jacqueline at the various mealtimes and for walks about the decks.

We arrived at Pier 90 in New York City and what a wonderful sight it was to see that New York skyline which I so well remembered from my visit in 1929. It is an incredible experience which one does not get by flying. Herbie and Mary Barton met us at the boat and booked us in at the Piccadilly Hotel on 42nd Street just off Broadway. It was fairly expensive but we did get approval to take £5,000 out with us, which we thought would last a good year if we were careful. The cost of food and hotels was quite low but we had to find something more permanent. We decided that we would use the British method of going to a main estate agent and we picked out the biggest in New York City according to the Yellow Pages. We found they were so big they were only interested in people who would buy a 40-storey skyscraper or an hotel, and when we said we wanted furnished accommodation in the White Plains area they considered the request quite incredible but, nevertheless, being American, they said "There is nothing we could do, but you should go to the agents in White Plains which is just a train ride, and this is the man you should see". I suppose that nobody had ever gone to that company asking for a furnished rental!

We duly took the train next morning to White Plains. What we did not know is that you had to go to Grand Central Terminal and take New York Central Railroad. We asked at the hotel how to get to White Plains and they said "You go on the subway". Well, the subway took us to White Plains Road, which I believe was in the Bronx, so we came all the way back and found out exactly how to go next day! In the meantime, of course, we spent time walking up and down Broadway, having our meals in various restaurants and, of course, seeing all the lights and all the advertising; the colossal waste of food in all the garbage cans outside the restaurants was unbelievable in that it could happen only a few thousand miles away from the complete scarcity in Europe.

We used to walk a lot during the day and on 45th Street there was in the window of a shop a gold-plated dinner service which looked magnificent. It had 96 pieces, including teacups, soup bowls, large dishes etc., and we went in and bought it for $500, about £100. Sylvia was by now seven months pregnant and the baby was expected either at the end of January or early February. Any onlooker would have observed the complete lack of planning in our emigration - a pregnant wife, a small child of four, temporary accommodation in a strange country, a gold-plated dinner service and no job!

We finally reached the real White Plains in Westchester County and found the agent recommended, who had a very nice house for rent in Rutgers Place, Hartsdale (the high part of White Plains) which was a winter rental expiring in April. The house belonged to a golf pro who went south to Florida during the New York winter.

We moved in on November 2nd and as the East Coast had had a very long hot summer the grass on the lawns was generally brown, but the most interesting thing was, of course, that delicious wild strawberries were growing in the garden - so different from our English Novembers which always seemed to produce, in those days, pea-soup fogs. Immediately we moved in the next-door neighbours came over and welcomed us and of course, being English, one starts off with a great advantage, most Americans like the English!

Arthur Levy knew of my arrival but with getting the family settled I had no chance of calling him to find a position in the Scophony Company. However, after settling in I called him and took the train to New York City and had a talk with him. He said there were problems as the company was involved with possible violations of the Sherman Anti-Trust Act. This was an Act to avoid monopolies and it affected a number of companies, the most apparent being Kodak because when one bought a colour film the processing was included in the purchase price and therefore you had to send it back to Kodak. Because of this Act they could not continue to include the processing and you were free to have the film processed anywhere, for which you paid. The Dupont Company, who had a major stake in General Motors, had to give up their involvement and General Motors became a separate corporation.

With regard to Scophony, Arthur Levy had got Paramount Pictures Inc., Television Productions Inc. and General Precision Equipment Corporation interested, and the Supreme Court ruled that Scophony Limited be subject to the Government's Anti-Trust suit alleging monopolistic control of television patents, although it had been declared by a Lower Court to be out of the jurisdiction of the Government's action. A full and interesting history of the Scophony company has been published by the Royal Television Society, written by Tom Singleton, former Editor of the RTS Journal, entitled 'The Story of Scophony' to which I contributed most of the technical information from my comprehensive files. Tom wrote a note to me saying that the book would never have been written without my considerable help.

The problems with Scophony were a big blow to me; Arthur Levy told me that the equipment which had been shipped from England was being stored in the factory of Freed Eismann in New York City and Arthur Freed, the President, was considering entering television production but Levy felt that he could overcome some of the problems and get Scophony going in the U.S.A. It was essential, therefore, for me to get a job. We thought the £5,000 that we had would keep us going for a good year or two - how wrong we were!

I saw an advertisement in a trade magazine and also in the New York Times from a company in Lindenhurst, Long Island, who were expanding and wanting engineers with a knowledge of radar. The salary being offered was $7,500 a year, which was about £2,000 at that time. I wrote to the company, The Servo Corporation of America, with a brief background on my experience, and as a result, after an interview, I was appointed.

Before I took up the appointment with Servo it was absolutely essential to get a car in order to take the New York driving test. I bought a 1941 Studebaker and applied to take the test. I joined a number of immigrants and we had to read a paragraph from the Declaration of Independence and go through a sight test and colour test before the driving test.

The day of the test it snowed the night before fairly heavily, nevertheless I waited at the test area and saw a man walking down in the snow towards me; he looked at me and said "You do not have snow tyres, you're not equipped, therefore I have just walked back from the last test drive and I am not doing any more walking". He went on "We are going to start by going up this hill, you are going to do a 'U' turn at the top and come down the hill and be able to stop". He continued "If you do not do that I will fail you and you won't have another test for a year". Well, of course, having driven in all sorts of mud in our various trials which we enthusiastically undertook in England, I thought there would be no reason why I could not get the Studebaker up the hill, do a 'U' turn, go down the hill, and stop when he said so. He waited for me to walk away but I did not. I let as much air as possible out of the back tyres and he said "That won't make any difference, we tried that". However it did make a difference and we went up the hill. He said "I want you to make a 'U' turn now"; unfortunately it was on the steepest part of the hill but there was no possibility of driving forward, having stopped, so the obvious way was to reverse, apply brakes suddenly, swing the front wheels over so they slid sideways, and the car then faced downwards. We got down the hill, he said "Stop!" and I stopped by driving into the soft snow at

the side of the road. He then said "What's the fishing like in England nowadays?".
I knew I had passed the test!

Henry Blackstone, President of the Servo Corporation, was a good engineer but my very wide experience in all aspects of radar allowed me to almost choose a project. They had a contract to produce a radar simulator for training purposes to simulate exactly the new height-finding radar where a 45° angle radar scanner in conjunction with the normal horizontal scanner would give height by interpolating where the two scans coincide on an echo. The specification was as follows:-

'The equipment to be developed is an improved height indicator and computer, which will provide a height indication in feet of selected targets on an oscilloscope.

The height indicator and computer to be housed in a console similar to that employed for the PPI Indicator of the AN/CPS-6B and to be operable with either the AN/CPS6 or AN/CPS-6B.

The indicator to show height up to 50,000 ft. and from 50,000 to 100,000 ft. with a relative error not greater than 250 ft. plus 2 ft. for each mile of slant range, and an absolute error not greater than 500 ft. plus 4 ft. for each mile of slant range. Small targets will be discriminated when separated 0.2 miles in slant range or 1 degree in azimuth. This accuracy and discrimination was subject to information of this accuracy being present in the Radar's video.

The indicator and computer will have to indicate the elevation of a target which will be manually selected by setting electronically generated crosshairs at the range and azimuth of the target on a PPI console of radar set AN/CPS-6.'

It was a combination of mechanical and electronic components. I was given two engineers to work with me, one a very practical engineer/draughtsman called Van Pala and Carl Sommers. The mechanical side could have been very complex and expensive but it was possible to buy a number of surplus equipments at that time, and one of them was a range-finding equipment for gun-laying used by the army. By suitable changes of the gearbox train a device fell into place very quickly, which had been expected to be the most difficult and costly, leaving only the electronics which were basically straightforward. It was, of course, essential to take into account the curvature of the earth and for this solution I wound a resistor on a former following the earth's curvature so that this signal could be applied in the display and compensate.

The U.S. Signal Corps were very impressed with the simulator and the speed with which it was designed into a working model. There were other projects in which I became interested, and one was a device to radar-scan the ground from an aircraft, using a rotating dish. This was mounted at an offset angle and, I believe, could be arranged to look down or forward to pick up other aircraft. The problem with the dish was the fact of the wind noise and loading and the necessity to compensate for vibration. I overcame this by arranging for the dish to be inside a cylinder; this gave automatic balance, and a patent was applied for in my name and that of the company.

The journey from our house in White Plains to Lindenhurst was a total of 67 miles and by that time I had purchased a Straight 8 Buick Roadmaster which did the journey very comfortably in one and a quarter hours without exceeding any speed limits. The driving in America (at that time anyhow) was without stress; no lunatics cutting you up on corners, nobody going at excess speed and when a slight mist appeared you were forced to drive behind a jeep with a large sign saying 'Follow me - Fog'. This, to me, was incredible because we had been used to driving in thick pea-soup fogs in London when, very often, the radiator mascot disappeared in the fog and the advantage of the Lagonda in those days was that you could fold the windscreen down flat, which improved visibility and at night, by mounting foglights with cadmium glass under the bumper so that the lights were only approximately 12 ins. above the ground, it gave a very good visibility of kerbs and general obstructions.

I used to enjoy the journey driving from White Plains into Long Island every day along the Vanderbilt Highway and could see the various seasons which, in America, seemed to be more accurate than those in England. Spring seemed to start at the end of February, Autumn certainly started at the end of September and we always had some sort of snow at Christmastime.

At Christmas the Americans, of course, just have the one day as a Public Holiday, not Boxing Day. I remember driving the Buick to Long Island on the morning of the 26th December 1947 with a few snowflakes falling, but the weather forecast was rain. During the morning at work the snow fell straight down with no wind, which normally is a sign of a heavy fall. It went on all morning until late afternoon, when I thought it right that I should leave and get home before it got too thick.

The Buick had the knobbly tyres fitted to the rear wheels, which was the normal thing the Americans did in the East, and I was happily motoring along the Vanderbilt Highway towards the built-up area of Queens. The snow was really deep and only by keeping going could I get traction. A bridge over the road had four arches, two for traffic in one direction and two for the reverse direction. I decided to pick out the second arch on the left-hand side where obviously there would be less snow. I managed to get up a really good speed of about 40 m.p.h. and entered this archway but came to a sudden stop, completely enveloped in heavy snow. I managed to back out but, for the first time in my life (that is, my motoring life) it was not possible to go forward or backwards after the initial movement. I got out of the car, walked through the heavy snow (by this time about 12-15 ins.), and found a garage down the side of the road where they had a tractor with which we towed the Buick onto their forecourt as such, and I had to find my own way home from there.

The Long Island railroad, realising the snow, had put on a steam locomotive and after a wait of about one hour this train came along going into New York City. It took approximately two hours to do a journey of not more than seven or eight miles. At New York I walked to Grand Central Terminal in heavy snow; the snowploughs had not yet started clearing because of the rain forecast. I managed to get a train to White Plains at about 2.00 a.m. and arrived home, including the walk from the station to the house, at 5.00 a.m. If only the Americans had kept Boxing Day I would have been saved that journey!

The snow carried on until we had 24 ins. and New York City was raving mad at the forecasters, deciding from then on to use a private organisation who guaranteed their forecasts would be accurate. Incidentally, when I got home the law says that every householder must clear the section of the sidewalk along his property because if it was not clear the householder would be responsible for any accident by any person slipping or having a problem in travelling along the sidewalk so I had to clear our section! Clearing 24 ins. of snow is no easy job, however despite that I took the train the day after and picked up the Buick, went to work and by that time the snow had been rolled flat in most places and in others it had been ploughed, but it was one of the worst snowfalls that New York City and that area had ever had, so I did not feel too bad about being unable to complete my journey.

There were occasional conversations with Arthur Levy who said he was still battling with lawyers and that Arthur Freed's partner, Eisemann, had left him so the company was therefore called Freed Radio Corporation rather than the well-known name of Freed-Eisemann. Freed's company had a very good reputation for high quality audio with designer cabinet reproductions of Sheraton etc. Arthur Levy told me he was interested in going into television utilising the cathode ray tube and Arthur Freed would be contacting me in the near future.

The call came within a few days and I met Arthur Freed in his factory which was on the fourth floor in a large multi-storey factory building in Hudson Street, downtown New York. Each floor had an area of approximately one acre and the elevators were capable of taking a truck to each floor. On the floor above us was a company called Bulova who had developed a watch utilising a tuning fork as a control frequency - nobody thought at that time whether you could get a quartz crystal in a tiny wrist-watch, which is now so prevalent today.

Arthur Freed offered me the job of Head of Research and Development in the company at a salary of $15,000 rising to $20,000. I had been with Servo a full year and in that time I had a very efficient secretary called Elizabeth Swain, so one of the conditions of joining Freed Radio was to have a personal secretary, and Liz agreed to come to New York and work for me although she lived at Babylon on Long Island.

I had a word with Henry Blackstone, President of Servo, and told him of the offer. He did not like to lose me because I was an unusual person in the field in which they specialised, but on the other hand I was also specialised in television. He wrote me a delightful letter when I left.

On February 2nd 1947 Suzanne Jane was born at the St Agnes Hospital in White Plains. Our next-door neighbours were always very interested in us and Eddie, the husband, asked us to let him know precisely when the pains started because he had always wanted to drive his car through all the red lights of the city to take Sylvia to hospital! The pains started late one evening so we telephoned him; he brought his car round immediately and drove all the way to the hospital but every light went green, to his great disappointment!

I should mention here an important factor - that in checking the blood types of Sylvia and myself before Suzanne was born it was discovered that whereas I was Positive, Sylvia had the rare blood type Rhesus Negative, so the possibility of a blue baby was then fully expected and as a result Sylvia was very heavily handled to get the baby out before a natural birth in case there had to be a complete blood transfusion. Fortunately the baby was a healthy normal child but the effect on Sylvia was to last a long time necessitating, some time later, a hysterectomy at the young age of only 32.

As soon as we got the house at Rutgers Place we contacted Mary, our help from England, and she booked a passage on a Swedish vessel. I picked up Mary from Pier 90 in New York City; she was very excited to see New York City as we drove along the Bronx River parkway to White Plains.

We also sent for Rex, our golden retriever, who had been living with my sister Freda in Old Windsor and he came over later on the 'Queen Mary'. When I knew of the arrival of this ship I went by train to fetch Rex. A law in New York City was that every dog must wear a muzzle and the immigration people gave you a muzzle, provided you pay for it, which I did. However as Rex had never worn a muzzle in his life he did not like it, so every few minutes I found this thing hanging at the side of his face and had to put it on! No taxi would take us, they would not have a dog, so we walked to Grand Central Terminal and there he had to go into the guard's wagon, muzzled, and I sat with him. Fortunately the guard was a dog-lover and a golden retriever likes people, so after a bit he was helping the guard eat the odd sandwich! I do not know how he could eat the sandwiches because during the five days journey on the 'Queen Mary' the Chief Butcher was responsible for the dogs and he liked Rex, so Rex must have been eating the finest steak for five days and I think the butcher was rather loathe to part with him!

By the time Rex arrived our rental at Rutgers Place was over and it was almost impossible to find anything, the only place we could find was a house shared with a family in Tuckahoe, which was south of White Plains. It was not a good arrangement because we had to share a kitchen with a couple who fried everything in a frying pan! It was essential to get Jacqueline into some form of school so she went to Public School No. 8. There was a so-called small garden attached to the house and we were there with Jacqueline one day when some other children came into the garden. She went up to them and said something like "Ger out o owr ya", so we asked her what she said. She replied "Well, that is American, I said "Get out of our garden". What she really said was "Get out of our yard"! It was impossible to stay in this house for long and a house in Church Street, White Plains, became available so we moved into 106 Church Street. This house was of wooden construction, typical of some of the American buildings in the east, because wood with cedar clapboard tiles on the outside made the house very warm in the winter and relatively cool in the summer. It was very near the shops, in fact it was necessary only to cross the road to go to a choice of two or three supermarkets.

My interest in cars was still very much alive and a short distance down a main avenue, not more than a quarter of a mile from the house, was a used car lot owned by a man called Paul Jernigan. He dealt in better quality cars and had an amazing ability to know a real buyer from just a 'looker'. I would very often go to him on a Sunday morning and was quite surprised at the very high quality of engineering and design of American cars; most of them in those days were of the pre-war designs based on 1941 models. It was amazing how little he knew of European cars and how little we in England knew about American cars - they were always known as 'gas guzzlers' with very soft suspension. It was he who took my Studebaker in part-exchange for the Buick Roadmaster and the hire purchase agreement had a very low interest rate of 2 or 3%.

On joining Freed, with a relatively high salary and a future, the time was ripe for us to buy a house rather than pay the usual rentals. It would also allow us to bring our furniture over which was in store in England. We found an ideal property in Hartsdale, a residential suburb of White Plains which, incidentally, is the administration centre of Westchester County.

It was a house typical of the area, constructed from clapboard with cedar tiles on walls and roof, with four bedrooms, three bathrooms and a shower. There was a very large two car garage integral with the house. It overlooked a permanent playing field and an additional building plot adjacent to the house gave a relatively large garden of one third of an acre. We bought the house from a Mrs Walters for $23,000. What is interesting in America is that there is no great delay while a search goes on for the title deeds; an organisation called The Guarantee Title Corporation takes responsibility, for which you pay a reasonable premium, and that guarantees the title to the property. Central heating was by gas and all services were in a very large basement with no outside plumbing, everything was routed through the centre of the house. One very useful gadget was a linen shute which came from the first floor straight into the basement where the laundry equipment was situated. Around this time we acquired a kitten which got on very well with Rex.

I joined Freed in September 1948 and his Publicity Department sent an announcement to most of the Press which read:-

'Joshua Sieger has been appointed director of research and development of Freed Radio Corp., manufacturers of Freed-Eisemann radio and television receivers, it was announced by Arthur Freed, president. Mr Sieger was formerly engineering chief of Great Britain's wartime radar program.'

Dr Alfred Goldsmith was President of the Institute of Radio Engineers in America and when the article appeared in the August 1939 issue of 'The Proceedings of the IRE' on the design and development of television receivers using the Scophony optical scanning system I got to know him very well by correspondence. He wrote:-

'It was pleasant to learn from your September 15th letter that you have now accepted a responsible post with the Freed Radio Corporation. I hope and believe that you will do well and that your career with this organization will be a thoroughly successful one.

One of the former members of that firm - Joseph Freed, now deceased - was a student of mine in radio engineering many years ago. He was a delightful and effective person who passed from us in most untimely fashion.

I agree that you should re-join the Institute of Radio Engineers and will be happy indeed to act as one of your references. And I hope also that you and I will soon find an occasion to lunch together. It will be pleasant to exchange views with you on that occasion.'

The general idea was to get involved in setting-up a research division independently from the radio and television manufacturing side. The Wright-Patterson Air Force Base at Dayton, Ohio, were interested in two projects:-

1. A display device for plan position indication (PPI) to give a full colour picture.

2. To use the dark trace tube (Skiatron) in conjunction with an image amplifier so that aircraft flying two or three times the speed of sound would be piloted by one who would have a picture in front of him from a camera in the nose of the plane.

Mrs Swain (Liz) joined me soon after I had started with Freed so that I could prepare the technical proposals which the Air Force needed. The first project would be based on the ultrasonic cell. A lot of technical publicity has been written on the cell and as recently as 1988 it is referred to as the Scophony spatial light column. The cell works on the principle of a crystal at the end of a liquid column, the crystal having a frequency suitable for the definition required and observation of the waves in the column to be seen by means of the Schlieren dark field optics. The column of waves in the cell acted as a diffraction grating with the usual appearance of fringes parting either side of the slot or bar. In the Scophony television system we maximised the sizes of the bar and slot to get the most number of fringes, and therefore more light. It was noted, however, that if the slot and bar were narrowed down to the space between two waves in the column of the crystal and therefore the spacing of the waves, colour fringes would occur, and this could be used for generating colour in the projected image purely by changing the frequency. I therefore proposed to the US Signal Corps that we could arrange the cell to be amplitude modulated for contrast and frequency modulated for colour. I managed to get Carl Sommers to join me at Freed so that work could start on repeating some of the pre-war experiments to show the Air Force scientists the viability of the system.

The announcement in the Press brought a response from Adolph Rosenthal, who was living in New York City. I was delighted to hear from him as he was the missing link in the second project and who could be better than the man who was responsible for the original invention. I did not know at that time, despite my association with TRE, that the Admiralty research were using the Skiatron tubes for projection ppi, these tubes being manufactured by a company called Cinema Television, and offshoot of the old Baird Company. Talking recently to the Works Manager, who now lives in Swanage, Dorset, he remembers making 18,000 of these tubes and he told me that he could still make one, given the right facilities.

It was essential to build up the strength of the research division and I advertised for a physicist with a wide knowledge of optics and a wide background in general physics. I found one who had a Ph.D from Massachusetts Institute of Technology (MIT) and also a Ph.D from Princeton University. He started work before I managed to get Rosenthal and I found his knowledge was book knowledge, no imagination, and he fell asleep most afternoons. I have come across this many times, particularly at TRE, where our brilliant entrepreneurs had low academic degrees but a wide knowledge and real imagination. The polytechnic is often the best place to find someone to work in a field which covered such a wide range of sciences, whereas the high academic type specialises in a narrow field. I hired two students from Stevens Tech. and found the right sort with imagination, drive and enthusiasm. Rosenthal joined in 1949 and in March 1950 I was elected Vice President of Freed Radio Corp. I received a confirming letter from Arthur Freed dated March 2nd 1950 and from the National Advertising Department of The New York Times I received a congratulatory letter dated March 7th 1950. I received many other letters, including one from Manufacturers Trust Bank.

With the research laboratory well set up, including vacuum and glass blowing equipment, and all essential apparatus necessary to manufacture the Skiatron tube and the precision machining facility to make the light cells, the contract with the Air Force was approximately half a million dollars and I did the complete costing and calculated overheads, making great friends with the two project engineers in the Air Force which formed a very co-operative team. The company was manufacturing high quality radiograms, special FM receivers for schools where school programmes were transmitted by some of the local stations and the sound from advertising announcements was automatically silenced by a signal that came from the transmitter which operated a relay in the receiver.

Freed started manufacturing some 12 ins. cathode ray television sets which were based on an RCA design and of mediocre quality. At that time RCA announced an entirely new cathode ray tube which was 16 ins. in diameter in a special metal construction of which only the viewing area and the phosphor were in glass. Arthur Freed asked me to look into the design of this unit and I found it was possible to get a very bright contrasting picture by having a higher voltage on the tube and other minor changes to the I.F. circuit than those specified by RCA.

It was so quick to make design changes in America at that time and if we wanted a new chassis we telephoned a company called Minute Man, took the thumbnail sketches to them, went away and the next day came a chassis all perforated with the holes in the right place. We re-designed the deflection yoke to give accurate focusing across the tube and the first demonstration of the unit was a considerable advance on anything being made at that time. Freed had a demonstration at the Ritz Carlton Hotel with a number of these 16 ins. T/V sets in the usual very high quality cabinets in which Arthur Freed specialised. It was difficult to get a good picture in New York City because the various transmitters came from different buildings and the ghost effect was unbelievable. We had to put a directional aerial on the roof of the skyscraper to look at one transmitter, another directional aerial for the second transmitter and so on, and feed them down separately to the demonstration floor. This all changed of course in later years when all transmissions came from the Empire State Building.

Just before the war Sagall managed to recruit for a short period a Dr Peter Goldmark who worked in television in Germany. As I remember he contributed very little to anything going on as we were well advanced in high quality, high definition pictures. He left to go to the United States, like so many others, at the start of the war and subsequently joined the Columbia Broadcasting System. The 33 rpm record was pioneered by CBS and Goldmark was given the reputation of devising them, although in the early thirties a British company called Broadcast Records were making 12 ins. 33 rpm records which were freely obtainable; I had a number of them which were of excellent quality.

There were discussions going on world-wide on television standards and the

US Government, through the Federal Communications Commission (FCC), organised a National Television Systems Committee (NTSC). Their programme was basically to look into the world television standards to get some form of agreement but, more importantly, to look at the present state of the colour television art. I was invited by Frank Bingley, Chief Engineer of WOR the New York Station and Chairman of one of the investigating committees, to be a member of this Colour Television Committee.

An international conference on standards was held in Zurich, Switzerland, in July 1949 and as a member of the NTSC I was kept informed of the negotiations of this meeting. As usual, each national government had its own ideas. America, which had gone from 441 lines (the pre-war standard) to 525 30 frames, tried to introduce this standard throughout the world. The reason for the 30 frames in America was because of their 60 Hz electrical power, whereas the majority of Europe and many other countries had 50Hz. They proposed, therefore, that whereas they would stay with the 525 lines, Europe could go onto 625 25 frames. These two standards are almost identical in that minor modifications to the line frequency would be required in the receiver to pick up either.

There was considerable disagreement; Great Britain and France were happy to stay with the 405 lines 25 frames for the band 41 to 68 mHz. France wanted 819 lines 25 frames for higher bands and higher definition and all other nations wanted the 625 lines 25 frames. With the sound channels seven nations voted for frequency modulation and two nations - Great Britain and France - for amplitude modulation. Britain maintained that the 405 line system provided a very satisfactory quality of service and they pointed out that in accordance with the recommendation of Lord Hankey's Committee in 1945, the British Government was committed to continue service on these standards domestically for a number of years. That, in my opinion, was one of the bad decisions because many years later, when the independent channels started, it was essential to go to higher frequencies and therefore the 625 line picture became standard.

We had a number of committee meetings in Washington and visited most of the laboratories, and because of the talk of colour television the sales of monochrome sets were getting basically low. The US Government asked the FCC to decide on a colour television system as soon as possible and make their recommendations. Almost out of the blue we saw an announcement that they had decided that the Columbia system of colour television proposed by Dr Peter Goldmark would be the standard. This created an uproar and I was interviewed by the Press because I had stated that the Columbia system used a standard cathode ray tube with a colour disc rotating in front of the tube, giving the red, blue and green colours. I pointed out that this method of colour television was very well known and had been tried many times before, in fact I remember seeing colour on a low definition picture at Bell Laboratories in 1929, using a colour disc. We had played with it at Scophony and it was not the way to do it. It would have been easier with our mechanical optical system but even so it would have been better to use three light cells rather than an optical disc to break up the colours. My statements were repeated and I have pages and pages of press cuttings about this British engineer and what he said! The picture quality, naturally on a 12 ins. tube, was quite good and it could be stated to be compatible but nobody realised as much as I did that the small picture would have to give way to much larger pictures in the home.

Dr Dumont of Dumont Television, who were manufacturers of cathode ray oscilloscopes and had an experimental station in New York, devised a test for the FCC to see a large screen 30 ins. colour television picture based on the Columbia system. He produced a 30 ins cathode ray tube, a major feat in glass-blowing, and in front of that was an 8 ft. diameter disc with the three colour transparencies. The FCC were invited to come and sit down to view the picture. Immediately the disc started spinning and a colour picture appeared for some few seconds, the lights in the whole building went out as he was using a 5 h.p. motor to drive the disc and that had to get to a synchronous speed which took some minutes. After two or three attempts with the main circuit breakers in the building going off (which, incidentally was pre-arranged by Dr Dumont) the FCC had to reverse their decision and the whole industry heaved a sigh of relief!

In the meantime of course, RCA had developed the shadow mask tube, an amazing perception considering the obvious difficulty of manufacturing such a device to such close tolerances. We saw a number of demonstrations with RCA and at Haseltine Laboratories and Dumont Television where three projection tubes with colour filters gave reasonable pictures but obviously quite unsuitable for the home at that time. RCA of course had gone very thoroughly into the whole of the system from the transmitter frequencies right through to line standards and commercial equipment, they were capable of doing the whole job from beginning to end and I still have an original copy of their proposal to the FCC dated June 25th 1953 which consists of nearly 700 pages. They pointed out in their petition that at that time there were 24 million black and white receivers already in the hands of the American public, and the shadow mask system would allow a completely compatible television set capable of receiving either monochrome or colour without any changes whatsoever. They stated that it satisfied all the criteria for a colour television system specified by the commission. They were prepared, if the commission approved their proposed colour system, to expedite production of colour receivers, tri-colour tubes, broadcast studio equipment etc. to manufacturers and broadcasters. The National Broadcast Company which is part of RCA would commence broadcasting compatible colour television programmes immediately and would offer to commercial sponsors and affiliated stations throughout the USA.

As a result of this incredible document and the strength of engineering behind the whole proposal, the FCC had to reverse their decision in favour of RCA and CBS had to be a licensee.

The considerable publicity given to colour television, which appeared to be round the corner, seriously affected the sales of monochrome receivers. Arthur Freed was most concerned and a considerable number of employees in the factory were laid off as orders were insufficient to set the production line going on black and white. Fortunately the Signal Corps contract was moving quite well and progress payments were made. A certain number of purchase orders on the components were sent to companies for the contract, when I was staggered to find that previous invoices had not been met and they were unwilling to supply.

At this time Sylvia was in an extremely depressed state and required many visits to have electric shock treatment which, if anything, left her much worse. Mary had left us to get married, living in New York State, and Sylvia found difficulty in handling the children. I had a request from the Signal Corps at Dayton, Ohio, to give a lecture in a university on the Scophony system of television. I prepared a number of slides based on the considerable information I had retained, and as the lecture was in the evening it was essential for me to stay at an hotel overnight and return the following morning. On my return Sylvia had managed to get a help to come to the house and stay with the children and I came home to find she was not there but staying with very close friends of ours in Scarsdale. I found her in bed and in a state of not wanting to see me or anybody else, a complete breakdown. All she wanted to do was return to England. Fortunately her mother and stepfather came over and took her back on the s.s. 'Coronia' to England.

The day she left for England arrangements had been made with the new help to take care of the children during the day while I was at work and I would deal with them on my return in the evening; at that time Jacqueline was eight years old and Suzanne three. On my return that same day I found the house empty and a note from the help saying that she could not come everyday and therefore the children had been taken to her house and she would look after them. I was very upset and arranged immediately to take the children back to our house, telephoned Mary to see if she could come, and she said "I will be over immediately", which was a great relief.

Mary's husband, Stanley, worked for the New York Central Railroad and he was very accommodating, would come over regularly and actually taught the children to ride the new bicycles which I had purchased for them. He was extremely good at table tennis and we would play in the basement playroom where we had a good table and a lot of frustration disappeared when playing this rather strenuous game!

I was interested, through Paul Jernigan, to exchange my Buick for a Cadillac. He loaned me one for the weekend and I was very impressed and tried to buy one but unfortunately they were in short supply and there was a waiting list of some many months.

However, when the announcement in the New York Times of March 1950 appeared, on my election as Vice-President of Freed Radio, a call came from the Cadillac Company stating that the car in which I was interested was now available!. It was a Model 61, 1949, which had been used by one of the Vice-Presidents of the Cadillac Car Division with about 2,000 miles only on the speedometer, and I bought it for $3,200 - at that time just over £1,000.

It was the first of the 8-cylinder overhead valve engines made by Cadillac with a 331 cu. in. displacement, approximately 5.3 litres. It developed 160 brake h.p. gross, very high torque, and had a standard 4-speed hydromatic transmission which even today, in 1990, is just appearing on some of the popular cars. They quoted in the book a performance of 100 m.p.h. as maximum speed and from 0-60 m.p.h. in 13.4 seconds. It is interesting to note that from that year on few Cadillacs had less than 200 brake h.p. and the engine size had gone up to over 6 litres. As early as 1959 all Cadillac models had h.p. ratings of 325 on standard cars and 345 on the Eldorados; all this was, as you realise, before the emission controls came into being in 1973 and all cars had to meet the government specifications so that h.p. was lost to meet these requirements.

When the Works heard of my car, which was left in the road outside the main factory, they came down in their break periods to look at it and, typical of Americans, there was no envy only the statement made by so many "One day we will get one of these".

The problems with Freed Radio would not go away and finally Arthur was forced to enter into Chapter 11 of the Bankruptcy Act. A friend of ours, Charles Carpenter, was an attorney in New York City and he advised me to leave Freed Radio as soon as I had got a certified cheque for salary, and write to the Signal Corps telling them of my decision. I had been having conversations with the owner of Ansley Radio and Television Corporation at Meriden, Connecticut, and he suggested that it would be extremely helpful if I assisted him re-start his television company which had lain dormant because of the loss of monochrome sales. At the same time my attorney was in conversation with the U.S. Signal Corps in New Jersey who had a problem and wanted to know whether I would be available.

The problem was a very old established company called J.H. Bunnell, a company founded by Jesse Bunnell who was Chief Telegraphist to Abraham Lincoln. He formed a communications company and Western Union Telegraph. The company had a number of military contracts but the President, Mr Dougherty, had died and his wife was acting as President but there were many problems, financial and technical. Would I be available to take over as Chairman and President?

My decision to leave Freed so quickly, an organisation which I built up with a strong staff, was probably a bad decision on my part, influenced by Charles Carpenter's legal advice. Lawyers will always give you the right legal information based on the possibility of litigation so that whereas the decision to leave was legally sensible, morally it was not. Arthur Freed was very disturbed and did not take it at all kindly and Mrs Swain even more so. I pointed out that I left an organisation with someone who could carry on precisely where I had left off - Dr Rosenthal; this was not enough to cool tempers, however the deed was done and I went up to Meriden to Ansley Radio & Television to see the factory and determine whether it was possible to rescue this company which had not got the reputation of Freed and basically was in the same position, with a complete lack of orders for monochrome television sets.

CHAPTER 9

PSYCHICAL RESEARCH

Before writing about my future plans I have to go way back to the 1920's to describe my extra-curricula activities in psychical research; all those with a scientific mind like to investigate the problem of psychic phenomena, of which there is no doubt, and I certainly was one of those. I bought a book by Harry Price, who was the Secretary of the National Psychic Research Society, and in that book he described various phenomena, which were recorded by witnesses. I also studied the work done by Sir Oliver Lodge and Sir Arthur Conan Doyle. Alan Hunter and I visited a number of spiritualistic séances and medium circles, and whereas I was deeply interested he felt the whole lot was phoney - with a journalistic mind he could not see any real facts to prove what he saw and heard.

The chief radiographer at St Thomas's Hospital, Dr Kilner, using the early Crooks X-Ray tube, devised a pair of spectacles where the lenses were covered with a coal-tar derivative Dicyanine. A coal-tar base such as Dicyanine or Anthracene have the ability to convert X-Rays and radio-active radiation to visible light. Dr Kilner was an experimenter and on one occasion he had the Venetian blinds of his laboratory drawn and was setting up his equipment to X-Ray a young patient. The sunlight came through the very small slits in the Venetian blind - through his spectacles he saw an aura around the whole body of the patient and the part where the aura showed very weak was where the particular physical problem was located. He wrote a book called 'The Human Aura' and the Kilner Effect is well-known, but apparently little research has been done to investigate this phenomena all those years ago.

At Scophony, Wikkenhauser seemed interested in some of the things I had done in the past and I arranged to take him along to a medium circle in London at the Spiritualistic Union. The medium in this case was a Londoner, a woman of about 45, very down to earth and, I would say, not particularly well educated. The circle started and voices came through, this woman's voice changing accordingly to those of the various people as she spoke to one or other in the circle. Suddenly she had a message and, believe it or not, it was in Hungarian and she spoke Hungarian to Wikkenhauser who answered back and the voice coming through was his mother! This, to me, was unbelievable, because the woman, even if she was a linguist in the more common languages, would not have known Hungarian which is a language of its own, based on the nomad gipsies who founded the country centuries earlier.

When Jefree joined us at Scophony I found another who had a very deep interest and he was a student of the Rudolf Steiner Institute. His New Zealand wife was an artist and she had painted many watercolours of her guide, whom she had seen on many occasions at various medium circles. Jefree was doing cancer research with the Institute and carried out diagnosis by the blotting paper technique. This consisted of blotting paper wrapped round a glass cylinder, then the end of the cylinder and the blotting paper were immersed in a very thin layer of the subject's blood. Immediately, by capillary action the blood crept up the paper and formed a crystalline structure at the top edge. This was analysed in some way, which I do not remember now, but the type of cancer and its location apparently could be discovered by this technique.

There were a number of long breaks in my study of this field until the early days of the war when, in disposing of Herbert Barton's furniture we found a ouija board. This was a small heart-shaped plate with a point, in the point was a pencil and in the rear end were two ball bearings, while the top of the plate was covered in cork. Sylvia and I put the fingers of our two hands on this plate and immediately got involuntary movement. I decided to make a board with all the letters of the alphabet arranged in a semi-circle plus a "yes" and a "no", with numbers from 0-9. We sat down one evening as there was no television and the radio was mainly news with some entertainment, and immediately got results. We found somebody by the name of Toofman who was a Dutchman, and he explained in some detail that the St Augustine monks discovered the south coast of North America, probably Florida, in the 12th century, two centuries before Columbus.

Toofman was a constant visitor to our house but he was interrupted on many occasions by somebody who said his name was Andrew Young. Andrew Young was a pirate in Poole, he was very concerned about a treasure in a steel box which he had buried in the area in which we lived. We discovered from him, after many evenings, that the grounds containing this so-called treasure were the garden of a house on the high part of the road adjacent to Poole Harbour. We knew the owner of the house very well indeed, a very active 90 year old with a son and a daughter, both in their late 40's, and they agreed to let us come round with our ouija board and get Andrew Young to point out precisely where this treasure was situated. This was done by Sylvia and I on the ouija board, and we had a long steel probe which we put into the ground in various areas until he said "yes". Where it was "yes" we found that about 2 ft. down this probe struck a box. Unfortunately that was too much for our friends and they said it would be unlucky to go any further; as far as we know that box is still there!

I had an idea that if we found another couple who had the same interests as Sylvia and I with the ouija board, we could use Toofman as a guide between to allow us to carry on a conversation. An engineer who worked with me at TRE and later at RPU, was Dr C.L. Peters and he lived in a house in Lilliput not far away. He was quite enthusiastic, but for some reason or other Toofman did not operate his board but all sorts of extraneous information came though which Dr Peters found difficult to interpolate and the experiment failed.

In the meantime we managed to hear of a healing medium in the area who was a car mechanic and he maintained, corroborated by his wife, that he had cured people of TB and various other diseases. A friend of ours in Pearce Avenue, adjacent to where we lived, had TB and the doctors obviously could do nothing. Various tests were taken which showed the TB was very active. We managed to get her to come to a circle we had at the house and be operated upon by this healing medium. He used beside him on a table a bowl of water and a towel and he put his hands on her and when he washed his hands afterwards in the bowl the water turned red. A test taken by the doctors a week later showed that all signs of TB had disappeared. I then had one difficulty in understanding because, stuck in the towel which the medium had used, was a small red gelatine capsule - in other words he had this faith healing ability but had to add a bit of theatrical colour to the scene!.

My investigations brought me in touch with a number of people working in the field and I wonder now how I had the time to do all the things I did. I read all Dr Paul Brunton's books - 'Search into Secret Egypt' and others - which intrigued me in the power of the pyramid, the interesting thing about the pyramid is its dimensions which are based on a sphere, and the diameter of the base of the pyramid from corner to corner is equivalent to the diameter of a sphere, and the height of the apex is the radius.

I had many conversations with a Mr J.J. Williamson of Hastings although no experimental work was done at this time apart from my interest in one of my colleagues at TRE who was working on remote equipment capable of disabling the ignition system of an engine at a reasonable distance. Reeves came to TRE from France, a well-known company called Le Materiel Telephonique, where he was working on centimeter waves. He, with others at TRE, was responsible for the very great advance of centimeter wave radar which was more accurate and more directional than the well-known CH system in the $1^{1/2}$ meter band or 20 mHz.

The more I investigated this immense subject the more I discovered the famous names working in various fields, generally under the heading of 'Radionics and Radiesthesia'. The simple occult investigations which we had done were not rewarding when it came into looking at the work done by very well-known scientists throughout the world. One interesting book was written by Mr J. Cecil Maby on research into dowsing and he was measuring the frequencies when searching for water or metals, to find out why a dowser with a hazel twig or any similar device would accurately determine the flow of water and its position. The French scientist Dr E.A. Maurey wrote papers and lectured on his research on the human electro-magnetic field, and the other was a paper read by Mr Larvaron on the earth and its effect on life.

A number of these papers appeared in 1950 in a publication on 'The Proceedings of the Scientific and Technical Congress of Radionics and Radiesthesia' which was held in London. A lot of publicity at that time was given to a Dr Abrams who invented a device called the Abrams Box where he could diagnose at a distance the cause of illness of people who were prepared to let him have a blood sample. The Electronic Medical Digest, published in the summer of 1950, described in great detail Dr Abrams and his work, with a full technical description of his equipment.

In that journal was a table of electronic disease classification where each of the ten buttons indicated particular medical problems. It is interesting to note that the frequency used was in the 43 mHz band and the difference between each of the ten buttons was approximately from 200 kHz down to 6 kHz. Abrams was not a pseudo-scientist but a highly qualified scientist who took his MD degree in Heidelberg with post-graduate courses in London, Berlin, Paris and Vienna. He was a Fellow of the Royal Microscopic Society and published prolific papers on electro-medical research. This information was published in 'Who's Who' in America.

The most interesting work was done by a chiropractor, Dr Ruth Drown, who produced remarkable pictures with what she called her Radiovision instrument; most of the work here was carried out in California in the 1930's. She maintained that there was a vital fluid-like life force flowing through the entire universe energising itself through all forms and each having a different rate of vibration. She went on to say that this fluid could be found in the blood plasma. She had a means of photographing the blood spot of a patient and incredible photographs were published of patients who had submitted their blood sample and the photographs were taken although the patient, in some cases, was living 6,000 miles away.

I became a member of the British Society of Metaphysicians and the more I investigated the field it became larger and larger and I realised that to investigate further was a lifetime objective.

We arrived in the USA in November 1946 and in April 1947 I received a letter from a Julius Weinberger. He was head of the Industry Services Division of the Radio Corporation of America in the RCA Laboratories in 5th Avenue, New York. The following is a copy of this letter:-

'Some time ago I read an article in one of the New York newspapers concerning research work in the psychic field which was being conducted by Mr J.J. Williamson, at Hastings in Sussex, England. I have been quite interested in this field (personally, that is - it has nothing to do with RCA), so I wrote to Mr Williamson and asked for references to any detailed publications which he might have made. He has replied to my letter, describing a method which he proposes to use for spirit communication, and also saying that you will be in charge of research along similar lines in this country, using a different method which he described as a 'beat frequency' method. He suggested that I communicate with you, relative to the formation of an American section of the 'Society of Metaphysicians'. While I feel, quite frankly, that it is premature to form societies before one has substantial research in progress and results to report, I would like very much to meet you and discuss this subject in a general way.

Would you care to do this, if so, would you call me up some time so we can agree a mutually suitable date and place?'.

We had a most interesting discussion and realised that we had a lot in common in our profession and our outside interests. He suggested that I contact a Mr Harwood White at Santa Barbara in California who was an author and a spare-time tennis coach. The three of us got together, had many interesting discussions and considerable correspondence, copies of which I have retained all these years. A fourth member joined our group, Arthur Young, who was the Chief Designer, I believe, of Bell Aircraft, one of the major manufacturers of helicopters. He devised the counter-rotating fan attached to the tail of a helicopter to counteract the rotary motion of the rotary wing. Before that time the helicopter was based on the work done by Cierva who devised the auto-giro which had a forward propeller and would drive the lifting rotor through a gearbox from the main engine. I was fortunate enough to fly in a Cierva auto-giro and it would fly in a straight line except as soon as you touched down the whole fuselage would rotate while the rotating blades would apparently be stationary. I flew in this aircraft from Hanworth Aerodrome, which is now Heathrow, and it was quite an experience to watch the traffic on the Great West Road some 500 ft. below me.

Our work was becoming known, and as I said previously, it is amazing how many people of scientific backgrounds were investigating all this phenomena and how important it was to get to know them all and find a common denominator.

One interesting individual, Mr Hieronymus, who was Chief Engineer of the Kansas City Power & Light Company, had carried out work on getting photosynthesis in plants in a dark cellar, turning normal plant leaves to normal green in the presence of sunlight. He arranged a copper plate on the roof of his house facing the sun and an insulated wire was brought through the house into the cellar and connected to the plate adjacent to the plant. He maintained, and proved it by practical tests, that the essential constituent of sunlight in the ultra-violet band could be transmitted by wire.

In order to show the type of person interested in this field Hieronymus was a typical example. He was a Fellow of the American Institute of Radio Engineers, Member of the Electro-Chemical Society, Member of the American Association for the Advancement of Science, and he was a registered professional engineer in the State of Missouri.

Beese White, as we called him, co-ordinated the work done by Hieronymus, Julius Weinberger, Arthur Young and myself. Amongst the interesting people we investigated was a Frederick Marion who wrote a book entitled 'In My Mind's Eye'; Fred Marion signed a copy of this book for us in April 1952. He was born in Prague and from an early age found he had an unusual psychic gift. He found that the entertainment side could be important and at the age of eighteen he undertook to test his psychic ability by finding objects somewhere in Prague, not knowing what the objects were or where they had been hidden. He stated that information detailing these objects, prepared by a committee to investigate his powers, was in a sealed envelope which had been handed over to the police headquarters in Prague.

Marion said that he arrived at a cafe and found a fleet of cars waiting outside and a crowd of immense size due to previous publicity. He entered the first car, accompanied by the Chairman of the committee, and the chauffeur was told to follow directions given by Fred Marion, whatever those directions were. He said that after a number of false moves where he found his concentration was missing, it fortunately returned when his conception of the physical situation disappeared and his telepathic intuition came into play. They arrived at a famous florist outside Prague where he left the car, went inside and at the far end of a long counter were several bouquets of flowers. He took out a particular one of these and returned to the car, almost having to fight his way through spectators crowding the pavements. He then told the chauffeur to head to the National Park on the other side of Prague; he carried the bouquet into the Park and laid it at the foot of a monument erected to the national poet Zeyer. He said his facilities were really warmed up and he told the chauffeur to drive to a certain restaurant. Here he took a bread roll from one of the tables, returned to the car once again and the chauffeur was told by him to drive three times round the monument in the centre of a square and then continue back to the cafe where they started. In the cafe there was a piano, he touched the soft pedal with his right hand and put the bread roll on the keyboard. Amid considerable excitement the sealed envelope was brought to the cafe by the Chief of Police, it was opened and the contents were read aloud. It was revealed that young Marion had carried out exactly to the letter all the instructions laid down by the committee.

He found he could speak seven languages, obviously Czech was his natural language but he stated he had never made the slightest conscious effort to learn foreign languages, he just managed to pick them up without problems. For many years Marion made his living in the music hall entertainment field and his book describes a large number of unusual telepathic occurrences. When he went to London he took part in a television programme of the BBC. The tests given to him were his ability to use crypto-thesis, that is the art of using some object as a medium for obtaining extra-sensory perceptions of a person who has been closely associated with the object. Apparently he made a very successful show and his abilities became quite famous.

We met him in New York and he came to the house where we lived in Hartsdale, north of New York City, where we conducted a very simple experiment which showed his powers. We had Marion in the dining room of the house with the door closed and in the lounge Beese White, my wife and I sat round a table with a pack of cards which were shuffled and shuffled by all of us in turn and then cut by all of us in turn. The cards were face downwards and the first card was turned up; we asked Marion, through the closed door, what it was and he gave the correct answer. We went through the whole pack of 52 cards and 49 of them he guessed absolutely correctly - three of them were not correct in that he went to the card below the one we had looked at.

Marion felt that my wife and I had the ability to do some of this work provided we were prepared to concentrate. He suggested a white card about 12 ins. square with a black spot in the middle. The card would be supported at the end of the bed and we should look at that spot until all other thoughts went from our minds, and to continue doing this for some months. With the pressure of work and all the problems domestically and otherwise which we had at that time, we did not do it for very long, certainly not long enough, but it was a most relaxing period to find that viewing a black spot could get rid of all sorts of extraneous problems in the conscious mind.

It was generally felt amongst our group that electro-magnetic theory could be applied and could solve a number of these mystic problems. It was natural that Julius Weinberger and myself wanted to produce a device which could prove this point. If the mind could produce a fairly powerful electro-magnetic atmosphere it should be possible, if one had a radiation source and a sensor, to interrupt the source of its emanations. We decided, therefore, to build two equipments, Julius to make one and me the other, both identical.

We obtained a source of radio-activity, Cobalt 90, and in order to detect the radiation we used an Anthracine screen which would convert the radiation into light with a photo-electric cell to pick up the light emanations and feed those into a chart recorder. Suitable shielding was needed to make sure that no external influence would affect the experiment and so we thought the best would be a copper shielding suitably earthed, this would keep out extraneous light and any radio frequency or other interference, although what to shield against we were not sure. I set up the equipment in the cellar of our house and by adjustment of distance between the energy source and the receiver, I obtained on the chart recorder a number of spikes which we professionally called 'grass'. Adjustments were made until the maximum deflection, almost about I" on the chart recorder, was obtained. I then tried putting the white sheet with black spot on the wall and concentrated on the spot, and after some minutes of concentration the 'grass' disappeared from the recorder and we had a straight line which meant that my mind, I believe, had transmitted sufficient energy to suppress the source.

Beese White knew of a famous medium in New York City who was a features editor of one of the well-known newspapers, who knew her powers but never used them for purposes of getting in touch with spirits who had passed over and wanted to speak to somebody in a circle. She agreed to come along and we asked her if she would get her spirit guide to produce letters of the alphabet from A-Z.

As soon as she came into the room and went into a trance the 'grass' reduced considerably and we had a letter 'A' shape and 'B' another shape and so on, but very difficult to really differentiate that it was an alphabet. It was a very disappointing experiment.

Beese White took the roll of chart paper to California and with the equipment made by Julius he repeated the experiment with a medium in Santa Barbara. The most interesting thing was that when the chart recording done in New York was compared with the recording done in Santa Barbara, using the same letters of the alphabet, these almost indecipherable letters were in many cases practically identical. Beese therefore decided to get a patent on the system, which quite honestly defeated the Patent Office and I had to sign an affidavit to say that I had witnessed the experiment; the patent was entitled 'X Energy Detector' and the design of the equipment was described in fair detail with drawings.

We left America and returned to England early in 1954, no further work was done, Beese White died, and I lost contact with my associates. The interesting sideline to this is that the New York medium was asked, at the time of our experiment, if she could in any way assist us in the design of equipment, and she kept on saying to me, via her guide, that she could see a sensor consisting of a shiny wire spirally wound on top of a piece of string, or what looked like string, and this was the way to go. We tried every possible way of deciding how this could be used but some years later when the gas detector sensor was born it was precisely where that description fitted!

CHAPTER 10

U.S.A. AND PRESIDENCY OF J.H. BUNNELL

After careful consideration of the Ansley Radio proposition it would have been an impossible target to make a success of the company, which had no staff, just a lot of half-finished equipment and a President/owner who was not in any way au fait with the market problems at that time. Charles Carpenter said the opportunity at the Bunnell Company was very good, the best thing for me, but it certainly had to go through the period of Chapter 11 Bankruptcy because they had an overdraft of something like half a million dollars with the Chemical Trust Bank in New York and a number of military Government contracts on which, because of the state of the company, no progress payments were being made. He suggested the best thing would be for him to find a qualified business man to take over and I could go in as Works Director.

He was not successful in finding a professional business manager and suggested that I probably could fill that vacancy, so he made arrangements with the then President of the company, Mrs Dougherty, to give me an agreement as President and Chairman of the Board and he would negotiate the Bankruptcy Act for a fee of $150,000. Mrs Dougherty and her brother John, who was working in the factory but unable to contribute very much in any way at all, thought the amount was too high and they contributed some of the money that Charles Carpenter wanted and I used Henry Hofheimer Jr. as a lawyer to look after my interests.

The factory was situated in Sand Street in Brooklyn, just the other side of the Brooklyn Bridge. It had been in existence since 1878. In 1880 the once small establishment which Jesse Bunnell started grew to a point where complete re-organisation was necessary and the Bunnell name had become nationally known. The new organisation was called J.H. Bunnell & Co. The Bunnell equipment was used extensively by the U.S. Government during World War 1 but in the 20's the art of telegraphy had radically changed and the Bunnell Company took on a programme of research to modify their range of communications equipment. By the time World War 2 had started Bunnell were then called upon to provide every type of standard communications unit for military and industrial purposes.

The Bunnell building was six storeys with very comprehensive equipment from precision machine shops to assembly and test. I moved in as President in

December 1951. The contract was for three years at a minimum salary of $20,000 per annum plus expenses and salary increases based on gross sales increases. I was given a good office - from the window I could look down on a small car park situated next door to the building owned by Jehovah's Witnesses. I could keep my eye on my Cadillac parked down below, although there never appeared to be any problems such as we have in this country with regard to vandalism.

The company's auditors were Scovell Wellington & Co. who produced quarterly accounts. Unfortunately I was not educated in reading into a balance sheet so I took a course of two hours each evening at a night school associated with Columbia University. Being an engineer I had to simplify a balance sheet for my own satisfaction, extracting certain figures essential for running a company on a day-to-day basis. The information I required was:-

1. What was our bank balance?

2. What was the amount owing to our creditors?

3. How much was owed to us by our debtors?

4. What were our total invoice values?

These figures, which are ideal for day-to-day operation, obviously did not include overheads, work in progress, stock, and all the other flexible figures which appear to go into balance sheets.

After a few days I realised I had an incredible job to do. The balance on December 31st 1951 showed total liabilities of over $840,000 with the total assets of just over one million dollars, with a lot of estimates including a goodwill figure of $50,000. The contracts for the Signal Corps and the Navy Bureau of Aeronautics appeared to be at a standstill due to problems of manufacture and performance. I discovered that the insurance policy of the company was so bad that I called in my broker, Joe Minden, who reported that we should change brokers immediately and get proper cover against loss and product liability despite the fact that we were paying very high premiums. He told me that our lack of protection against losses could be of catastrophic proportions if we did not adequately cover.

Meanwhile I received a letter dated March 10, 1952 from Dr Alfred N. Goldsmith reading:

'I feel that I should congratulate the J.H. Bunnell Company on having secured the great advantage of your guidance of its activities through the coming years. I am confident that under your wise and experienced direction, this well-established and highly-regarded organization will become an   increasingly important factor in the fields of its activities.

I wish you all personal success and contentment, and hope from time to time to have the pleasure of seeing you.'

The factory was a completely Union shop with the International Brotherhood of Electrical Workers. This was well-known as a Communist led Union and I was warned to be very careful with my handling of such a powerful organisation. Within a week of my appointment as President I had a visit from the Union Negotiator, a very smart well-dressed individual, who appeared to be quite friendly. He said to me that he had two propositions, the first that he would meet my payroll for six months completely, with no interest, just to keep the company going under the terms of the Chapter 11 Bankruptcy. I should explain that Chapter 11 was an arrangement whereby the creditors would agree not to pursue their claims and the company, with new management, could be allowed to turn the losses into a profitable state within a year. The second point he made was that he wanted a five cent per hour increase for all employees and suggested a meeting should be held with our lawyers and the Union's lawyers round a table; they would demand ten cents an hour and we should argue strongly at the meeting, and if we shook hands on the five cents that would be the deal and they would agree. The meeting went exactly to plan and we agreed on five cents.

I then looked into the complex problems on the Air Force and Navy contracts and I first dealt with the US Signal Corps where a contract for a number of high-powered transmitters was in a state of semi-manufacture with test results showing the difficulty of meeting the very stringent specifications.

The company had a Chief Engineer called Taylor who, although he was quite good at the engineering of morse keys and sounders, had little knowledge of high performance electronic equipment; under him was an engineer called Malcolm Reader. In talking to him I found that he could get nowhere with Taylor and if I could remove Taylor the electronics side of the business could materially improve. I had a conversation with Taylor and, with a suitable payment, he was quite prepared to leave the company and I appointed Reader as Assistant Chief Engineer and gave myself an additional title of Chief Engineer. At the same time the Signal Corps Supply Agency installed a resident industrial financial advisor, a Mr John Vicedomini.

I received a letter dated 25th June 1952 from the Office of The Commanding General asking my opinion, through experience of recent contracts, on conditions which could be improved to give earlier deliveries of equipment.

It was essential, therefore, for me to talk to Brigadier General W. Preston Corderman and after an extremely friendly meeting he sent another letter dated August 13th 1952 saying it was a pleasure to have had an opportunity for discussion and he was aware I had many problems but he was willing to assist in order to expedite delivery of the equipment.

It can be seen that in a very short time I had made close friends with the people with whom I would have to deal and they, in turn, invited me to make suggestions whereby the Supply Agency could improve its liaison with manufacturers.

At a Board Meeting held on April 10th 1952, in my report as President, I made the following comments:-

'My investigation of the Company in the four months I have been President has been one that has demanded the utmost of my attention. Very considerable clean up has been necessary and is still not completed. The very fact that the company did not use monies it made in the past years toward development of up-to-date communications equipment has left us with a business of replacement equipment of devices designed 25 or more years ago. There was practically no "know how" amongst the engineering side of the company which could be usefully employed in making up the considerable elapsed time of many years to bring the Bunnell Company in the forefront of communications equipment manufacturers. I have every intention of concentrating in this direction to make use of every new development in the field, and developments which I, personally, have in mind in the facsimile field which I believe to have a great future. Whatever I do, however, from an engineering or production point of view must be backed by adequate working capital. This we do not have and it is almost impossible to get sufficient working capital out of profits which are subject to taxation. It appears that a minimum financing of $100,000. is required to enable us to bridge the pressure period so that we may continue in production with only a minimum degree of financial safety.'

Another contract we had with the Navy Bureau of Aeronautics was for a communications receiver which, although approved as a prototype, was not approved when production started and deliveries commenced. The trouble was a switch which instead of being made of coin-silver was made of silver-plated brass. After life tests on this switch the silver was rubbed off and brass filings tended to short the switch; all units were sent back for modification. At the same time it was found that the bandwidth was too narrow due to the intermediate frequency coils being of a higher Q than should have been in the design. It was discovered that Litzendraht wire, which is a multi-strand wire, had more strands than necessary, which gave this narrow bandwidth and high gain. The changes were fairly straightforward and in the same report of April 10th I said the following:

'I am presently negotiating with the Bureau of Aeronautics for 300 Radio Receivers of exactly the same type that the Company has produced at a value of approximately one million dollars. This procurement I am informed is to be definitely placed with us as we are today a sole source. This contract will commence delivery in about October or November of 1952 and go on for 10 months thereafter.'

As you can imagine, my visits to the Bureau of Aeronautics at Washington were almost on a weekly basis. I would usually fly there early in the morning, return in the afternoon, dictate a report for Mrs Dougherty and be home by 7.00 p.m.! This went on for many weeks while I re-negotiated contract prices, deliveries and design. On other days I was paying visits to the Supply Agency of the U.S. Army and with the assistance of Lt. Colonel Boynton and a Colonel Couch we managed to modify the contract requirements, which were physically impossible to meet, and also to re-negotiate a price more accurately determined than the original figure quoted by Bunnell a year or so previously. On some of the visits I was accompanied by Malcolm Reader who was a very great help.

Meanwhile our golden retriever, Rex, which we had in 1940, reached the twelve years of a big dog's lifespan and he was suffering with the usual kidney trouble and weakness in the back legs which meant he could not walk; it was heartbreaking to take him to the vet and have him put down. After this very distressing visit we got in the car, went straight round to the local dog compound and found a dog there who looked at us with appealing eyes, and we decided to have him. He was a mongrel but did not look it; he was obviously a cross between a collie and a terrier, black and white with long hair, long legs, well proportioned, and he had the name Laddie. He was incredible in his dislike of police cops on motorbikes. He would be sitting in our lounge with either the radio or television on and for no reason at all he would suddenly sit up, lift his ears and make for the heavy steel door between the house and the garage. He would push this open and be out like a shot and we could then hear the motorbike coming along the road, being chased by Laddie! This was a standard occurrence and fortunately the cops did not seem to mind!

During this time I had problems with John Dougherty - although he received a good salary for doing very little he was perpetually running short of money and we would make loans to him against his salary from time to time. He produced expense sheets which were very doubtful but to begin with I approved payment as well. Mrs Dougherty's secretary was a Miss Noonan, who was also of Irish descent. She did not like John Dougherty and I had many problems with her in order to keep him happy - after all he was a shareholder.

By June of 1952 I managed to get the lowest deficit figure of just over $180,000 compared with the $350,000 of December 1951. The bank loan from the Chemical Bank at December 31st 1951 was nearly half a million dollars and by June 1952 it was down to $78,000.

I introduced, with Malcolm Reader's help, a complete schedule for technical reorganisation of the Engineering Department, starting proper inspection, incoming goods inspection in particular, and quality control. This allowed me to make use of a number of reasonably qualified people in these new positions.

I never realised, in dealing with the Dougherty family of shareholders, who were of Irish descent, how much they disliked the British. We certainly did not have that feeling in England and in general we got on very well with the Irish, but of course every country in the world has a belligerent minority that make much more noise than the stable sincere majority. I remember driving home from Brooklyn on a Friday night on Riverside Drive; that road is four lanes of traffic wide and it was full of cars. We were all driving along at slightly over the 35 mph limit because to go slower would cause the car behind to hit you, or by going faster you would hit the one in front. Approaching the Washington Bridge I was waved down by a motor-cycle cop who managed to get me to the side of the road and said, with an Irish accent, that I was exceeding the speed limit and gave me a ticket. I said it was impossible to go slower or faster and therefore 1,000 other cars were also exceeding the speed limit. He replied "Well we always find Cadillacs a problem and now I hear your accent it is a bigger problem". I had to go to the magistrates' court in New York City and explain to the judge what had happened, and he immediately dismissed the charge.

On another occasion I was followed in heavy snow on the way home by a police car driving about 10 yards behind me. I pulled into a gas station as I was due to refuel and the attendant there said "As you have a Cadillac you have a cop following you and he'll pick you up whatever happens". I meticulously kept to less than 35 mph and finally the cop pulled up behind me and sounded his siren for a stop. I stopped, he came up to me and said, again with an Irish accent, "You've been driving at 50 mph all the way". I said "In snow you don't drive at 50 mph". He replied "Well I have got you clocked at 50 mph all the way, I am giving you a ticket". It was interesting, on that evening I had on the back seat of the car the chart recorder and equipment I was using for my research into psychic phenomena. I said to him "I can prove I did not exceed that limit". He answered "No way". I went on "Well, I have on the back seat a recorder which was recording my speed precisely". He looked at the back seat and said "Oh, well don't do it again", and drove off!

The loans I was approving for John Dougherty had to stop and he was very upset as he had commitments which only a further advance of salary could get him out of a difficult situation, however I stated that we could not keep on doing that as I was trying to pull the company out of a real mess within the year, as given by the Court under the Bankruptcy Act. I then noticed he had numbers of meetings with his sister-in-law, Mrs Dougherty, and spent quite some time in her office.

Henry Hofheimer was my lawyer who looked after my interests and the employment agreement I had with Bunnell was for three years, to be renewed after the first year, with one important clause - that the total number of directors on the Board should be five and no more. The new agreement was drawn up by Henry Hofheimer to date from December 14th 1952, which was one year after I joined the company. t was agreed that we would have a Board Meeting an November 18th to confirm the appointment and the agreement. I sent a memorandum to John Dougherty, who acted as Secretary of the company, on the 5th November:

"The present situation is slowly reaching a climax.

I would like an informal meeting with you and Mr Hamburger on Thursday, November 6, 1952, at 1 o'clock in order to determine our future relations.

A memorandum of new employment was submitted to you on October 16th and I must know by Thursday just what we have in store."

As no meeting was held I sent him a further memorandum on the 13th November and at the same time a memorandum was sent to Mr John Vicedomini, with copies to Mrs Dougherty and John Dougherty:

"A Board of Directors meeting is called for November 18th at 11 A.M.

I should appreciate it if you could be available to attend as certain matters are to be discussed which will have a direct bearing on our performance of the balance of the Signals Corps contracts".

The meeting was held at the factory on November 18th and Mrs Dougherty presented to the Board two newly elected directors; this of course was against the original agreement of a maximum of five. Hofheimer agreed that these two members could sit at the meeting but they would not be allowed to take part in any vote. At the meeting my new contract of employment was discussed. As I could not vote, nor Hofheimer or the two new directors, the only members who could vote were Mrs Dougherty and John Dougherty. They voted against continuation of the contract. As a result it was decided to reconvene the meeting on Tuesday, November 25th.

Meanwhile I received a long memorandum from Malcolm Reader entitled "Progress of the Company's Engineering Department during the period of your management". The first paragraph read:

'Events of the recent days lead us to conclude that certain major changes in management are imminent. Inasmuch as many of the plans for this company are long range in nature, their present status is that of being started but nowhere near completion. It is the purpose of this memorandum to outline the steps anticipated for the completion of those plans. It is my hope that some future management may be aided by the knowledge of the nature of these plans and their state of completion as of this date and that this memorandum will be available to such persons.' He then went into details.

At the meeting of the 25th November the Board of Directors were unanimous in discontinuing my term as President and I had no alternative but to resign immediately. On the morning after the meeting I had my secretary send letters to my friends in the Signal Corps and the Bureau of Aeronautics, and then I got into the Cadillac and went home! My letter to W. Preston Corderman read as follows:

'For some weeks now negotiations have been taking place with the Board A Directors of J.H. Bunnell & Company and myself with respect to the continuation of my term as President of the Company, which expires on December 14th. At a meeting held on November 18th, at which the principal stockholders and directors of the Corporation were present, two additional directors were presented to the Board having been elected at a previous stockholders' meeting at which I was not present. This meeting to discuss the continuance of my term was held over for a meeting held November 25th at which the new directors and the principal stockholders and directors of the Company were present. At this meeting an agreement was reached by the above not to continue my term as President, and as such I had no alternative but to resign effective immediately, and a new President was therefore elected.

I wish to place on record the fact that as you so well know and have access to the information, the financial condition of the Company when I took over December 15, 1951 has been radically improved and that shipments of GR-8s and T-5 equipment have been made and in some days from now the whole of the GR-8 contract will have been completed and 85% of the T-5 contract has been shipped. The Company has shown profits and a considerable debt to the Chemical Bank has been almost liquidated due to my turning the inventory of raw material into essential shipments for the Signal Corps.

During my term as President I have had the most delightful cooperation from yourself, and in particular Major Savage, Mr Vicedomini, Mr Forrest Crain, Colonel Boynton, and Colonel Couch. Without this cooperation my achievement would have been almost impossible.

As most of those I have just mentioned have indicated satisfaction of my administration of the Bunnell Company, I would like to feel that my professional engineering standing and administrative ability could be verified by such a person as yourself or other members of your Agency, should it be necessary at some future date.

Please be assured that should you wish to call on me in any connection with the completion of the contracts, you will have my complete and absolute cooperation.'

I received a reply on December 2nd 1952:

'I sincerely appreciate your interest in advising me, by letter of 26 November

1952, of your resignation as President of J.H. Bunnell & Company.

I am fully cognizant of the difficulties which confronted the firm at the time you assumed office. The marked progress accomplished on the Signal Corps contracts since that date is, I am sure, attributable in great measure to the leadership and direction you provided. Your efforts, on behalf of the company, to cooperate with representatives of this Agency have served to create a more fundamental understanding and appreciation of each other's problems and viewpoints.

If at any time I may be of service to you as a reference, please do not hesitate to call upon me. I wish you every success in any endeavour in which you may engage and thank you for your kind offer to be of assistance in the future.'

From the same address, and dated the same day I received another letter from John Vicedomini's boss thanking me keeping him advised and for my comments regarding co-operation by Mr Vicedomini and giving best wishes for the future. In addition I had a letter from John Vicedomini himself dated 5th December 1952:

'Our association, during my stay at the J.H. Bunnell Company as Resident Industrial Financial Adviser, has always been most pleasant and I sincerely regret your decision particularly in view of the fact that under your able guidance, technical as well as administrative, J.H. Bunnell is now emerging in a very satisfactory position from the state of financial distress and production inertia prevailing at the time you took office in December 1951.

Let it suffice to say that during your tenure of office, the J.H. Bunnell Company has fully completed one of the two major Signal Corps contracts under performance and is presently well on the way towards total completion of the other. Financially, the company's condition, as at 30 November 1952, discloses a Working Capital position of $171,000, far improved when compared to the one existing in December 1951; Net Profit of $71,000, an appreciation in the company's Net Worth from $623 as of December 1951 to $129,000 and a decrease of the company's Deficit position from ($351,000) as at December 1951 to ($222,000) at the end of November 1952.

I look forward to the pleasure of meeting with you again in the near future and want to convey to you my very best wishes in any new enterprise which you might contemplate undertaking at this time.'

From Lt. Colonel R.W. Couch at the same address I received the following:

'I would like to wish you the best of luck in any future undertakings that you might have as a contractor doing business with the Signal Corps. I wish that all of the relationships between the Signal Corps and Industry were as pleasant as ours.'

Finally, I received a handwritten letter dated 4th Dec. 1952 from Major Douglas Savage:

"I was very sorry to learn of the termination of your contract with Bunnell. It had been a real pleasure to work with you. So much so, that I felt I must sit down to let you know your efforts were much appreciated and to thank you for your splendid cooperation - oh! and I think the Sig C also got some needed equipments.

My very best personal wishes for your future success and happiness."

It was a great disappointment to me to leave Bunnell and I remember crossing Brooklyn Bridge in the car and wondering what destiny was in store, because here at Bunnell I had been successful and carried out a major turn-round of a company where I had improved the finances almost entirely by getting the engineering right and shipping equipment out through the door. I had a reputation of being a financial wizard, and I thought that I could capitalise on that reputation by setting up as a consultant and helping companies which had been mismanaged; management is always the cause of a company failure, it is management policy and their understanding of the employees which produces a team and final success. I have said many times that "employees" really is the wrong term because good management has people working with it and not for it.

I had a friend called Brook-Flowers; he was the son-in-law of Sir Alan Gordon-Smith, head of the big S. Smith & Sons company in England. Brook-Flowers had an office at 45 West 45th Street, just off Fifth Avenue, which was a showroom for the Smith products such as timing clocks, clocks of various descriptions, instrumentation etc. He worked with one secretary and as he had a spare room I could use the room and dictate to his secretary any work necessary for my business, but he of course had priority. As he was quite often out travelling this was an ideal arrangement for me. When I set up my office in this room I received many congratulatory letters including Manufacturers Trust Bank, Chemical Bank and the Signal Corps, wishing me success.

Another friend, Jack Kramer, who was President of a small company called White & Co., which made all sorts of equipment, basically as sub-contractors, had a job for one of the hospital bed manufacturers to convert a bed to an electrically operated unit so that the patient, who had very little power in the hands or fingers, could change the various parts of the bed with minimum strength of movement. The bed was the usual three handle type, one handle to wind the bed up and down, one to lift up the centre so that the patient's knees could be lifted, and the third to raise the back to a vertical position to allow the patient to sit up. This was not a difficult conversion job and he gave me a West Indian, who, incidentally was a British subject from Jamaica, as a mechanic to do the work.

I managed to motorise the bed with a single motor and solenoid-operated half-nuts which would engage on the various screw threaded rods which controlled the bed. The solenoids were operated by three micro-switches, a device which required almost no pressure to obtain minimum contact. This work was completed within three weeks and went into full production.

A very wealthy man, Ted Berner, whose name was derived from the interest his family had in the town of Berne in Switzerland, asked me to look at a number of companies and report on them.

He owned a company called General Precision Equipment inc. and they had a method of putting wiring onto an insulating board by a photographic process and depositing copper and silver electrically; this was the origin of the printed circuit board. I also looked into two large public companies and I had the ability to walk through a plant, talk to the people who were working there and discover the reason for the difficulties, and usually these were in the lower management area. By suitable suggestions to top management my visit was normally very successful.

I carefully analysed myself at the time and realised that I had two avenues to take; one was to concentrate on consultancy, which of course would mean taking on technical staff and covering a very wide field, or returning home to England where Sylvia, without doubt, would be very much better. There was a third alternative, and that was to go to the West Coast, to California, where perhaps the climate would be so much better than that of New York City so that Sylvia maybe would have liked America enough to stay. After almost one year of consultancy we decided in 1954 that we would sell the house and go back to England.

CHAPTER 11

RETURN TO U.K.

It is a major planning job to move residence from one country to another, although 3,000 miles is nothing today. There are the schools for the two children, the animals and the furniture.

When we had agreed the sale of the house it gave us one month to pack up the furniture and find homes for Laddie and our cat. A very nice individual came round and said he would have them both so they went off quite happy in his car. However, two days later there was a bark at the back door and there was Laddie, happy to be back home - he had travelled some 22 miles! We gave him a good feed, telephoned the new owner, who came almost immediately, and with great regret he was taken away.

We arranged to have our furniture collected and packed for shipment to England and we booked passage on an American vessel 'The Constitution' owned by American Export Lines. When we left the house and everything was organised we stayed at an hotel in Scarsdale, Westchester, until the date of sailing. I can always remember giving the Cadillac a final wash and polish at the hotel at the end of February in warm sunshine. We drove to the port, I believe it was Pier 90 in New York City, and the Cadillac was loaded into the hold of the ship by crane. The ship left New York and went over the South Atlantic route, stopping at Gibraltar with a port of call at Cannes in the South of France. We were very pleased with this arrangement because we wanted to drive through France and return home after having a break.

'The Constitution' was a very modern ship, fully air-conditioned and very clean with good food. The children had a cabin with two bunks, one above the other. There were a certain amount of problems there as to who would have the upper bunk. Suzanne did not feel too well for the first few days due to the motion of the ship, the reason being that there was a problem; the problem was that although it was a twin-screw vessel one screw was out of action either due to engine, propeller or propeller shaft, I never found out, so the journey took eight days instead of seven. When we anchored off Gibraltar many small boats appeared and the occupants were very busy trying to make sales of their various products. They would throw these up onto the lower deck where we were standing, followed immediately by the crew throwing everything back!

We arrived at Cannes on March 9th 1954. 'The Constitution' dropped anchor about a mile out in the bay and a raft ferry came alongside. The Cadillac was hoisted up by the ship's derrick and dropped carefully onto the raft, the wheels suitably wedged. We got on with all our luggage and entered the old port of Cannes. Enough petrol was left in the tank of the car to allow us to drive about a mile; on the way to the hotel where we were to stay the car suddenly stopped (very unusual for a Cadillac). On lifting the bonnet I found that the battery had been disconnected whilst in the ship and the cables had just been pushed onto the battery lugs to allow the car to be started, but they did not tell me that they had not tightened up the clamps and so one of these cables came off. We filled up with petrol and then drove to the hotel adjacent to the Carlton, owned by a Frenchman who had been in the Resistance movement during the war. It was recommended by Paul Cherney, an American friend of ours with a Hungarian background, German speaking, with an English wife. He had a large photographic distributing company in New York City and was very active in the photographic industry. During the war his background and his ability to speak German gave him a good position in the U.S. Army as an interrogator. He had visited the hotel in Cannes many times and also gave us an address for a famous underwater photographer. We received quite a welcome from the owner of the hotel who, together with the bar tender, spoke good English as our school French had not had very much practise. It was a nice warm day with hot sunshine.

Whilst in Cannes we visited the office of the underwater photographer, and were surprised to see that the various secretaries in the office wore bikinis and this was in March! Something we certainly remembered when we drove up through France to return home to England.

We had been told that we would probably have trouble in France driving an American car with a New York licence plate; for one reason or another some of the French did not like Americans. we found the exact reverse - we were welcomed wherever we went and parked the car, which shows that you cannot always believe statements of that sort as it usually is an opinion of one person and one incident and that can be amplified every time it is repeated.

We stayed three weeks and decided to slowly drive up through France to reach Boulogne. Our first stop on the way back was Montelimar - well-known as the town from which the famous nougat takes its name and the nougat can be bought in any shop, any hotel, in fact anywhere in the town. It was rather a pleasant hotel, the name of which I do not remember, alongside the river, and it was nice to walk in the country around the area and certainly along the river bank. We had very good food at the hotel and, incidentally, the manager and all the staff spoke English.

We continued to motor slowly up through France and as there were no motorways in those days we travelled on the Route Nationale No: 7 which of course we knew very well from pre-war days. We headed for Paris and from our pre-war visits we seemed to know our way around, a very different thing today when, if you are in a car and do not know where you are going you will be swept off the road by passing motorists who know exactly where they are going! We stayed at Swiss owned hotel which we knew, and decided to spend a day or two in Paris so that the children could see some of the sights. One of the most famous of course is the Madeleine, and we parked the car in the square opposite and walked across to it. We returned to the car only to find that I had locked the keys inside! A Cadillac is a very difficult car to get into and therefore you usually carry two sets of keys, one you leave in the car and one you have in your pocket, and maybe a third set you hide somewhere on the outside of the car. Quite a crowd stood around the car and watched me trying to find a way in with a piece of wire which I had in the back of my car, trying to lever a window up. The 1949 Cadillac had a quarter window which was hinged, and by means of a certain amount of bending I managed to get a screwdriver in to slip the lock of the quarter window, open it up and then obviously get my hand in and away we went!

We decided to pick up the cross-Channel ferry at Boulogne, which could be done easily in the day from Paris, and stay the night around that area which, in pre-war days, was famous, particularly Le Touquet which had magnificent hotels. There was no need to do any previous booking because we were quite sure there would be no problems, and after an uneventful drive with very little trouble we arrived at Le Touquet only to find the whole of this resort and its hotels completely shut. There was no way we could get into any hotel, they were all shut, either for ever or for the winter, we never found out which, so we drove on to Boulogne and chose an hotel there which managed to find two rooms for us, they had just opened after being shut for the winter. We had a reasonable meal there and went to bed, then found the beds had never been aired and were all damp so we slept in damp beds that night and were very glad to get out of there next day and turn the heating on in the Cadillac to dry ourselves out! Only a few weeks previously it was lovely and warm in the South of France and here, although it was Spring in a way, it was very cold with no sunshine, just grey.

We took the ferry in the morning and as usual the Cadillac went into a cradle, was hoisted up over the ship and dropped into the hold with the ship's own derrick, and we did the short journey to the White Cliffs of Dover. There appeared to be no unnecessary formalities on arrival and we managed to get away fairly early and thought we would have time to drive to an hotel called 'The Hog's Back' on the hill of that name just outside Guildford. We had no trouble booking rooms and were in time for lunch, and the lovely smell of Spring air on the top of the Hog's Back was most refreshing.

We had friends in Parkstone whom we had known for many years, the husband, George Havill, being head of a plating company called Pender Plating Ltd. He was extremely popular during the war because, with a plating facility, various motor traders had the bumpers of their cars re-plated etc., which of course was completely illegal, and as a result, when the war was over, George Havill went into the motor trade. We kept in touch with him while living in America and he arranged for us to stay at an hotel in Canford Cliffs or, if that was difficult, he would find an apartment we could rent temporarily. When we arrived at his flat, typical of a motor trader he was on the 'phone for a good half hour before he could say "Hello"! He showed us the flat he had taken for us, which was not far away. We took one look at it, did not like it and immediately went to the Branksome Court Hotel and booked up there full pension, where we stayed for something like one month.

We enjoyed staying at the hotel, which was extremely friendly with very good food, quite inexpensive, whilst we searched for a more suitable rental and finalised on a house on Cliff Drive, Canford Cliffs, owned by a Mrs Cyril Beale, a relation of the family who owned the well-known department store in

Bournemouth. We moved in on a six months tenancy which we thought would be adequate to get firmly established. The first thing we did was to get a dog. We got in touch with a Colonel in Woodside Road, Parkstone who bred golden retrievers, and managed to get an eight week old puppy which we called Rusty. It was fortunate that it was a furnished house we rented because this puppy thought anything that had four legs in the way of furniture was not right, either one leg should be chewed or all four, and we were constantly having to correct him, getting rid of his excess energy and chewing by buying him rubber bones and giving him old shoes to chew.

Meanwhile we got the children settled into local schools - Jacqueline went to Uplands School in Parkstone and Suzanne first to The Haven School and later to St Christopher's in Poole.

As our accommodation appeared to be assured for six months I had to immediately set about finding something to do, meeting some of my old colleagues in order to create an income. We probably had enough cash, having sold the house in America, to live comfortably for two years but it was obviously dangerous to go too far without being assured of an income of some sort.

I rejoined the Radio Industry Club which had formal luncheon meetings in London and came across my old friend Sidney Bird, whom I had helped way back in the early 1920's by using his variable capacitor in one of my wireless sets, the details of manufacture being published in 'Amateur Wireless'. He was delighted to see me and said his company was considering moving the factory from Enfield, where they had been since its inception just after the First World War, to Poole. Well, I happened to know of a building which was empty, utilised during the war as a sub-contract engineering unit, situated in Fleets Lane, Poole. Fleets Lane at this time was partially an unmade road but the road was made up to this factory.

Sidney came down to Poole and we both looked at the building and he decided that they would move lock, stock and barrel into the area. In the meantime he told me that they were in the small component industry as 'Cyldon' named after his two sons, Cyril and Donald. Cyril was now Managing Director but Donald unfortunately had died some years previously. They were interested in making a television turret tuner similar to the Americans, and they had a sample which they wanted to copy, would I act as consultant? This was the opening for which I was looking.

Sidney gave me the sample turret tuner - I had one look at it and said "Where did you get this from?" He said "I do not know, we managed to get it from the States". I said "This one comes from Freed Radio where I was Vice-President, and this is a unit which we designed and built suitable for selling to television manufacturers, and fixing holes were universally drilled to fit some of the well-known makes like Emerson, Philco, etc.". They had no idea how to go about manufacture, which was fortunate as it gave me scope to utilise my knowledge. They had a Chief Engineer there called Ganderton who did not like the idea of a consultant, which was natural, so the co-operation was not very good. He had developed a means of testing the tuners by a variable condenser driven by a motor and scanning a frequency so that the band pass effect of the tuners could be measured accurately. Well of course this method of changing frequency by a variable capacitor had not been used for some time in America; we had devised a neat system where the 50 cycle mains were fed into a transformer and the low voltage side of the transformer was fed into a coil wrapped around a ferrite rod. Another coil, adjusted to the centre frequency of the band width required, was also situated adjacent to the variable magnetic coil. The change of inductance induced by the magnetic changed on the 50 cycle mains gave a very simple sweep circuit which could be adjusted for any type of radio frequency equipment.

The main trouble with the Cyldon company was that they did not plan their marketing and production facilities. Apart from components for the radio industry they made bell chimes, spent a lot of money on developing an electronic organ, and most of their other components were based on copies of that which was already on the market. When I looked at their bell chime I was staggered; every time a button was pressed it took about 3 amps out of the dry batteries, which they did not like for long. Nobody had taken the trouble to re-wind the activating coil to be more effective, and when I re-designed that we had a good bell chime consuming one tenth of an amp only.

I wrote letters to both the BBC and to what was about to be formed, the Independent Television Authority, pointing out my many years in television in England and my years in America as a member of the National Television Systems Committee in Washington, my experience of ultra high frequency transmissions and, of course, colour. I cannot remember whether I had a response or not, but if I did it was the type of response which you immediately put back in the envelope and throw it into the filing system on the floor! I decided, therefore, that my best bet was consultancy, it would give me freedom to work where I wanted to live.

I went regularly to the Radio Industries luncheons in London with Sidney and met many old friends, among them Basil Ferranti, and Ted Rosen of Ultra. These visits were important to me because having had nearly ten years in America, business life and methods are so different in this country that I had to become acclimatised without losing my American 'nationality'.

In no time at all our six months tenancy of the house in Cliff Drive was due to terminate and it was essential for us to find somewhere to live permanently. We did find a most magnificent house in Branksome Park called 'Greystones'. This house was built of Purbeck stone in 1911 at an enormous cost of £14,000! It had mullioned windows with bronze casements, all oak doors hand-made with hand-made hinges and locks, oak and maple floors - a dream house. The agent said to us that it was a very sticky house to sell, it had twelve bedrooms but nobody would buy it because one and a half tons of coke a week had to be used to heat the boiler for central heating. It had five acres of ground but unfortunately the garden was neglected due to the death of the previous owner, and no attempt had been made to at least keep the garden tidy. The servants' quarters were ideal as a first-class laboratory for me as they were separate from the main living quarters, particularly as a fully glazed tiled pantry would make an excellent chemical laboratory.

The house was going up for auction and as we knew the reserve price of ££7,500 we were rather concerned that we should not go to the auction - as we were known to many of the estate agents in our search, they would be aware of

Laboratory at "Greystones"

our bidding and think because we had just come back from America and had a big Cadillac we were very wealthy, so it was possible that they would push the price up. One of the main estate agents in Bournemouth was Ormiston Knight and Payne. Tony Ormiston was an auctioneer and we gave him a cheque for 10% of the reserve price and told him to get the house for us. It paid to use a professional as he sat in the front row at the auction and the moment the reserve price was reached he was at the rostrum with the cheque and we got the house.

Naturally a number of changes had to be made to the house; for instance the whole kitchen had to be brought up to our American standards, all the white glazed brick walls had to be chipped away, an Aga cooker dismantled and removed, new lighting installed, and a refrigerator which, incidentally we brought back with us from the States. We also installed an oil-fired boiler to replace the original coke one. We could now get our furniture and this finally arrived in an enormous crate which contained our washing machine, refrigerator, and other niceties which the Americans had and we certainly had not in England at that time. A most interesting thing happened - we had a three-drawer canteen of silver cutlery as a wedding present and when it arrived in America one teaspoon was missing and we thought it could be stolen or just one of those things, it had disappeared. When the crate was brought to 'Greystones' and emptied of all the furniture, amongst the straw was that one teaspoon and we never knew how it got there, it must have been stuck in the cabinet somehow and dislodged itself during the return journey to England!

The servants hall was converted to a laboratory, in fact conversion is wrong because the built-in furniture was absolutely ideal and the beautiful hand-scrubbed kitchen table 8ft. x 4ft. was a perfect instrument table in the centre of this parquet-tiled room. I bought some essential test equipment, particularly an Avo meter, the tool of every engineer at that time, a signal generator which was Government surplus, inductance and resistance bridges - again Government surplus, and so on.

Whilst I was re-designing some inductances for Cyldon for their frequency modulation discriminator circuit which was an over-coupled coil giving an ideal 'S' curve, a letter arrived from the States. It was from a company of patent attorneys who worked for the Servo Corporation of America (my first job out there), asking if I would be interested in undertaking pure research for a client of theirs called Aircraft Marine Products Inc. The product was the crimped terminal which was slowly taking over from soldering in a number of major equipments. Would I pay a visit to their headquarters in Harrisburg, Pennsylvania, all expenses paid, to discuss terms and meet the principals.

We booked on the 'Caronia', a most beautiful ship of the Cunard Line, which was painted in a very pale Spring Green colour and although only 40,000 tons was a real luxury vessel. In the five day trip to New York we met a most interesting number of people, with some of whom we are still in communication after thirty-four years. We also called up many friends in New York on arrival and then took the train to Harrisburg.

The head of research at Aircraft Marine Products was a Dr Wells and a Mr Whittaker was President of the corporation. They all insisted on giving me the title of 'Dr' which, despite my disclaim, continued during my whole association with AMP. An agreement was being prepared which was finally dated November 1956 and I offered the full facilities of the laboratory at a fee plus expenses, and decided, with Dr Wells, that two good physicists would be required as staff and one mechanic.

We returned to England and during a visit from Dr Wells we had a meeting in the Westbury Hotel in London, interviewing applications replying to the advertisement for the jobs by AMP. We settled on two, Dr Rowland and Jock Mackenzie. Rowland got his Ph.D at Bristol University and Mackenzie received his B.Sc. in Glasgow.

It was essential to obtain specialist equipment and I first modified the large pantry with a fume cupboard and installed a Myford lathe and other associated equipment. The laboratory needed a very accurate balance which was an Oertling, meters, inductance bridges, resistance bridges and probably most important was a vibration generator. This latter was a major purchase as in the testing of these crimped connectors it was essential that vibration would be a central part of the procedure. I had a conversation with Goodmans, my old friends from pre-war days who made the vibration unit, and a company called Brian Savage responsible for the high powered amplifiers and frequency generator. The vibration unit weighed about three-quarters of a ton. It was decided to put this in a room in the garage on cork and other cushioning material and the electronic drive unit was a 6 ft. rack with low frequency generator and amplifiers. When this was started up at a frequency of about 500 Hz. it could be heard some distance away and certainly in the house; radical soundproofing had to be carried out in the room and finally we had to use this at selected times of the day!

A secretary was important and we settled with Mrs Daphne Watson who was very fluent in French and some German. When she left we had a Mrs Joyce Bell who had been educated in Switzerland and she was fluent in German as well as French and was sufficiently interested in the subject of crimped connectors to go to the central library and obtain reference books important for the work.

One of the tests on crimped connectors was their suitability under severe atmospheric conditions of salt air etc. and the American MIL Spec. gave figures which were sufficient for me to design and have built a test chamber and this was made up by a local firm, Ridouts, in perspex and I always remember that despite using all the right salts at the right temperature the crimps performed perfectly, but if we put them outside the window in the garden, in one week they became corroded!

Quite a bit of the correspondence between lab and Dr Wells was by tape; he would record certain things of interest to the lab plus, I remember, some of the first recordings of Elvis Presley which appealed to Rowland who was an amateur guitar player. We had a fair amount of fun in producing a tape covering a day in the lab, with all the right noises. It started with a car approaching up the gravel driveway and coming to a sliding halt, doors banging, a typewriter going at very high speed, telephones ringing, plus the various lab sounds, and an immediate silence after more door banging which meant it was five o'clock!

AMP were a very live-wire American company and they set up manufacturing plants in various parts of Europe. They decided to hold a sales conference in The Hague in Holland and we were invited to go there and meet the various people, and certainly to visit the factory at s'Hertogenbosch. We stayed at a magnificent hotel in The Hague and learnt a lot at the high pressure sales meetings which kept everybody, except me of course, making copious notes; meetings which lasted a full day from early morning until early evening.

After returning to England we hired a mechanic called H.V. Greenwood who spent his time machining bits of metal. The important part of research of the crimped connector was what happened when the connector was crimped to the wire. It was believed that a cold weld took place and it was essential to find if there was a temperature rise and how much. I managed to obtain a good thermo-couple and built a transistor amplifier utilising two of the only transistors available on the market, a green spot and a red spot, and recorded the temperature rise when the crimp was put under controlled pressure and recorded on a sensitive chart recorder. It was discovered that the faster the pressure was applied the better the crimp, and to prove the effectiveness of this we joined 100 crimps with a wire between each connector and measured resistance change accurately when a string of crimps was put either outside the window or in the room under controlled conditions.

I realised it would be of very great advantage if the Bournemouth 'Greystones' laboratory was approved by the Air Registration Board to undertake type approval work. This would give us the advantage of having the various specifications for cable terminations which, although not essential for our pure research, at least it helped to know the full parameters for which the terminations were used.

The AMP Company in London were at Kingley Street in London W.1 and Mr

J.C. Collier was the Chief Design Engineer. In association with him we managed to obtain approval from the Air Registration board on the 1st January 1957.

It was impossible to have all the equipment really necessary but fortunately SRDE (Signals Research Development Establishment) at Christchurch, whom I knew very well, were prepared to undertake tropical exposure tests on the AMP connectors over a storage period of 84 days. The results, which were certified by the Establishment, were very important and were passed to Harrisburg.

Dr Rowland did not like working at 'Greystones' and I had to agree; although the facilities were absolutely first-class for research, it was nevertheless part of a private house and to make any changes to provide a separate entrance, as I mentioned previously, was not on. Dr Wells felt that, under the circumstances, as I had initiated the whole programme, the time had come to move either somewhere else locally or to London. Rowland pressured for London and it was decided therefore to terminate the agreement that I had with AMP by December 1957. Rowland moved and at the same time Greenwood left. Morrison stayed until about May to complete some of the work he was doing.

The specialist equipment which I purchased for AMP was slowly, within the next two to three months, moved to London; the last to go was the vibration generator. Nevertheless a considerable amount of test equipment which I purchased and used working for AMP stayed in the main laboratory and all the chemicals (which belonged to me personally) in carefully labelled bottles, although a considerable number which were used in our research programme stayed in the chemical laboratory. The fume cupboard remained - I realised how valuable this was to be later on.

'Greystones' had a very large hall which was our main sitting room, it also had a drawing room almost 30 ft. long and 20 ft. wide and this I used as my acoustic high-fi laboratory where I did a fair amount of work for various companies in re-designing high-fi amplifiers and loudspeaker enclosures. Being somewhat versatile I was asked by a friend of mine, John Clark, to install a complete high fidelity system on board his luxury 500 ton yacht 'Anadan' which was being re-conditioned at Appledore. I installed a complete console using a Wright & Weare tape recorder, a belt-driven turntable and a multi-band radio made by the Hacker Bros. in Maidenhead. In the main saloon I installed a very large Tannoy cabinet enclosure using their new 12 ins. co-axial loudspeaker. The aft deck I equipped with loudspeakers suitably waterproofed. Loudspeakers were also installed with individual volume controls built into the panels in the dining room and staterooms, and a modified Tannoy amplifier with distribution network was in the console. This took me about three or four weeks and installation was basically done by the electrical contractors who were re-wiring the vessel. The 240V AC supply to run the equipment came from a motor-driven alternator in the engine room. At the time I did this installation there was talk of stereo records; very few had been produced and Tannoy made a pick-up (which was not marketed) working on a moving coil principle, but it was too heavy so that the installation did not include a stereo system, which would have been possible two or three years later.

A friend of mine, Royce Turner (Lady Docker's brother) was having a 55 ft. yacht 'Sherina' built by Randall & McGregor at the Royal Motor Yacht Club. He wanted a complete radio/telephone installation and a telephone system between all cabins, wheelhouse, engine room etc. I purchased from Woodson in Aberdeen the radio telephone equipment, and from Gents in Leicester the intercom telephone system.

I bought a book entitled 'Sound Reproduction' by G.A. Briggs. His company, Wharfedale in Bradford, made some excellent loudspeakers and he was quite an authority on these. I contacted him and we became close friends. I let him have photographs of my equipment when I started testing loudspeakers in 'Amateur Wireless' in 1924/25, which he published in his next book called 'Audio and Acoustics', and later on he published a book called 'Audio Biographies' in which a whole chapter was given over to the work I did in the field. He had good connections with EMI and Decca and would keep me well informed of the excellent recordings which were available to demonstrate full high fidelity equipment. In the drawing room laboratory we had a full French concert grand piano and Gilbert, who had written a book on 'Pianos & Sonics' told me that we had one of the best examples he had ever heard, and as he had owned some twenty or more pianos at one time he certainly was an authority. Unfortunately he died some years later and the company was taken over. Wharfedale loudspeakers have always been extremely good but a considerable amount of scientific research has gone into acoustics in general and many companies now make very good products.

Another friend of mine, a dentist, was an expert amateur in recordings and he liked making tapes of the big steam railway locomotives either at high speed going through a station or starting off on a gradient, and I remember once he went to Poole Station to record the London/Weymouth express going through. He took in his equipment, set it up and then tried to find an AC power source; he did not know there was no such thing at Poole Station, all the lighting was by gas!

I used one of his tapes at a cocktail party we had at 'Greystones'. In the big hall I had two loudspeakers, one at each end. The cocktail party was with many friends on Christmas morning and Sylvia was anxious that they should not stay too long as we had a turkey dinner to eat. I overcame the problem by putting on the steam engine tape at full level and with a fader I faded from one speaker to another and this locomotive appeared to run through the house, after which everybody left!

It was during this period, one of the important periods in one's life, that between Christmas 1957 and May 1958 there was a major change in my working life. A friend of mine, Walter Rayner (always known as 'Tom Rayner') an Australian naval architect, whom I had met through his wife, Denise Rayner teaching PT at Suzanne's school, St Christopher's, had a number of very successful designs to his credit. I introduced him to Guy Fountain who had a large 45 ft. Osborne cruiser which required some modifications and the possibility of building a new one.

Tom Rayner came to me and said that there would be a need for a sensitive gas detector for small boats to give early warning against petrol leakage and/or Calor gas. He said that Guy Fountain had a unit on board which did not work and he tried it with all sorts of petrol and Calor gas to no effect. So many explosive fires had occurred due to the fact that most hydrocarbons have a molecular weight two or three times that of air, and therefore they tend to sit in the bottom of the boat and any small spark from whatever source produces ignition, and very suddenly it goes up with a big bang. Guy Fountain's gas detector was one made by a company in Scotland, so I purchased a unit straight from them. It was a very heavy brass casing and the principle of operation was by osmosis; gas entering the unit via a fine molecular screen flowed into a cavity with a flexible diaphragm operating a contact. In the presence of gas the pressure in the cavity changed, operating the diaphragm switch which could be connected to any alarm system. It had many problems, it did not like vibration, it did not like major atmospheric changes, and whereas it would work sometimes on propane or butane gases, on some of the low grade petrol it did not work at all.

At this time I was still visiting Cyldon on a regular basis. Cyril Bird had taken on a joint Managing Director, Cyril Adams, to improve the production facilities at the factory. He called in a firm of management consultants and they immediately revised the whole factory procedure. They first of all made a major change in that nothing was to be manufactured without a drawing, and the drawing office therefore had to be considerably increased. What they did not know was that although drawings were available for most of the components being manufactured, it was known by the Stores and by the factory management that nothing was ever made to the drawing but made by knowledge of the changes which had taken place but had never been recorded. The major change made by the consultants was to produce complete chaos and old Sidney Bird said to me he was very worried about things, so between us we agreed that I would not act as consultant any more because it would be a waste of time and money. As a result, in December 1957 I gave up the work.

CHAPTER 12

INVENTION OF GAS DETECTOR

I realised I had been a successful consultant with both AMP and Cyldon but in order to expand my operation it would mean travelling to different parts of the country to find other opportunities for consultancy. I was not too enthusiastic, in that having had the policy of working where I wanted to live I did not intend to spend my time away from home for some days every week. My policy, therefore, had to be that if I was successful as a consultant to other companies, who would be more appreciative than myself, so I would be a consultant to myself, develop ideas and market them to companies who could carry out the manufacture.

In the meantime Guy Fountain of Tannoy, who kept his boat at Poole, suggested that as I had been some years with the radar research group of the Air Ministry, wasn't there something which I had developed at that time which could now be used commercially. He had already succeeded in getting a claim through a government department for his own company. He introduced me to the individual who prepared the various statements and I told him of my specific invention of a time delay device, invented at Scophony some years previously before the war, and my proof of the invention was the letter which Sol Sagall sent to me telling me to get in touch with our patent attorneys, Reddie & Grose, and have it filed. This was before Tom Brown joined us at Scophony as our own patent man.

The ultrasonic light cell which I had designed and developed for Robert Cockburn, Divisional Leader of the counter-measures section at TRE, proved to be the very device he was looking for, as described earlier on in this book. What I did not know when I made my first application was that the head of that area looking into patents was Tom Brown, and I could not understand why he should have been so against the invention which really was a considerable improvement over the two loudspeaker system which he cited as having been patented in 1928. After much correspondence I found I could not win so gave up the attempt.

I thought that working on a selective system to measure any flammable gas would be my first project as my own consultant and immediately I went about two things simultaneously, firstly to contact the Board of Trade in London to provide me with information as to the world-wide market for a gas detector for petrol driven motor boats, secondly to ask the patent agents to carry out a search going back fifty years on gas detection equipments. This was decided as a reasonable period in that Sir Humphrey Davy had discovered the reaction of a flammable gas in the presence of heated platinum early in the nineteenth century. The patents were carefully read, and in general the equipment described was mainly based on the detection of mine gas where the danger appeared to be most prevalent.

The Board of Trade, who were exceedingly helpful, produced an analysis of the number of small petrol-driven boats in the world, which they did by contacting the various Consular Offices who, in turn, obtained information on Yacht Club membership and boat builders; the total world market of that time appeared to be about one million vessels. This was enough for me to enter into a research operation, knowing full well that the market was likely to expand rather than contract. Fortunately Mrs Joyce Bell had stayed with me to cover my secretarial work.

There were one or two companies in the gas detection field; the well-known American company called Mine Safety Appliances (MSA) used a catalytic system which consisted of a helix of platinum wire heated to a high temperature but nevertheless consuming high current, and certainly unsuitable for the limited current available on a small boat. Their equipment depended on a pump aspirating gases to the sensor which would be in a control unit. Another was, of course, the Scottish company already mentioned, the manufacturer of Guy Fountain's unit.

What was needed, therefore, was a sensing device which could be remotely fixed in the danger area on a boat, with a control unit in a safer and more accessible area - it had to have low current consumption and be selective to flammable gas and not any other incidental effects such as pressure change, humidity, etc. Looking through the history and patent literature of devices to detect flammable gas, the majority used the ability of a heated platinum wire in the presence of a mixture of gases and air to increase temperature by combustion and therefore change the resistance of the wire. Some of the early patents before the First World War utilised the platinum wire, but in some cases they were wrapped around the bowl of a mercury thermometer and the presence of gas was indicated by a rise in temperature, seen on the capillary glass tube.

Early in 1957 experimental set-ups were constructed using platinum wire to measure more accurately the temperature, and therefore the resistance change, under measured amounts of gas. It was advisable at this time to use commercial Calor Gas, which was butane plus a percentage of carbon dioxide; it was always necessary to shake the bottle vigorously before testing. A test rig was constructed where a number of helically wound coils of platinum could be assembled and put in a chamber into which a given amount of gas was inserted and resistance measurements were made, having first applied current to each sample, until combustion occurred. It was noticeable that the turn spacing of the helices was significant and this would be expected, in that the closer the spacing the more initial heat would be generated for a given wattage, therefore combustion taking place earlier.

Experiments of this type went on for some twelve months but the difficulty in repeating the tests was due to the fact that the wound filaments would vary their spacing after being heated by combustion, and therefore inaccuracies in measurement occurred.

A complete study was made of the various noble metals in oxide form that would act as catalysts, and it was a natural step to overcome the problem of the sagging filament by winding it on a former to which other catalysts could be added.

The theory of noble metal catalysts was not sufficiently examined at that time but it appeared, by the experiments being carried out, that the larger the surface area of the catalyst the more responsive it would be to an applied gas. In order to support the winding, therefore, it required a very porous or multi-fibred former which would hold the platinum wire helix in position and allow other noble metal oxides in liquid form to be impregnated. Some experimental tests were made and immediately it was noted that combustion took place on low current, therefore filament wattage went down, which was important.

The next step was to carefully analyse various supports. Work done by Dobereiner in the early nineteenth century on carriers utilised platinum black which was made by adding zinc to chloro-platinic acid. He found that substances in a very fine state of dispersion, such as potter's clay, asbestos, pumice, kieselgur, cellulose, cotton, etc. were all suitable. The decision was made to use asbestos string to support the platinum helix as the fibres were extremely small in diameter (a few microns) and therefore a very great dispersion of the catalyst could be obtained. Most important of all was the fact that asbestos had a fine crystalline construction giving a surface area many times larger than the original size of the fibre. Utilising the original jig, a number of filaments were wound on asbestos string of various diameters, and tests were made with no catalytic application but purely to repeat the original test done without support carriers. It was noted immediately that the results were repeatable.

Various applications to the samples were tried, utilising chloro-platinic acid in a weak solution of hydrochloric acid finally dried off at various temperatures by applying current to the platinum wire. The result of these tests showed that it was very important in the winding of the platinum wire that the turn spacing should not be less than one wire diameter and not more than three wire diameters. The current consumption of these filaments supported on an asbestos carrier impregnated with the mixture showed immediately to be 50% of the straight helix, utilising the platinum wire as the catalyst itself.

Investigation was made into the literature, particularly the Journal of Physical Chemistry in 1927, where active platinum was obtained by reduction of platinum chloride with formaldehyde. A.W. Gauger in the Journal of the American Chemical Society in 1925 proved that the extent of surface of the catalyst was extremely important, but when using glass wool as a carrier the catalyst became inactive, although it was possible to remove the poisoning as such by high temperature application. Considerable literature was discovered on catalysts where the need was for refining by hydrogenation of hydrocarbons.

Some thousands of samples of filaments wound on asbestos were made, and the most effective was platinum wire on a platinum catalyst with formaldehyde in solution. The platinum wire used in all tests was of a diameter of 0.003 ins. - the reason for this size being that it was easily obtainable from British Drug Houses as a standard diameter for calorimeter testing.

The primary reason on designing a sensor for the detection of gases or vapours in a boat was that it should draw little current from the batteries - in the past the platinum wire helix had a consumption of some 6W, i.e. 6V at 1A, and as the average boat battery had an 80 A/H capacity, approximately 7-8 hours of operation would mean the battery became incapable of starting the engine. It was necessary to reduce the wattage still more, and experiments were therefore made in different wire diameters.

One of my boating colleagues was John Simpson, Managing Director of the British Diamond Wire Co. Ltd., and it was possible for him to draw down the 0.003 ins. wire to various sizes, finishing at 0.00l ins.. The general physical dimensions, which were ease of construction, determined the best diameter was 0.0028", being the standard wire gauge of 45. The construction therefore was changed, in that winding the helix onto asbestos string gave a varying diameter due to the unevenness of the string; in addition it was difficult to duplicate precisely each filament. The modification consisted of a helix wound with a given length of wire on a l mm. mandrel; after removal the asbestos string, suitably twisted to a smaller diameter, was threaded through the centre, anchoring the ends of the helix to an exact linear dimension, then the string was untwisted so that the fibres protruded through the turns of the platinum wire which held it in position; this gave an accurate repeatable winding. It was necessary to determine now the type of circuit most suitable for measuring the resistance change of the filament and the Wheatstone Bridge was the obvious solution. This demanded a second leg of the bridge which had to be insensitive to gas or vapour, and it was obtained by a similar winding of the platinum wire but on a 2 mm. mandrel, and asbestos string used in the same way but unimpregnated. The smaller diameter of the sensitive filament and its impregnated catalyst would respond much earlier to gas, in that the platinum wire was running at low current on the non-sensitive and therefore was not activated.

The next point of the design was to decide at what level the alarm should be given, and this had to be a percentage of the Lower Explosive Limit of Calor Gas (i.e. Butane or Propane) or petrol. Between 25% and 30% appeared to be the practical sensitivity which represented approximately half percent by volume of gas/vapour mixture. The use of a meter was considered to be undesirable at that time and therefore it was a choice of using a very sensitive relay in the bridge circuit to switch the alarm light or bell, or utilising a transistor amplifier and an inexpensive relay. The latter was the choice, and as transistors at that time consisted of only one or two germanium based types, it was decided to use a single transistor in which the base was connected to the sliding tapping of the high resistance potentiometer on the opposite legs of the sensitive and non-sensitive filaments, the emitter connected to the centre of the two filaments, and the relay in the collector circuit. Only two types of transistor were available, so called Green Spot and Red Spot; the Green Spot, which cost l/-d. (one shilling = 5p), was chosen as it was easily available from most manufacturers.

Having got this far the construction of the sensor and its flashback arrestor was given special attention, and the first sensor design utilised a small tubular assembly, the filaments connected across a Bulgin 3-pin waterproof plug and socket. The flashback arrestor consisted of mono-metal gauze 50 mesh 36 swg. wire; 5 concentric cylinders were made and assembled, and the whole unit measured 1¼ins. diameter x 2 ins. long.

Early in 1958 sufficient facts were available to produce a comprehensive patent and the patent agents, Johnson & Burgess, a local Bournemouth company, produced a provisional specification. This was passed to Reddie & Grose in London, whom I knew personally to be qualified in technical patents, to arrange for the complete patent application.

It was not the general intention at that time to be a manufacturer of gas detection equipment but to design the unit complete to a production phase, arrange the production by a contractor who would manufacture and sell, and I could then go on to another project so that the research laboratory would have minimum employees, preferably not more than one and a qualified secretary. As a result, my first visit was to Peter DuCane, Managing Director of Vosper Ltd., Portsmouth, who was highly enthusiastic, and the first six units were made by him in a true Admiralty fashion, the sensors being manufactured by myself in the laboratory.

It was necessary to carry out more practical tests on the equipment and fortunately another of our yachting friends, Royce Turner, being a meticulous person, was anxious to have protection on his new yacht 'Sherina" for his Calor Gas system which provided the cooking facilities in the galley. Two 32 lb. cylinders were arranged on the aft deck in boxes, with a detector in each box, and detectors were arranged under the hot water geyser and under the cooker; catching trays were provided and a pipe from the catching tray went into the side of the sensors so that no spillage would occur without early warning. The alarm relay controlled a magnetic valve which shut off the gas supply. It was so connected that it was normally shut and opened only when the unit was switched on and not in alarm; the installation was highly successful.

Knowledge of this device spread around other members of the Royal Motor Yacht Club and a second installation was made for a yacht being built by Cousins & Co. at Weymouth which had petrol engines and Calor Gas cooking facilities. It was the detector on this latter vessel 'Nigola III' that gave the alarm when there was a genuine leak and the owner wrote a letter to this effect, which again created more publicity. Over 100 vessels were fitted with gas detectors in Poole Harbour only.

Vospers at that time were building the 'Brave Borderer' Class of motor torpedo boat, utilising aircraft type jet engines for propulsion, and they decided it was more important to concentrate on those vessels than, in addition, go into gas detection as a product. Also, during this time, a decision was made that the elaborate design of Vospers for the gas detector control unit was too expensive for the yacht owner, so a complete re-design of the unit and the sensing head was made to allow for higher production. The sensor was changed first - the gas flashback arrestor was made in the form of a dome with double thickness gauze and the filaments supported on pillars fixed to a plastic base. The control unit, which included a bell, was re-designed into an aluminium box with a suitable nameplate incorporating red and green warning and running lights and was designed for 12 and 24v operations. Practical tests showed that the varying voltage of the battery supply on a small boat could cause false alarms if the variation was greater than 10%, and it was essential, therefore, to control the voltage more accurately. The simplest way to do this of course was to use a barrettor, and an ideal barrettor was a tungsten filament lamp which would also act as an indicator that the equipment was on, and would go out should there be a break in the connections or filaments. The tungsten lamp changed resistance with changes of voltage and tended to give a constant current to the filaments in the sensor; this compensated for wide ranges of voltage on the unit.

During the work with Peter DuCane of Vospers a problem occurred with the 'Brave Borderer' Class of motor torpedo boat; these used three Proteus gas turbines for propulsion and Peter asked me if I could detect water in diesel fuel. The answer, naturally, was "yes" but then I discovered the reason causing the problem - during the refuelling testing of one of these vessels sea water was pumped into the tanks by mistake from the tender and the three engines were ruined. I did a considerable amount of work on the detection of water in fuel oils and contacted my old friend Gordon Vokes of Streamline Filters at Guildford, who were a major company in filtration. The engineer from that company assigned to this project was Alan Thrower, and an immediate liaison developed which was extremely successful.

Some water in fuel oil does not detract from the performance, in fact at times it can be helpful, but too much water of course is a problem. I designed an equipment based on the specific inductive capacity of water and oil; fortunately water is 80 times the value of oil therefore its detection could be relatively simple. I used a high frequency circuit approximately 10 mHz, the detector was a series of blades in the form of a capacitor in the main fuel line and the capacitor was part of the tuned circuit. Detection was by a frequency modulation discriminator which would give a linear output to the measured readings. Having spent a long time with Alan Thrower and Streamline Filters and found problems due to the fact that specific inductive capacity of the oil varied quite considerably according to the type of oil and temperature, it looked as though it would turn into a major research project. When I mentioned this to Peter DuCane he was only interested in a device that would ring a bell showing that water was in very large quantities in the fuel oil, therefore there appeared to be no purpose in continuing development of a device of this sort with obviously a limited market. Alan Thrower was a meticulous engineer and he, like myself, was a perfectionist. Neither of us was ever satisfied that we had produced the best device!

CHAPTER 13

PURCHASE OF POOLE FACTORY

'Greystones' was a very large house with five acres of grounds. It had an expensive upkeep so we put the house on the market. During our residence in 'Greystones' we had purchased a plot of land in Crichel Mount Road at the top of Evening Hill, Poole, with the intention of building a house for ourselves, but a short distance away in Bury Road was a smaller house designed as a Spanish villa, originally called 'Santa Lucia' but renamed by us after purchase 'Westbury' based on the fact that it was between Western Avenue and Bury Road. There was no room for a laboratory but there was a space at the side of the house which lent itself ideally to building an extension. This we did, and built in benches and cupboards, making it an ideal place to work being adjacent to the house but with a separate entrance.

One of my friends at the yacht club was Brian Gyles, he had an hotel in Bournemouth and was also a brilliant amateur mechanic; we knew him because he married Pauline, the daughter of Stoddart Fox of the real estate agents Fox & Sons. He sold his hotel and said he would love to come along and assist me as he had a small machine shop at his house and as an amateur mechanic he could save me a lot of trouble. It appeared to me to be a delightful combination and he helped me set up the lab in the new extension at 'Westbury'.

The first thing we designed was a cabinet so that we could accurately measure gas and vapour percentages in testing the sensitivity of the sensors. Brian was a genius and in order to obtain accurate figures he made a large 12 ins. diameter drum in transparent perspex; each end was sealed and one end had a sliding drawer in which a sensor could be placed and put into the atmosphere in the cabinet. Measured gas was put in by a calibrated manometer. A fan which fitted the inside of the drum had a motor drive which turned it very slowly to be sure the gas was properly mixed. In addition a small metal dish, which was heated electrically, allowed us to put in a few drops of various liquids which would vaporise and mix, and therefore we could cover the range of gases and most liquid vapours.

The laboratory at 'Westbury' was not a suitable place for manufacture and a small company in Poole, Communications & Electronics Ltd., were invited to manufacture the sensors and the control units. As each sensor was manufactured it came back into the laboratory and the processing by various catalysts took place. C & E, although highly efficient, did require almost daily visits to observe the manufacture because of the necessity that a catastrophic warning device had to be completely free of any service problems - the reliability had to be 100%.

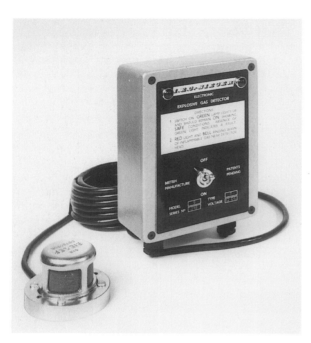

Mark 9 unit.

The unit, in the redesigned form with built-in bell, called a Mark 9, appeared to be ready for proper marketing but as I was not really interested at that time in manufacture, discussions were held with the Firth Cleveland company in London and in South Wales, and with the well-known company Siebe Gorman. No sensible arrangement could be made in those directions and it was therefore decided to continue the manufacture with C & E but to tie up with an international marketing company for sales. During my period with Scophony before the war it was essential for our high speed scanners, which were running at over 30,000 r.p.m., to have bearings which were so precise that there was no intermittent friction at those speeds. Robert Saville-Sneath had a company called International Engineering Concessionaires Ltd. in Parliament Street, London, and he had a house in Balcombe Road near to where we lived in Branksome Park. After a meeting with him he was particularly interested to get involved in selling the gas detector for marine purposes. This was the ideal arrangement, a small company to manufacture and a marketing company to sell, it left me free to carry on with the research facilities to continually examine the processing and reliability.

One of his secretaries, Jennifer Taylor, dealt almost entirely with the gas detection side and I would dictate technical replies to correspondence, not only to do with gas detection but other devices IEC were handling. I remember her getting on her bicycle with brown paper parcels containing gas detection units and cycling to the Post Office to mail them to various customers!

A company was formed on the 31st July 1959 called IEC-Sieger Ltd. and an important policy decision was made at the time, that the export market was more important than the domestic market and the expertise of IEC could be used to set up distributorships in some of the major countries. In the previous year, 1958, most patents had been applied for in the major world countries and complete specifications were accepted some time later; these covered Australia, Britain, France, West Germany, Italy and the U.S.A.

By now a few hundred units had been sold and through IEC the first 50

First factory and offices, Stanley Green Road.

marine units went to New Zealand. The BBC Home Service gave adequate publicity to the devices, and one programme went out on the World Service of the BBC. A significant factor occurred when a telephone call was received from Unilever in London; apparently a Director had installed one of the gas detector units on his boat and wanted to know whether the sensor was capable of detecting ammonia gas. As the very nature of the catalyst, and the way the developed sensor had been designed, meant it was capable of responding to all flammable gases or vapours, a request was made for me to visit London as soon as possible to demonstrate a unit; this was the start of a most successful liaison in conjunction with Unilever.

The possibilities of providing safety equipment for the big ammonia compressors of Ross Foods, Birds Eye, Walls, etc., opened up a sophisticated market requiring more advanced equipment which had to be approved by the Factory Inspector as Intrinsically Safe. In conjunction with Unilever a Code of Practice was prepared for ammonia compressors and detection equipment, and discussions took place with the Safety in Mines Research Establishment at Sheffield to obtain approvals for operation in hazardous atmospheres. A modified unit to meet the safety specifications was called the Mark 7; it was granted approval and Unilever became a good customer.

Continual development work was taking place, and it was found necessary to manufacture personally and not through a sub-contractor, so in June 1961 a building was purchased in Stanley Green Road, Poole which had been constructed as a car showroom but was never completed, therefore it was possible to re-design the interior with proper laboratory facilities, production area and two offices upstairs, the builder retaining a flat in part of the upstairs premises. At the same time Sylvia was not happy at 'Westbury' which was rather dark inside as it was in the middle of pine trees in Branksome Park. We decided, at the same time as the Stanley Green Road property was purchased, to buy a house we had always liked - 'Tinkers Revel' in Crichel Mount Road at the top of Evening Hill, Poole, which had a lovely view across the harbour and was next door to the building site we had purchased a year or two previously with the intention of building a house for ourselves. The house was modified fairly extensively and a swimming pool built in the garden.

Jacqueline had taken a Home Economics course at Bournemouth College when she left school and then was a hairdresser at the famous Raymond salon in Bournemouth until a dust allergy forced her to give it up. She took a riding instructor's course, but again found the allergy would not let her follow this career. Because the working hours were shorter she became a model at Beales, a well-known department store in Bournemouth and was runner-up to Ann Sidney in the 'Miss Bournemouth' competition. She also did modelling work for Derry & Toms in London for a time and was 'Miss Kensington'. After we had occupied 'Tinkers Revel' and the various modifications to the building were completed, she fell in love with a boy living across the road, and shortly afterwards they were married. She temporarily lived at his mother's cottage opposite before Sylvia bought a house for them at Corfe Castle.

Meanwhile Suzanne had left Wentworth Milton Mount school in Bournemouth and at first worked as a dental nurse at a local surgery. Here she became interested in the production of X-Ray photographs of teeth and decided to take up a career in photography so she served an apprenticeship with a well-known photographer in Bournemouth for some years until she decided to start her own business as an industrial photographer, calling her company Industrial Photographic Services. Initially at Stanley Green Road she was given a dark room and took photographs of all the Sieger equipment and then took photographs of industrial equipment for many of the large companies in the area.

All sales of gas detection equipment were made through IEC, London, but there was a strong realisation that the individual unit, whereas ideal for a small installation such as on a boat or in a small compressor plant, would develop ultimately into major control systems, the only competitor at that time being Mine Safety Appliances who used an aspirated technique bringing the hazardous atmospheres into a central console. The advantage of my system was the individually sited sensors which could be at considerable distances from the control unit situated in a safe area. It was only due to my visiting old colleagues at the RRE Establishment, Great Malvern, to find them breaking down a number of marine Mark 9 units and building them into a multiple console plus the fact that a Mark 9 unit sold to the National Physical Laboratory at Teddington was completely unsuitable for that particular application and exploded, that made me realise IEC were marketing with no technical selling and it would be essential to take over marketing and selling with qualified engineers, as well as manufacturing the equipment. This is a policy which stayed with the company throughout.

The original agreement with IEC stated the minimum amount of sales per year must be £5,000, and this was exceeded by only a few hundred pounds each year. With difficulty the arrangement with IEC was broken and a new company, J. & S. Sieger Ltd., was formed in August 1961, although the selling arrangements were not formally under direct control until August 1962. IEC refused to part with their customer list so it meant the company had to search old records for any details of names and addresses mentioned in correspondence with IEC, together with advertising in trade journals in an attempt to advise customers that the company was in a position to offer direct sales with complete after-sales service and advice.

The only way to break the agreement with IEC was to pay £3,000 in compensation and purchase back all the units held in stock, and it was agreed to pay them 20% more for these than the original price. This reduced the liquidity of the company very considerably and it was essential to borrow working capital from a bank. Mr Gerry Ward, the Manager of Williams Deacon's Bank (of which there was a branch in Poole at that time) was very receptive and always took an interest in the business, but the collateral necessary was quite considerable - the house and the factory. An overdraft facility of £7,500 was obtained, which continued until Mr Ward retired and the new, much younger, Manager of the bank was not interested in increasing the overdraft facility without even more collateral. As those with considerable experience of banks will know, it is the Manager and not the bank who is the essential person. As a result I joined Martins Bank Ltd. in Longfleet Road, Poole, where the Manager was Mr John Myers, whom I got to know at meetings of the Wessex Export Club (which I will mention later). He was quite happy to take the account as he had a personal interest in companies involved in export, and the facility was increased to £100,000 which, incidentally, was very seldom used, but nevertheless took financial worry away from me. Mr Myers paid regular weekly visits to the company, which was appreciated as the proper function of a good Bank Manager. Martins Bank was in due course taken over by Barclays Bank plc, with whom the company remained until 1983.

The Mark 9 marine unit was selling well, it cost £18 and a trade discount of 25% was given. A number of units were made for display and these were exhibited at the marine exhibitions as working models. It was interesting to note that in the days of petrol lighters an alarm could be given by holding the wick of the petrol lighter against the sensing head. Members of the public tried this to such an extent that finally the staff on the stand had to turn the bell off. The unit could be designed with one or two heads and as a result of making the display units for various exhibitions a power supply was designed to give a ripple-free constant voltage on the normal mains input. It appeared as though this would make a good marketable proposition so these power supplies were advertised and sold. Detailed instruction leaflets were designed and printed showing all types of installation on a vessel, including the use of shut-off valves to close down the supply of gas or petrol at source. The choice of a magnetic shut-off valve was somewhat difficult because the unit had to be fail/safe - in other words, when the unit was on the gas was on, and in an alarm condition the gas would be shut off. It was essential that the valve should take minimum current otherwise the batteries of the vessel would run down. The total current taken by the unit and the shut-off valve was usually about 400 mA on a 12V supply.

Transistors were appearing on the market, a few silicon but mainly germanium, and it was decided to build a very small gas detector, 2 1/2 ins. square, using a 2-transistor circuit (our first attempt at making our own printed circuit board, the artwork being done in-house), with a separate bell which would ring in pulses, increasing in speed as the level of gas rose. The cover was transparent perspex with the name 'Mark X' embossed in the moulding so that the components could be seen through the cover and, of course, a separate sensor.

There was a quiet period between giving up our IEC connection and starting our own manufacture and sales while we tried to contact former customers and advertise as widely as possible. Our success with the printed circuit board for the Mark X prompted us to make a straightforward transistorised amplifier as we had calls from two sources to ask if we could fill what they considered was a dire need. One requirement from a company who manufactured pilots' headsets of soundproof construction with microphone, was to produce a unit which could be used in noisy situations, particularly airfields, where up to four sets of headphones and microphones could be connected and would allow conversations between four people despite the environmental noise. We produced such a device in a very short time and sold a number to Vickers at Weybridge, which were very useful during the building of the VC.10, when a man could be on the ground at the tail and another in the cockpit checking the various controls so that they could communicate easily without the usual arm waving which used to go on.

This diversification of products is typical with a small company, but fortunately it was realised that concentration on gas detection should be the goal and the other equipments were slowly phased out.

CHAPTER 14

INTERNATIONAL MARKETS

The Sieger name was becoming well-known. Shell International contacted me as they were interested in protecting a white oil storage depot at Gibraltar. The request from Shell International to quote for a complete protection of the white oil storage tanks in the Rock meant that although Intrinsic Safety would apply, a Buxton Flameproof Certificate was also required, and immediate steps were taken to visit Simplex in Staffordshire who manufactured flameproof enclosures. The equipment was designed to fit these enclosures which then had to be approved by Buxton. A second visit was made by me early one morning to Simplex with the equipment in the car, and they arranged for it to be inserted into their flameproof enclosures, taken to Buxton for certification, and the same day it was possible to bring the completed equipment back to the factory.

In June of 1962 I spent two weeks in the Rock of Gibraltar with Shell International, supervising the testing and installation of the system. The sensors were protected by heavy iron shields against falling rocks but there was a problem with the furthermost sensor which was some 5,000 ft. inside the Rock situated outside the steel door of the most distant white oil storage tank, as it created false alarms which were difficult to explain. Discussions with the engineers solved the problem - it was found the Spanish labourers working there were using that corner as a toilet below the site of the sensing head and the methane given off in that area was responsible!

The year 1962, on looking back, was the major turning point in the company changing from an operation which was intended to make small marine units to one where sophisticated industrial safety equipment opened up an enormous market and the first certificate of Intrinsic Safety for the Mark 7 had been received in 1961. As a result of my visit to RRE in Malvern, mentioned in the previous chapter, an order was received for 120 hydrogen units with metered readouts. Orders were also received from the National Coal Board for a special sensor designed to detect methane, from Midland Silicone for another special sensor designed specifically for hydrogen and ammonia, also from The Distillers Company for detection of alcohol leakage in their storage warehouse, so it was necessary now to increase staff.

For some two or three years the most valuable assistance was given by Brian Gyles who could make equipment for production purposes, such as filament winding machines and gas measuring cabinets. Most of his work was done at home during the night hours, and a sleepy Brian Gyles would come in by ten o'clock the following morning with a completed unit; this enthusiasm was very

Alan Thrower.

essential in the build-up of the company. He finally left to go into his own business. It was also necessary to have adequate secretarial facilities available. The payroll, petty cash and book-keeping were carried out by Sylvia, but with the increased load of marketing abroad Rosemary Adams was hired in April 1962 to provide knowledge of export procedures, covering all accounting, UK and export invoicing and general secretarial procedures, remaining with the company until 1982.

The necessity to increase staff when Brian Gyles left made me think immediately of Alan Thrower, the engineer whom I had met at Streamline Filters, Guildford. A job was offered to him as Chief Engineer, together with the flat upstairs where he could live with his wife Joy and small daughter Carol until they found a suitable house in the area, and he joined the company in autumn 1962.

At this time the dome type flashback arrestor was changed to a zinc casting with mono-metal gauzes installed and sealed, a design which is still in evidence today known as the Type 800 head, the difference at the present time being that it is now made from stainless steel.

The sensing head, as previously described, was a platinum coil wound on an asbestos string. The original units installed on m.v. 'Sherina' in 1959 began to show signs of drift, and on examination it was found that after three years of operation and the vibration which occurs on a vessel of that sort, the asbestos fibres dried out and the centre of the wire helix had no support where the asbestos had broken away. It was obviously essential, therefore, to find a substitute for asbestos which would have the equivalent surface area and yet be incapable of destruction at temperatures which, when the catalyst was in the presence of gas, went to 800-900°.

From the earliest days it was apparent that a portable unit was an essential part of the system - this, therefore, was another reason for the necessity to find a substitute to asbestos. A portable would allow a proper survey to be made of major installations and would also be quite useful on a boat so that a check could be made of any possible gas or petrol leakages before engine start-up. The portable would obviously need to have a low consumption catalyst as it must run from self-contained batteries.

I contacted The Chemical Insulating Company who made a material called Refrasil composed of pure silica fibres 10 microns in diameter, which were manufactured in yarn or made into a woven tube. Tests were carried out using this material, and the performance was found to be in every way equal to the asbestos, with a more rigid construction during the winding process, capable of running at high temperatures without damage.

The first modified sensors were made by using yarn, and a special winding machine was built which would hold the yarn under tension whilst the winding was made. The tension of winding was highly critical and the machine had a number of devices to ensure a fixed diameter of winding without compressing the silica fibre. The manufacturers of Refrasil were very co-operative and after some hundreds of sensors made with the yarn, tests were carried out on the woven sleeves which simplified the winding construction and gave a more accurate mechanical device. The use of the sleeve permitted a winding machine to be made, where the sleeve was pushed over a mandrel which fitted exactly. The winding was then put on accurately in turns and length and the whole assembly removed from the mandrel, it then being mechanically and electrically sound. All sensors, therefore, from 1962 and 1963 onwards used this Refrasil technique and asbestos was discontinued.

It was decided that the ideal portable would have the sensor on the end of a semi-flexible arm of approximately 2 ft. long, but when held in the hand with adequate cable attached a person of normal height could reach 8 ft. high and also be able to measure gas down manholes or at ground level. The size of the sensor would have to be limited to 15 mm. diameter so that it could be pushed down boreholes looking for gas leaks on pipe runs. The filaments were wound on Refrasil and supported in a micanite plate with two holes, one at the top and one at the bottom. The sensitive filament was placed at the top across the hole and the non-sensitive at the bottom. The configuration would slide into a tube of special stainless steel gauze which had been treated to have the same effect as a sintered metal tube

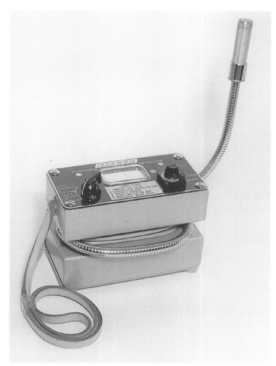

Portable unit.

and acted as a flashback arrestor.

The control unit for the portable needed a design which would have two compartments, one for the batteries and one for the circuit and meter, suitably separated to comply with the Intrinsic Safety recommendations. It was also necessary to find a way of storing the cable and the flexible tube which was fixed to the sensor head. The electrical conduit box of those days was mainly made from sheet metal and not castings as they are today, and by using two conduit boxes, one for the batteries and one for the control circuit with a spacer between the two boxes, the space so made allowed the cable and flexible tube and sensor to be wound in what finished up as a slot, and enabled the portable to be put into a case without the necessity of finding a special area to place its attachments.

The low consumption filament was highly successful and the portable in that form, known as a Type I, together with other portables of a more advanced design was still being manufactured and sold today at the time of writing. Despite little advertising it was sold world-wide with considerable numbers going to Unilever, ICI, CEGB, Rolls-Royce, British Oxygen and other similar companies in the United Kingdom. Over 80% of production was exported, the greatest number probably going to France, Holland and Australia. In 1967 35 units, designed for the detection of LPG, went to Peking in China; this was our first major contract in that country. It was believed that quite a bit of the success of the company in that country was due to this portable.

Market research is a common technique nowadays, an essential part of trading. The need for a portable was very apparent, but it is interesting to observe that if the manufacturer/designer is aware precisely in a practical way of the type of equipment best suited, that product can continue for a long time without any major design changes.

The rapid growth of the company makes it difficult to chronologically set out the various moves which were made. Two of the major distributors appointed by IEC were firstly a company in Paris called Compagnie Intercontinentale de Distribution and, secondly, a company called Panelectra AG in Zurich. The Paris company was started by Mr Ollie Kanitz who, before the war, had been Austrian Ambassador to the United States. During the war years he went to Black & Decker where he became their top marketing man, returning to France in 1955 to set up his own company. He was most enthusiastic, and the sales to France exceeded those of the United Kingdom. He had a flair for meeting only the top people, with the advantage of being a multi-linguist, and one of the major contracts due entirely to his efforts was the equipping of some ships of the French Navy.

Mark 7 control equipment was installed on a trial basis in the French aircraft carrier 'Foch', where it was necessary to detect the vapour from hydrocarbons, specifically pentane. The tests proved to be significantly successful and a report was written and published in booklet form. It was these successful tests that resulted in orders being received in 1965 to equip 20 ships of the French Navy and the aircraft carriers 'Foch' and 'Clemenceau'.

Ollie Kanitz organised a demonstration in the refinery at Notre-Dame-de-Gravenchon near Rouen where 30 units were installed in a control room and 30 sensors in the open air arranged in a semi-circle, 15 of them at 100 metres and the other 15 at 300 metres. At the centre of the semi-circle propane was allowed to escape from a pipe situated I metre from the ground, with the wind coming from behind the propane pipe to blow the gas straight to the centre of the semi-circle. The demonstration was to show the possibility of a major leakage in a refinery and where to site the sensing heads. The wind was approximately 10 miles an hour but the first warning came from a sensor at right-angles to the source 300 metres away, followed closely by the centre of the semi-circle and not, as one would expect, in the centre first of all and evenly distributed on either side. It was interesting that some two or three hours after the demonstration it was possible to take a portable unit and measure gas above the Lower Explosive Limit some four or five centimetres above the ground surface, covering quite a big area. This refinery demonstration created many enquiries. The engineer who worked for Ollie Kanitz was a Guy Legrand who had good imagination and engineering, and they were solely responsible for the company in France becoming one of the first members of the team which, as will be explained, grew international.

Possibly as a result of this demonstration, interest was taken by the Kodak Company in Vincennes, and engineers from Kodak came over with Guy Legrand bringing certain liquids, the composition of which they would not disclose, to carry out tests in the laboratory to see if these vapours could be detected. It was discovered later that these solutions were part of film stock and the necessity for detecting vapours was in process control. Tests were highly successful and orders were received from Kodak.

The second company, Panelectra AG, under the direction of Richard Buchschacher also, for a small country, did exceedingly well and the first really major system was installed at Gebrüder Sulzer in Winterthur, consisting of 20 circuits and 40 sensors situated in their big methane engine testing laboratory.

1962 turned out to be an incredible year where the future of the gas detection market showed the enormous range of applications. The many advantages of the Sieger system, as it was now being called, brought a visit from Ken Hudson of the BBC early in October and the BBC broadcast a ten minute description of the equipment, which was repeated by the overseas service and broadcast on shortwave throughout the world. The value of these broadcasts was considerable as enquiries came in world-wide and, as to be expected, every enquiry needed a special application and design. A small laboratory cum factory has its advantages - modifications can be carried out within hours, photographs and rough drawings made for record purposes, and delivery could be within a few days.

The Government Establishments became interested and in October three scientists from Harwell discussed the possibility of a multi-circuit hydrogen detection system which was constructed from individual Mark 7 units, and the whole project was completed within some weeks, with Harwell doing the installation. The UKAEA were delighted with the installation and its facilities, and as a result we had a visit from members of the Rocket Propulsion Establishment for whom further equipment was designed and installed.

Towards the end of the year Hay's Wharf in London had a major problem in a whisky bottling plant so equipment was designed and installed in this area to give immediate warning when a bottle was either overfilled or broken.

The flexibility of the bank loan allowed a positive financial policy to be instituted; every invoice received was paid on that day. It was only when the company became much bigger and the problem of part-deliveries occurred that the policy changed to immediate payment on receipt of a statement. Our relationship with suppliers therefore gave us an advantage in that we would have priority for items in short supply.

CHAPTER 15

EXPANSION OF COMPANY

By 1963 the company could look back on a year's trading entirely self-motivated. The sales were nearly £19,000 of which £9,000 was exported, compared to a maximum of £5,000 turnover in conjunction with IEC.

The detection of methane was becoming extremely important, and CHERCHAR, the Mining Research Headquarters in France, contacted Ollie Kanitz to test our sensors. The test procedure was very elaborate, followed by a period of testing which continued for six months. For our early tests we did not buy methane gas in cylinders because Brian Gyles knew the engineers at Kinson Sewage Works, Bournemouth, and we bought two or three very large beach balls which he would take in his MG sports car to Kinson, have them filled with methane and bring them back to the laboratory. It was quite an arresting sight to see this little MG with a large beach ball as passenger and another lurking in the back! We found that the methane gas from Kinson was different from other sewage farms, in that about 30% was CO_2 and the rest had methane plus impurities.

We received a major order from the Barking Sewage Works of London County Council, and samples of their gas taken in our beach balls showed a constituent which tended to reduce the sensitivity of our sensor, known even at that time as a form of poisoning. Running the sensors at higher temperature and adding cerium and calcium to the multiple catalyst gave the sensors a much longer life. The beach ball technique became extremely useful in that a reasonable brick on top of the ball gave a fairly constant output, and when we received a very special order from the Russian Trade Centre this method was used.

The specification called for by the Russians was a sensing system which would detect 98% hydrogen in 2% oxygen, and 2% hydrogen in 98% oxygen. These mixtures are highly lethal and no company would make the mixtures for us without incorporating nitrogen or CO_2; we decided, therefore, to do precisely what the Russians asked. We had two beach balls, one with oxygen and the other with hydrogen, and we borrowed from the Gas Board Research Laboratories in Poole two flowmeters - rather large devices which give an accurate indication of flow volume. Setting these to the right levels with a single pipe from the mixture to the laboratory was sufficient for Russian inspectors to approve the equipment and sign the certificate. It should be mentioned that the two beach balls and the flowmeters were well outside in the car park, so that any explosion which occurred would cause the minimal damage! We believed the Russians were impressed by the string and sealing wax method of measurement, but nevertheless it was an accurate way of carrying it out which they appreciated. Little did we know that in 1968 we would receive a contract from Constructors John Brown for detectors to measure exactly the same hydrogen/oxygen mixtures for their electrolyser which was used in the Polaris submarines.

As Ollie Kanitz was doing so well it was arranged that he would act as the main European contact and appoint additional distributors to come under his wing. At this time our existing distributors were in Australia, New Zealand, France, Holland, Italy, Switzerland and the United States. Although sales were made to chemical plants in Germany and Norway there were no arrangements with either country and therefore no service facilities. Ollie Kanitz did a complete analysis in Germany and made arrangements with a firm called Schmohl KG in Munich, who were in the fire detection business, to handle our products. Sadly, before the arrangement was finalised, Ollie Kanitz died. His company continued in the hands of an administrator and Guy Legrand, and was re-named Sciences et Techniques Internationales.

Through the Swiss distributor, Panelectra AG, a recommendation was made to appoint G. Karlbom AG in Sweden, and A/S Garek in Norway. Karlbom in Stockholm was a very able engineer and a good salesman, and the time was arriving where sales in Germany, Denmark and Sweden would need approval certificates. Without this approval companies in those areas could not purchase safety equipment unless it had received the approval of DEMKO in Denmark, SEMKO in Sweden and PTB in Germany - these authorities had to test the equipment and satisfy themselves, through a stringent programme, that the equipment was completely safe to operate in hazardous atmospheres.

At about this time a telephone call was received from the British Embassy in Copenhagen. They stated that an individual they knew very well, who was an engineer with the Danish Gas Company, wished to start on his own to handle gas detection equipment because he had these excellent connections with the Gas Company and naturally was able to install and service. This individual, Helge Schmidt, came over to England and it was found that he had good intelligence and understanding, following the policy of the company which was to appoint engineers who could sell and service rather than just salesmen. The problem with Helge Schmidt was (as with all new businesses) providing finance, so an advance of £250 was given to him and it is worth recording that within a year the sales were such that the initial payment was repaid.

The Danish authorities were also concerned about approvals and they did not like a straightforward gauze flashback arrestor, they demanded a sintered cylinder or disc. More than that, they required approval for each equipment installed rather than issuing an initial certificate giving approval for all future sales. Realising that the time would come (despite the efficiency of gauze as a flashback arrestor) when sintered metal would meet many of the difficult European specifications, a number of manufacturers in England and Germany made sintered bearings and two companies in England could produce sintered cylinders in brass or stainless steel which would be suitable. A new sensing head was therefore designed, built and submitted to the Danish authorities for approval. This was accepted and fortunately the DEMKO approval was also acceptable to the Swedish authorities for SEMKO. Gunnar Karlbom was most helpful in his knowledge of the authorities and their wishes.

It was apparent that to continue our high export it was going to be essential to meet the approval criteria of each country and this would mean different types of sensing heads. It is essential here to jump to 1966 when the DEMKO head was submitted to Physikalisch-Technische Bundesanstalt (PTB) in Braunschweig, Germany, for approval. Despite many meetings with them, together with our distributors Schmohl KG who were the translators, it was found that still further re-design was necessary as the specification was extremely difficult, in that any device with an exposed heater (and this of course was our heated catalytic filament) has to be completely hermetically sealed; this was an anomaly because if it was completely sealed there was no chance of detecting any gases as they could not enter the enclosure! Considerable discussions were held at Braunschweig and we devised a sensor with a large porous cylinder similar to those we had developed for Denmark and Sweden. The construction was massive, the connection box at the base of the unit had to be made to an increased safety specification and the porous cylinder was clamped between the connection box base and the top cover with six holding down bolts. This sensor was known as the Type 726 which happened to be our drawing number. The sensor filaments were mounted inside with special porcelain type feed-through explosion proof connectors. It was originally estimated it would be some four years before approval could be given, but approvals from PTB were then applied for via Scmohl KG - the name Sieger (in German 'victor') plus the fact that Schmohl was a German registered company seemed to help very considerably,

Various type sensors L to R: 800 with casting mounted on conduit box,. PTB, 800 stainless steel, DEMKO.

and approval was granted in 1967.

A further performance approval, for which tests were carried out in Berlin, was also granted. The performance testing produced some interesting reports which showed that the Sieger filament was highly resistant to some of the well-known catalyst poisons such as lead and silicones. Receipt of the approval opened up the market in West Germany again and it was interesting to note that by 1970 it was estimated 60% of the West German market had Sieger equipment. At this time Lloyds also gave us an approval letter covering our equipment for installation on ships.

The single transistor used in the original gas detection systems, whilst quite satisfactory for giving alarm indication of many gases between 10 and 30% of the Lower Explosive Limit, was not satisfactory for a meter readout. Transistors coming on the market at that time were becoming more sophisticated and had a greater range, and it was necessary to find a circuit which would give greater gain, absorb little power and yet be positive in its switching.

The General Electric Company were manufacturing transistors and the problem was given to them to suggest the circuit and the transistors to go with it; they came back with a circuit and the first units were built and sold. Alan Thrower then investigated in some detail the Schmidt trigger circuit which used three discreet transistors all of the same type, which GEC had suggested, and re-designed the values of all the components to use less circuit current. Also a temperature compensating copper coil was discontinued in favour of a diode. The new unit, called the Mark 7 Series 2, was developed towards the end of 1963 and early in 1964 was in full production. The original single transistor circuit of the Mark 7 was used only for the Mark 9 marine unit. On the 31st March that year the Intrinsic Safety Certificate was received for the Mark 7 Series 2 and in October the Intrinsic Safety Certificate arrived for the Portable Type 608. At the beginning of 1964 a visit was made by representatives of the Royal Aircraft Establishment, Farnborough, who were looking for a contractor to develop a fuel vapour sensor for military aircraft. They informed us that they had made a considerable review of the type of system which would meet their complex specifications and in their opinion the catalytic method would be the only approach. Many companies were interested in this contract and two companies remained after technical analysis - the English Electric Co. Ltd. and ourselves. Our company was awarded the contract on merit. A special laboratory was set up for this purpose and additional technical staff employed. We also received a letter from Shell International Petroleum Company Limited recommending us for the supply and installation of gas alarm systems, and a copy of this was forwarded to Farnborough.

The specification for the sensor required accurate operation from -40° to +200° and to work in wind velocities approaching fifty knots. Detection would be from the vapours of aircraft fuel Type JP4, Avtur and Avgas, and a number of sensors were required to be installed in the wings where storage tanks and supply pipes were situated. This contract gave us the opportunity to carry out further research on various types of catalysis and the most successful was the use of combined noble metal oxides specially deposited with added calcium which gave very stable repeatable results.

The Mark 7 Series 2 circuit was designed as our first attempt to use printed

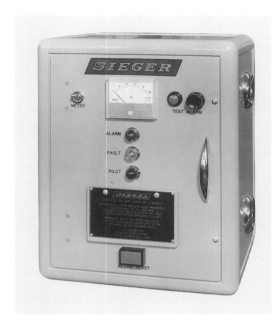

Mark 7 Series 2 unit.

circuit board techniques with discrete components and the plug-in facility allowed the construction of multi-circuits. Our French associate, S.T.I., received a contract from Societe Française des Techniques Lummus in France for a 40-point system in the pumping station for oilfield gas at Hassi Messaoud in the Algerian desert. This pumping station was situated 400 miles south of Algiers and a second contract was received from SN-Repal for a 12-point 3-level alarm system for an additional pipeline from the desert to Algeria. The gas from these sites was liquefied at the port and shipped by tankers owned by Gaz de France to Le Havre. The Gazocean ships were fitted with multi-point consoles with the sensors situated adjacent to the frozen gas storage tanks. It was of great interest to realise that we were responsible for protection from leakage of gas with equipment installed at the source in the desert, on the pipelines, and on the ships right to the port of Le Havre.

The technical superiority of our sensors was becoming so well-known that competition was having little effect on our expansion. A special unit, shock-mounted with recorder, was installed on the methane tanker 'Jules Verne' which was being built at Ateliers et Chantiers de la Seine Maritime and it is interesting to record that later, when a fault occurred on this unit due to a relay failure after the ship was in service and berthed at Le Havre, it was Rosemary who went to Le Havre with the necessary replacement spare on her way to holiday in Paris. It was this type of immediate service which we were able to provide as a small company, everybody being part of a team - one of the secrets of our success.

The satisfactory working of our installation for UKAEA in the Rutherford High Energy Laboratory at Harwell prompted a good order from CERN, Switzerland, the European Organisation for Nuclear Research in Geneva.

The year 1963/4 was showing a rapid expansion and equipment was designed and built for Dowty Fuels to measure leakage of their high pressure pumps used for supplying fuel to jet engines. Apart from Hay's Wharf, alcohol detection equipment was designed and built for Strathleven Bonded Warehouses (storing whisky) outside Glasgow, and this was installed and working for their opening day.

Towards the end of 1963 into 1964 equipment was provided to the National Coal Board, ICI at Billingham, Manchester, Middlesbrough and Welwyn Garden

City, British Oxygen, the Gas Board, BP Research Centre in London, The Steel Company of Wales, as well as numerous small installations.

A meeting was held at the Central Office of Information headquarters in London to promote exports to the USA which I, amongst ten other industrialists, attended. One of our most successful distributors was an organisation called Case-Smith-Jesse in Los Angeles. The departure of Mr Case and the untimely death of Harry Smith left Norman Jesse to carry on the American sales. He was an ex-pipeline man from Kansas City and had entry into the major pipeline companies of that time. One of the largest orders received from him was for the Great Lakes Pipeline Company (later called Williams Bros. Pipe Line Co.) for 123 Mark 7 units. Because of the basic simplicity of this unit minimum service was required; as the pipeline stretched many hundreds of miles cost of service was extremely important to the Americans. The installation triggered off orders from many other pipeline companies in the States.

America is a very big country and a lot of the basic purchasing came from Houston, so Norman Jesse appointed The Condit Company to promote sales in that area. It was interesting to note that some of the early platforms installed in the North Sea were equipped with our gas detection equipment in Galveston and towed across the Atlantic to the North Sea sites.

During one of my visits to the U.S.A. I was in New York City when a call was received from Poole stating that Atlantic Richfield Oil were interested in a

First assembly section, Stanley Green Road. L to back: Marion Mitchell, Joy Denman, Margaret Davis. R to back Sheila Sinnick and Gwen Maidment.

quotation and discussion. I went straight there, to their very great surprise, as they had only telephoned the enquiry through the day before and the next day the Chairman and Managing Director of the company was on their doorstep!

The year 1964-5 showed a total sales of over £40,000 of which £32,000 was export. The company had been able to participate in the five-fold increase in ethylene capacity in France, where some 86% of the total productive capacity in 1970 was from petroleum and oil. The first of the large ethylene leak detection alarm systems was sold to Technip-SNPA for a new plant near Pau. The unit consisted of two complete systems in one console, each system continuously monitoring twelve detection points, giving alarms at two levels of gas/air mixtures. Hydrogen detection equipment was supplied to Norsk Hydro-Electrisk Kvaelstofaktieselskab.

Final approval of Sieger equipment was received from the French National Navy and the Royal Australian Navy. The Royal Australian Navy, after investigating all gas detection systems available on the Australian market, indicated that Sieger equipment was the most acceptable; this was after much deliberation on the merits of the various units offered, which included American detectors. Twenty-six units to detect leakage of petroleum vapour were fitted on the 'Empress of Australia', a 10,000 ton vehicular ferry operating between Sydney and Tasmania.

Our first woman operative, Mrs Joy Denman, joined the company in 1964, shortly followed by Mrs Marion Mitchell and then several others. With all the extra work a Foreman was needed for Production and Alan Thrower met a Mr Reginald Stride. He found, on talking to him, that Reg was a very practical individual who then decided to take a year's course in electronics and finally joined the company later in 1964 to take charge of the Production operation.

The company was growing rapidly and essential modifications were made to the building in Stanley Green Road, adding offices and, as Alan had moved, converting the flat to research and sales and later adding an 'L' shaped extension.

On the many visits I and others made abroad it was sometimes necessary to combine service to equipment, which made it essential to train people who could fulfill this function. A previous associate of Alan, Gerald Moore, joined the company and they worked very closely together developing the module system, as against the original equipment designed, where multi-circuits were built into an enclosure which could not be expanded or contracted. This modular system, known as the 1300 Series, was a great advance and reliability was such that no change in design occurred until 1981. It was a major order in 1982 for a Russian pipeline (causing an international stir) which specified Model 1300 units as the control equipment due to its known reliability. In 1965 S.T.I. in Paris obtained from insurance companies in France a reduction in insurance premiums on establishments equipped with Sieger gas detectors.

The need for technical sales engineers grew in importance and whereas our distributors did an excellent job outside the UK, the UK operation was weak. A former Petroleum Inspector, with a very sound knowledge of the industry, Emlyn Thomas, was appointed, situated in Glasgow, His personality helped to build up a reputation with ICI who at that time were becoming major customers, and the need for a London base was later covered by using the services of Geoffrey Davis - this latter appointment, as will be seen later, became another turning point in the company's success.

For many years I personally processed every sensor head and records were kept of every unit. Running an expanding business and acting in production on test was impossible and I had to delegate. Catalytic and Electrochemists were employed.

It was realised that our system for detection of flammable gases to protect plant and personnel, despite the rapid growth, would one day be involved in competition with many other companies - in fact some competition already existed in the UK and USA. Gas detection became an 'industry'. It was essential to cover detection not only of flammable gases but those which were of danger to life. Apart from carbon monoxide various gases and vapours used in industry, petro-chemical plants, solvents used in paints, plastics and many others, sensing had to be in many cases in parts per million. Therefore the recruitment of an electro-chemical chemist was to pursue ideas in this field and research started in 1966. The result of producing an oxygen sensor was shown on a film produced by the Central Office of Information, shown over television.

John Stallard, who finally became our Chief Draughtsman and then Manager of our Ministry Contracts Division, joined Alan Thrower as an assistant and a Drawing Office was set up with three assistants. A Quality Control Inspector was also appointed.

The policy of having control of production in all its forms demanded the use of a machine shop capable of making every part to do with our sensing heads and sheet-metal enclosures for the equipment. There were not many companies who were carrying out paint spraying at that time so an expert car sprayer was employed, firstly in a small hut and then accommodated in the extension at the rear of the factory. Two brothers, one of whom built special enclosures, covered the sheet-metal work, and a very unusual Polish instrument engineer joined the company, who could make anything using only a Myford lathe with attachments. A number of components were obtained from local wholesalers and an individual from one of these companies became our storeman. As production was increasing purchasing became a major operation, and it was fortunate that during one of the redundancy sessions at Sydney S. Bird, Ted Daley became available and was our Chief Buyer. He was absolutely professional and his buying saved the company a considerable amount of money compared to the early days when Radiospares and other wholesalers were meeting our needs.

Any equipment which is manufactured has to have good, very technically orientated promotion leaflets and clearly written manuals. Again it had to be mainly an in-house procedure and technical leaflets were written by Alan Thrower but had to be printed outside until the necessary equipment was obtained in the late 1970's when a qualified engineer came in and took over our printing section and a Print Room with an offset printer was set up. It was then possible to print in full colour and produce leaflets in French and German.

It is essential not to leave out the clerical side which was originally covered by Rosemary Adams, but as the volume of business increased two shorthand-typists were employed and an accounts and wages clerk who learnt despatch procedures from a 'bible' on export documentation produced by Rosemary, and she was later joined by two invoice typists. Most of our equipment despatched abroad was sent by air freight via a daily collection from the factory.

Our auditors at that time were Thornton Baker and one of the partners, Harry J. Smith, was responsible for the company's audit and accounts. He left Thornton Baker to join us and financial controls of purchasing and production were introduced, so essential to convert a small individually owned company where memory played an important part, to an intermediate sized company with plans for growth.

CHAPTER 16

TESTING EQUIPMENT AT SEA

The rapid expansion world-wide of gas detection systems under a very great variety of environments, particularly massive changes in the North Sea, caused some concern that false alarms could be given due to extraneous circumstances - simultaneous combination of various external interferences could not be duplicated in the laboratory. It was observed in laboratory experiments that radio frequency signals picked up by the sensor leads could, at certain frequencies, produce an alarm condition. It was also observed that transient signals, in the case where equipment was fed from the mains electricity supply, in rare conditions would also produce a false alarm. It was decided that with the very large number of units now supplied for marine purposes and off-shore platforms it would be essential to obtain a vessel where the control units could be installed and checked and, at the same time, external sensors could be subjected to the usual atmospheric conditions. Poole Harbour has been known for some time to be an excellent testing place for corrosion and at one time most manufacturers would have floating rafts alongside Brownsea Island, in the middle of the harbour, where samples were left for a period of time to study the effect of atmospheric damage.

In June 1966 a vessel called 'Laelia' was purchased, based on a Scottish fishing trawler design, 52 ft. long with a dry exhaust system from the main diesel engines and a single funnel amidships to give an opportunity to measure exhaust gases. The vessel was installed with a 100W transmitter covering the marine band frequencies, a VHF transmitter which worked on the 150 mHz band, a diesel generator providing I10V DC and an AC inverter to give AC power from the DC batteries to run various equipments, echo sounders etc., as well as a 24V DC supply for ancillary equipment.

The gas detection equipment could therefore be tested with all equipment in operation, and it was found that under certain conditions a false alarm could be obtained when the main radio transmitter was working at full power with the aerials adjacent to the cables feeding the sensor heads. A 1300 type rack was installed, making it possible to test various units, and as a result minor design changes were made to overcome these problems. The vessel was used for this purpose continually from 1966 until 1974, when a new vessel called 'Environist' was built, designed precisely for the purpose with additional equipment, which will be described later.

The company was aware of the value of publicity and the vessel 'Laelia'

"Laelia"

found extra-curricula activities which promoted the marine side of the business. I was a long-time member of the Royal Motor Yacht Club and became involved in offshore power boat racing as Race Controller, particularly the Daily Express Cowes/Torquay race, and other races organised by the Club from 1966-1974. It required accurate control of all the power boats taking part by means of a fleet of enthusiastic yacht owners who took on the job of patrol and rescue throughout the whole course of the race. The VHF and MF radios were brought into full use and a plotting table was designed and built for 'Laelia'. Links were made with the Coastguard, with Cowes Control and all vessels throughout the whole course, including the VHF installed in the Royal Motor Yacht Club at Sandbanks. A Sieger Cup was given to the Cruiser Class of one of the races with gas detectors given away as prizes - in many cases won by Fairey Marine who fitted Sieger gas detectors as standard anyhow!

Alan Thrower visited Helge Schmidt in Denmark to sort out a problem he was having with a unit installed in a Gas Works. It continuously gave false alarms and Alan found the relays were buzzing; using a 'coathanger' as a stethoscope he could hear the relays singing and the voice coming over was plainly Shirley Bassey! It turned out that this was due to a high-powered FM transmitter in the next field causing pick-up on the wiring. Modifications were made on site and changes necessary were incorporated in future units.

1966 was an interesting year in that we were growing from a very small company to one which was gaining international importance. We received an order from Imperial Oil of Canada Limited for equipment to be installed at six of the Interprovincial Pipe Line Company's stations using units with, usually, 6-8 sensors from each console. A big system was sold to Parsons Powergas for an installation in Iraq. In addition orders were received for multi-circuit systems for ethylene gas in both Rumania and Turkey and from Continental Engineering in Amsterdam for eight 10-circuit systems for two chemical plants in Russia. We also supplied equipment for the Tyne Tunnel Project, the Tyne Tunnel Mid River Sump and the Harbour Crossing at Lowestoft.

An application for employment was received early in 1967 from a Mr Roland Cunnell who had recently been made redundant from Cambridge Instruments and as we still had only two salesmen trying to cover the UK market, he joined the company as Sales Manager. Because he required a bi-lingual Secretary a Swiss national was also employed. He was a very effective salesman and did much to expand the business in the Iron Curtain countries, so in 1968 he was made Sales Director.

At this time an award to exporters was initiated entitled 'The Queen's Award to Industry'. No indication was given in the invitation as to what the requirements were, apart from showing three consecutive years of sales figures indicating an increase in export sales each year. The second year a section was included for Technological Achievement. As we were continually exporting 70%, sometimes reaching 90% of our production, Rosemary spent some three months in conjunction with the Chief Accountant, Harry Smith, in preparing a magnificent document to apply for the award. It was therefore a great disappointment when we received a letter stating we were not successful in obtaining the award as it was left to the discretion of the panel of selectors who, although they visited other companies, never visited ours. We applied again in future years until 1969, when we were informed by the then Board of Trade they had pushed the company forward with a high recommendation, but still we were not accepted. The Board of Trade arranged for me to receive the OBE for Services to Export in 1970 - although this was gladly accepted it went to the individual and not to the company, all of whom were responsible for our success. Applications for the Queen's Award continued until 1979, still without success.

With 50 employees more space was required so we rented a factory of approximately 2,000 sq. ft. at the rear of our building and modified it to our requirements.

Due to our diligently sending out Press Releases when any major order was received, we had a lot of publicity both in the local newspaper and in various national publications. In August 1966 the BBC broadcast on the World Service a ten minute programme entitled 'Raising the Alarm' which mentioned the granting of our German PTB Approval. Because of this publicity I became involved in extra-curricula activities and one of these was our local airport at Hurn, where my interest was due to my wartime association. In addition Mr Karlbom, our Swedish distributor, had a personal aircraft and on visiting us found he could not land at Hurn because they closed their doors at 17.00 every day, so he had to fly to Heathrow and make his own way by car to Poole.

It was learned that the Board of Trade, who were responsible for the Airport, were being persuaded by the owner of Southampton (Eastleigh) Airport to change the grading of Hurn to a B Class, which meant that Immigration & Customs would not be available. As our exports and those of other companies depended on communication to the rest of the world, an Airport such as Hurn was an essential part of our operation, so a meeting was held and the

Bournemouth Hurn Airport Association was formed with two Public Meetings held in Bournemouth Town Hall. Sir Alan Cobham became President of the Society, I was Chairman and Sylvia was Secretary, and the meetings were based on proposing Hurn Airport to be the major Airport for the South. It was as a result of these meetings and the persuasion, particularly by Sir Alan Cobham, that the Board of Trade accepted the seven hundred and fifty thousand pound offer for the Airport by Bournemouth and Dorset Councils. The Association actively attended all consultant meetings of the Council until 1974, and considerable correspondence took place in those years, the files making up folders almost 6 ins. thick.

We had enquiries from one of the major food storage companies, Sainsbury's, for a freon detection system to cover their main warehouse in Basingstoke. The normal catalytic filament was not capable of detecting freon, so immediately an experimental set-up was designed which consisted of a heated copper catalyst which, in the presence of freon gas, produced a green flame. The copper was heated by a very small flame from a propane cylinder. This could be measured photo-electrically and we found that it would be easy to detect leakages as low as 750ppm. Sainsbury's required 92 points of detection and a major console was constructed with an aspirating pump drawing in air through nylon tubes from various parts of the warehouse. The magnetic shut-off valves, which were timed, were in each line where a 5 second sample was taken sequentially. A paper chart recorder was arranged to have contacts so that when a pre-determined leakage limit was set it would operate the alarm condition. The importance of the installation was an economic one; firstly, should a leak occur and the temperature level rise in the warehouse a considerable amount of food would be destroyed and, secondly, the cost of freon gas is infinitely higher than the ammonia commonly used, so it paid to have a very early warning of the smallest leak. A number of these refrigerant leakage consoles were made and installed in the UK.

CHAPTER 17

CONFERENCES, AND PUBLICITY

It was decided in 1968 that we would ask as many of our overseas distributors as possible to a meeting in London where our engineers and sales staff could get together with them, giving us an opportunity of showing our latest equipment. The Excelsior Hotel at Heathrow was ideally situated and on the 26th February our first International Distributors' Conference was held with a total of 28 distributors present. It was possible at that time to show additions to our new equipments - the PTB Approved sensing head as well as a special head which we designed for measuring toxic concentrations of carbon monoxide. Our 1300 system, developed and in production, was also shown as the first flexible system where individual plug-in modules were controlling each sensing head.

In July the BBC again broadcast from Bush House on the Model 1300, a programme entitled 'New Ideas', and as a result the British & Industrial Trade News published a full description of the unit, printed in Chinese. There was no question we were world leaders in flammable gas detection, but by discussing our five and ten year plans, which we did quite often (many times with a change of mind), we realised that giving a warning of possible explosion danger in a boat or a factory did not necessarily protect an individual. The detection of toxic gases, many of which are not flammable, and the extremely low levels of detection required, allowed us to set out a programme of research into other sensing devices.

Our electro-chemical chemist was given the job of looking into electro-chemical cells and the Development side were looking at other methods of detection. A visit by an engineer from Dunlop Rubber was fortuitous, he had developed a system where a paper tape immersed in a chemical solution would produce a colour which could be detected by photo-electric means. Their main problem was detection of TDI, an iso-cyanate used in the manufacture of polyurethane foam. The manufacture of this material was usually done by somebody pouring a bucket of TDI into a container holding the polyurethane, which immediately foamed up to many times its volume. It had been discovered that inhalation of this iso-cyanate affected the liver, and many cases were reported of this incurable illness. This was the very lead we needed, and we took a licence from Dunlop and from ICI who made this specific tape. We redesigned the equipment where the paper tape was in the form of a cassette and would last for 168 hours, and engineered it to a very reliable unit. Other tapes were devised and our sales in the UK and USA far exceeded our expectations. Of the many tapes devised for various toxic vapours and gases, all gave alarm conditions and/or meter readouts well below the MAC (Maximum Acceptable Concentration).

The Mayor of Poole at that time was Alderman Fred Rowe, a well-known builder/developer, and he was approached by an official of the Board of Trade who explained to him that Export Clubs were being set up throughout the country and as there was not one in the Poole area suggested he might sponsor a luncheon, bringing all the manufacturers involved in exporting together, to see whether an Export Club could be formed. A luncheon was held at the Haven Hotel, Sandbanks, in March of 1968 and more than 100 people attended. Various names were proposed and companies agreed to co-operate. I was appointed Chairman of what was to be the 'Wessex Export Club', a position I held until 1985 when I became President.

The first meeting of the Club was held at the Antelope Hotel in Poole on the 16th May 1968, when I and two members of the Bristol and West Exporters' Club gave short talks, followed by a business meeting during which the Rules of the Club were proposed, seconded and accepted, sub-committees appointed and a decision made that Club meetings would be held on the last Thursday of every month. The 70 member companies of the Club have continued with monthly meetings from October to May, producing a family atmosphere covering many companies, all with a single purpose in mind - to improve the British image abroad and export.

Norman Jesse of Los Angeles, as explained previously, was a pipeline man with many associates. Two of these, Charlie Keane and Steve Bergman were both resident in Kansas City. During a visit to England I was told of a need for a very simple domestic gas detector as a friend of theirs, Larry Winn of Winn Senter Enterprises, was a major developer and was about to build something like one million houses in the State of Kansas. He wanted a domestic gas detector which would be reliable and give a warning in the presence of leaking methane gas. A unit was developed almost overnight; it used the 800 type head (the original) and the sensitive and non-sensitive filaments were connected as one side of a Wheatstone Bridge, the other side being the low voltage centre-tapped transformer provided with a suitable low resistance adjustable control. The bridge output, connected to a full wave rectifier, consisted of four diodes rectifying the 50 cycle supply, the output fed to a sensitive relay. The bridge circuit was extremely efficient because of the low resistance of the two sides. At 30% of the Lower Explosive Limit of methane gas the current into the relay was in the order of 100mA; the sensitivity was such that it would always give an alarm at about 30% of the LEL. The warning device was a buzzer operating from the 50 or 60 cycle mains. Our calculations showed that this could be built at a material cost of about £4, a labour cost of £2 and a selling price of between £10 and £15. With the quantities envisaged by Larry Winn considerable savings could be made to both material and labour costs.

A sample model was sent straight to the USA for evaluation and early in October Sylvia and I visited firstly New York City and then spent a week in Kansas City. McAllister, an associate of Larry Winn, had an electronics factory and made an excellent pre-production unit of the Domestalarm with ABS moulded cover; the unit was working in their offices, surprising many people that a device could be so sensitive without using a single transistor. The exercise, however, was a wasted effort in a way as the gas companies did not like the idea of detection equipment fitted in alongside their appliances, giving the impression explosions were quite likely if such a device were needed. This was not a new reaction, our local gas company reacted in the same way.

America being a very large country the tour of the States was intended as a look at other possible distributors to cover a greater field than just the pipelines and petro-chemical plants. After Kansas we visited Houston and discussed projects with various companies, including the Dresser Company, main suppliers of control equipment for offshore platforms. We then went on to Miami where discussions were held with the Miami Fire Service Company who appeared to be the major manufacturers for fire fighting equipment in Florida. We also visited the Underwriters Laboratories in Chicago - America had no equipment approvals system in operation but Underwriters Laboratory checked all electrical equipment and gave approvals. One organisation was Factory Mutual, a consortium of insurance companies giving approvals on equipment in hazardous atmospheres.

They, at that time, had little facilities for proper testing and the object of the visit to the Underwriters Laboratories was to get them organised, based on our SMRE (Safety in Mines Research Establishment) at Sheffield, the Flameproof Establishment at Buxton, and the German PTB Approval. Some days were spent at U.L. describing in detail the sort of testing facilities they needed.

The Groningen field in the southern part of the North Sea was beginning to produce large amounts of natural gas and the pipeline came into Holland. Our distributors in Holland, Regulo Nederland n.v., obtained a major order from N.V. Nederland Gasunie for equipment which was installed in six compressor stations.

An enquiry received from the Swan Hunter Group who were building two container ships to be called 'Atlantic

Installation on one of the 'Atlantic' vessels.

Causeway' and 'Atlantic Conveyor', was of sufficient interest for Alan Thrower to visit the shipyard and discuss the installations. We received the order for equipment on both these vessels - later to be involved in the Falklands War.

The Sales Department was strengthened by two qualified engineers who were fluent in German, French and Russian. To all exporters true success lies in being able to converse freely in the language of the country - we all know that most people speak English, but nothing gives more understanding than a salesman reasonably fluent in the language of the country and it gives confidence to the buyer.

CHAPTER 18
FACTORY MOVES TO NUFFIELD ESTATE

In January 1969 Southern Television (at that time our local station) came to the factory and the results were shown on March 6th in their programme 'Facing South'. Meantime Sylvia realised her wish and a Bassett Hound puppy which she called 'Copper' arrived at home, joined in 1976 by a black kitten called 'Octo', both getting on well with our older dog 'Rusty'.

At this time we looked carefully into the possibility of using Switzerland as the main distribution area for all European sales, and in conjunction with Richard Buchschacher of Panelectra AG, our Swiss distributors, we investigated the formation of a company in the Canton of Zug, which held considerable interest due to the advantageous taxation position.

Special discounts were given to all our distributors and the German business was growing very faSt When we examined their selling prices and the prices they paid for equipment we felt the time had come when the main company should form its own selling organisation in West Germany and maybe manufacture. In September Sylvia and I, with Roland Cunnell, went to Germany and, in conjunction with Mrs Ernesta Schmohl of Schmohl KG and Mrs Schestag of Ingenieurburo Rudolf Schestag, formed a company called Sieger-Gasalarm-Systeme GmbH. The greater part of the finance came from myself with a small interest by Mrs Schmohl and Mrs Schestag; Ingenieurburo Rudolf Schestag, incidentally, were the manufacturers of the sintered metal flash-back arrestor used in the PTB type sensor.

The management of the company had to be left to Schmohl KG as we had nobody available to live over there, and felt it should be run by a national. The name 'Sieger', which has an Austrian origin, was a valuable name and we looked forward to considerable success. We tried assembly, shipping over all the component parts for the 1300 series of equipment, and Schmohl hired a production man and two women to do final assemblies for orders in their country. When we carefully costed the operation, we found that the assembly women received something like two and a half times the pay of equivalent workers in England and were something like 20% slower in their work. The thirty thousand Deutschmarks capital invested in that operation was completely used up in the first year and it was decided to wind up the company, pay all charges legal and otherwise, and carry on with Schmohl as distributors. We then realised we should have arranged for a company employee to be in charge of the operation, which would have separated it from the original Schmohl distribution agreement. The only advantage that came from the German company was the fact Schmohl realised they could lose a valuable income and hired an excellent salesman called Werner Remmel who, within two years, had managed to obtain 60% of the West German market in gas detection against major competitors such as Draeger and MSA-Auer.

We had appointed at that time a very good agent in Israel and the Israel Petrochemical Enterprises Ltd. in Haifa asked for a reference from ICI, Welwyn Garden City, on the suitability of our equipment for ethylene plants where a number of equipments had been provided. An excellent reference was received from ICI stating the satisfactory performance of Sieger detectors installed in gas analysis rooms on the Wilton Polythene Plants and a number of other factories operated by the Plastics Division, and this enabled us to obtain the order.

Roland Cunnell demonstrating the 'Cosign'.

In view of the legislation which had proved such a problem in the United States over exhaust emission, particularly in California, it appeared to us at the time that in order to maintain exports to the United States our cars would have to be considerably modified and the emission levels from the exhaust of carbon monoxide and oxides of nitrogen should be seriously limited. We therefore designed and tested a portable car analyser called the Cosign, using our 800 type catalytic filament which was connected to the control unit by an aspirating pump and a meter readout showing the level of the carbon monoxide. A number of these units were made and some were sold but, as one would expect, without legislation the market was extremely limited and the system was shelved despite the fact that there was a very good write-up in the 'Sunday Telegraph' and the equipment was demonstrated by Roland Cunnell to Barry Westwood on the BBC's 'Tomorrow's World' programme.

At the end of March we had our second International Distributors' Conference and the success of the one held at the Excelsior Hotel in London the year before prompted us to hold it at the 5-star Carlton Hotel, Bournemouth. We

Conference at Carlton Hotel, Bournemouth. French, German and Swiss distributors.

End of conference dinner, Carlton Hotel.

designed and built a display unit containing working models of all the equipment we manufactured, made specially for easy construction and disassembly so that it could be transported to trade and industrial exhibitions; this was installed in the Carlton Hotel ballroom. Twenty-two representatives from twelve countries attended the Conference and by very careful organisation of their flight arrival times we had a coach at Heathrow to pick them all up and bring them to Poole without too much waiting time involved. We knew a very good taxi driver from Bournemouth and he undertook to drive the coach and bring them back to the Carlton. He was an unusual individual who took the delegates through the best part of the countryside and stopped for lunch at a well-known public house en route.

After the Conference the coach took the delegates to Sainsbury's refrigeration plant in the food storage warehouse at Basingstoke where they could see our system of halogen gas detection in operation. This Conference was of extreme value to our distributors and to our own engineers, researchers and technical sales, and Conferences have proved time and time again to be a most valuable exercise in market research. The new display unit was sent to Germany and installed at the ACHEMA Exhibition in Frankfurt in June 1970, the largest chemical engineering exhibition in Europe.

The British National Export Council (BNEC) and the Council of British Manufacturers of Petroleum Equipment sponsored an Inward Trade Mission from Canada. Four members of the Mission came to the factory and were impressed by the work we had done and our world-wide reputation; the small company in Poole was gaining a name for pioneering gas detection covering safety and measurement throughout the world.

Units installed at Sainsbury's, Basingstoke.

The advantage of our research and development vessel 'Laelia' was reflected in the orders being received for equipment for the North Sea rigs and platforms engaged in the exploration and recovery of gas and

Phillip's Petroleum Model 1300 unit.

oil. Credit for creating the base for sales of our equipment in this area must be given to our distributor, Mr Geoffrey Davis, owner of a London-based company who, with his contacts in the natural gas and oil industry, was able to obtain many of the first orders for gas detection equipment. We were confident of the performance of the equipment due to long-term testing on our vessel. At this time Alan Thrower took the opportunity of visiting one of the Phillips North Sea rigs to gain information on the performance of the equipment on site; the first of many visits made by various members of staff. In later years a large Service Department was built up, many Service Engineers becoming familiar with the operation of these massive expensive enterprises. In the late 1970's/80's offices at Aberdeen and Lowestoft were set up to maintain local contact with the oilfields.

It may be worth relating some of the hazards the Sieger staff had to undergo during visits to the North Sea rigs. On one occasion Alan Thrower and Bill Simons (who took over from Alan as Chief Engineer in 1975 as will be seen in a later chapter) arrived too late at Aberdeen to fly out to the oil rig on the helicopter they had intended. They boarded the next flight and, landing on the rig, found that the helicopter they missed had hit the platform coming in and lay upside down on a pipe barge anchored to the rig. To make matters worse, whilst they were lifting up the injured, using a massive rig crane, the clutch on the crane burst into flame - this set off the automatic fire extinguishers on the rig which drenched everything. To cap it all the crane jib jammed over the heli-deck with their helicopter still grounded. After carrying out their work they had to go back to shore as there was insufficient accommodation to stay overnight, however the helicopter could not move because of the crane jib in the way. It started to get dark and a Force 8 gale began blowing up; still the jib was over the helicopter but they had to get off.

They were ordered into the helicopter and sat wondering what would happen. The pilot started up and tried a few practice hops, but what with the wind and the chopper blades only a few feet from the crane jib things were beginning to get nasty. Alan Thrower got out a book and tried to read to take his mind off the events, whilst Bill Simons sat looking extremely pensive. A few more trial hops and whoosh - the helicopter went off backwards and sideways, the illuminated rig reeling away at a drunken angle, but the helicopter was off safely. At one time the staff all looked forward to visiting rigs for a few hours away from the office!

The company's reputation as a major exporter of safety warning equipment was recognised by the British National Export Council, a Council formed to advise the Government on any problem, making constructive suggestions straight to the Minister of Trade. I attended meetings, having direct access to the Minister, and in December 1969 lunched with Roy Mason, then President of the Board of Trade; these meetings were extremely valuable.

A famous individual from Texas, Red Adair, the world expert in putting out wildcat fires during oil drilling operations, wrote saying he used our semi-portable equipment to find gas leaks, in many cases before ignition took place, stating Sieger gas detectors were a very great help and they were proud to have them on the job.

Major technical journals were continually giving editorials on the company's progress, and a fairly comprehensive write-up in the journal 'Electrical Equipment' described installations on two natural gas rigs, a terminal platform in the North Sea 40 miles off Great Yarmouth and two other natural gas platforms in the Bass Straits off the Australian coast. It is worth recording here that between 1963 and 1970 the company received write-ups (in many cases several times) in 105 technical journals and newspapers. The company ran its own advertising campaign until about 1970 when a professional advertising agency took over.

At this time we had distributors in the following countries:-

Australia, Belgium, Canada, Rep. of China, Denmark, E. Europe, Eire, Finland, France, W. Germany, Ghana, Greece, Hong Kong, India, Israel, Italy, Japan, Malaysia, Netherlands, New Zealand, Norway, Pakistan, Portugal, Singapore, South Africa, Spain, Sweden, Switzerland, Turkey, U.S.A., W. Indies, also 3 UK representatives based in Bristol, Glasgow and Leeds.

When the Queen's Birthday Honours were announced in June 1970 I was awarded the OBE for Services to Exports and in November of that year I went to Buckingham Palace for the investiture, accompanied by Sylvia and our two girls. I remarked later that the 25 seconds I had talking to the Queen seemed like half an hour she was so well informed on the company. To mark this event the staff presented me with a table lighter and scroll drawn up by the Chief Draughtsman and signed by all the employees on the company, numbering 61. I told them they were all responsible for our success.

Space was now a desperate problem and we heard through estate agents of a factory on the Nuffield Industrial Estate near Fleetsbridge leased by a company called Technivision (a subsidiary of Englehard Industries) who had gone out of business. It was available to lease completely equipped. I went to the factory on a Saturday morning and met a Director of Englehard Industries. The building

Buckingham Palace after OBE presentation. L - R Suzanne, Sylvia, myself and Jacqueline.

Presentation scroll. L - R Sylvia, myself and Rosemary Adams.

contained over 100 metal benches with integral lighting, seating, a complete machine shop and stocks of components, cable and other expensive parts, and I made an arrangement there and then that I would take the lease over for the remaining nineteen years and purchase the total contents for £10,000, which was gladly accepted.

We realised that the office accommodation was insufficient, being only a single storey section in front of the typical warehouse/ factory, so plans were drawn up to put a second storey onto the existing office block. Agreement was reached with the owners, Confederated Life of Canada, that the cost of the addition could be added to the revised rent, as our policy was to use capital for the business; the agreement was signed at the end of August. The whole of the Production, Packaging and Drawing Office departments moved early in October into the 15,000+ sq. ft. factory area of this building; two days later the Test Department moved but it looked as though we could never fill the space.

As can be imagined, a lot of time and petrol was used in keeping communication between the two premises that winter.

As mentioned in the letter of recommendation from ICI received by the Israel Petrochemical Company, we were the main suppliers to ICI olyfines plants. One of these had 500 sensors mounted round the perimeter at various levels of the whole plant. ICI engineers devised a steam curtain - this consisted of a pipe surrounding the plant with equidistant holes facing vertically throughout its length. In the case of an alarm in any section, processing steam would be diverted into this pipe and the steam pressure produced would lift the gas up into the atmosphere and therefore prevent it becoming a hazard, as most of the gases were of a high molecular weight and therefore likely to move along the ground and be ignited by any ignition source. ICI were anxious to publicise this and we contributed £8,000 towards the cost of the publication describing the system. As a joint advertising effort (the small Sieger company with the great ICI conglomerate) this was an achievement in itself. The publicity for our company was magnificent; whereas the steam curtain idea was not a process but could be easily copied, the Sieger name associated helped us in selling equipment to Japan and other petro-chemical plants who were not previously customers, due to the gas detection system having this very high recommendation. A special film was made by ICI showing the equipment and the steam curtain in operation. With associates I visited the plant at Billingham, taking Dutch and German visitors to witness a complete demonstration. Of course the ICI maintenance engineers were not happy on these various demonstrations because it was their process steam plant that provided the steam and pressure was lost very quickly!

There was a need in these petrochemical plants for a portable which could be used in the open area giving a positive alarm for leakage so that any work done on pipes would not result in ignition from a leak in the vicinity of the work. A unit called the 1601 was devised; it had to be extremely rugged and stable. The ideal form was that of a pyramid and this was made of coated sheet steel with a battery system in the base and the alarm system at the peak of the pyramid, consisting of the sensor, a flashing light, a polycarbonate lense, and a loudspeaker giving a pulsating 1,000 cycle note. This model was an extremely expensive unit to manufacture as the case had to be hand-fabricated and

ICI Billingham, steam curtain in operation.

ICI Billingham, mounted Sieger gas detection heads.

attempts were made to reduce the cost without success. A decision to increase the price was made in the hope that the big companies who could afford such a safety warning device would be the likely customers and so the loss made on each unit could at least be brought up to break-even point. Fortunately when the price was increased the orders increased - it was known in the factory as 'The Dalek'.

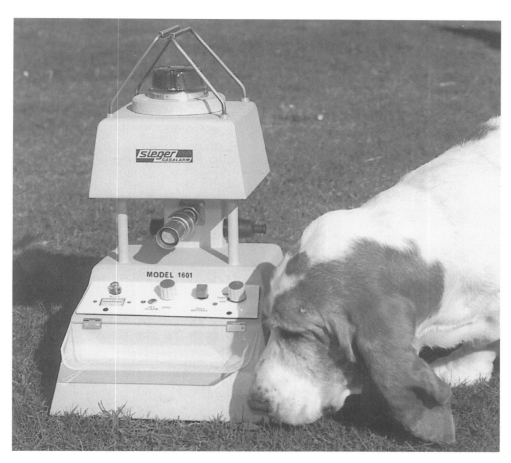

1601 Portable unit with Bassett Hound 'Copper'.

CHAPTER 19

OFFICES MOVE TO NUFFIELD ESTATE

At this time in the company, whilst we had a few indentured apprentices, there was no 'Off the Job' training available, and apart from attending the local Colleges for part-time day and evening classes, all training was carried out practically by moving the apprentice to various departments in the company. When the Engineering Industry Training Board was formed the apprentice training was monitored by a member of the Bournemouth, Poole & District Group of the Industrial Training Foundation.

Apprentices received a day release to College per week plus evening classes. Companies were encouraged to apply for exemption from the 2 1/2% levy placed on their payroll by the EITB, so yet more paperwork had to be produced by Rosemary Adams and a certain number of apprentices had to be taken on each year to comply with these requirements. In due course Don Nichols, who was already the Safety Officer for the company, undertook the additional task of Training Officer and arranged for module training which had then been introduced, achieving exemption from the Industrial Training Levy each year from the time he took over training.

The Wessex Export Club had continued to flourish with meetings being held in various hotel and club locations and speakers on subjects of interest to exporters, from representatives of the Department of Trade & Industry, BBC Overseas Broadcasts, Ambassadors to various countries, and, in later years the local Member of the European Parliament. From time to time speakers were arranged on local areas such as Poole Harbour, Hurn Airport (now Bournemouth International Airport), the proposed building of the Bournemouth International Centre (BIC) in Bournemouth etc. Forums were held to allow local exporting companies to present a short description of their activities and to answer questions from the audience. Normally a meal was served first, thus enabling members to exchange views or gain knowledge from other exporters, and speakers were introduced later in the evening.

Subscriptions were kept low, sufficient to cover the cost of an evening meal and the expenses of the speakers who often had to stay overnight if coming from a distance. A monthly newsletter was sent out to each member company and publicity was sought by sending reports and sometimes photographs to the local Press. One year a Mission from the Club visited South Africa and a model of the Wessex Griffin (the Club symbol) was made in felt and given to the group as a mascot on departure.

Wessex Export Club meeting, 25th September 1969.

The Club played a significant part in the local developments as a questionnaire was sent to all members when the building of an hotel on the Quay was proposed so that companies would have the opportunity of stating what type of hotel was required in the area to accommodate the needs of their visitors and conference facilities. This method was also used on other occasions.

That Spring Sylvia and I took the opportunity to take a world trip, visiting Japan, Hong Kong, Australia, Fiji and the USA. This visit was of great importance - in Japan new distributors were appointed and we were entertained royally by the ICI staff in Tokyo. Visits were paid to the various petro-chemical plants extolling the virtues of the steam curtain and the Sieger system of gas detection. During that visit Dr Taguchi, who devised the semi-conductor sensor, was visited and I was offered the rights to sell and manufacture in the United Kingdom. Samples were brought back and tests were made of the device, but it was not considered sufficiently accurate for anything but a basic warning system, therefore no action was taken. The visit to Hong Kong was most hectic; in the eight days there were only two hours spent in so-called sight-seeing, the rest of the time was spent with various companies in conjunction with our distributor, Golden Coin Trading Company run by James Lamm and his wife, part of the Wormald organisation in Australia, selling their fire detection and prevention systems together with our equipment.

Mr Hanbury Brown, who was working with our London agent Hazard Controls (formerly G.C. Davis) before he joined the company, negotiated personally the contract for providing gas detection equipment for the Hong Kong vehicular tunnel which went from Kowloon to Hong Kong. Under the main roadway were two large gas mains and two types of detection were essential. At each end of the tunnel air compressors forced air into the pipeline enclosure and the air escaped through gulleys in the roadway. The extremely diluted air which came up in the roadway was detected by highly sensitive flame ionisation units to give alarm in the case of a leakage of the very diluted gas. In addition a large number of sensors were placed in the tunnel itself to monitor gas leaks during periods when the main air compressors were not in use such as during service periods.

We went on to Australia for a visit of ten days exceedingly hard work, in that Wormald Brothers, a very big organisation in the country (and our distributors), were not getting the business which was available. For example, next door to the Wormald main factory a brewery was looking for ammonia detectors and it was only my visit that created a very good order. Lectures were given to various Wormald personnel who came in from all over the country, and visits were paid to Botany Bay where there was a large ICI petrochemical plant which had trouble with our sensors. Investigation showed that the steel covers which had been fitted over the sensors to keep off the rain, had been mounted upside down so that rain filled the cover and the sensor, naturally, could not breathe under water.

Whilst we were visiting abroad information was received, following an application for the BNEC Export Award for Smaller Manufacturers, that we had been successful as runners-up and on March 3rd Roland Cunnell went to London to receive the certificate. During the day the television unit visited the factory and the programme went out on 'Nationwide' in the early evening. This sort of event was received with great enthusiasm by all the staff, and the team atmosphere was such that everyone shared in this success.

In the light of mounting world concern about occupational safety, health and air pollution, I decided in the late sixties - as mentioned in the previous chapter - that Sieger would enter the field of toxic (as distinct from flammable) gas detection and analysis, and in 1971 a separate company, Universal Environmental Instruments (UK) Ltd., was formed to market a new range of instruments in the industrial hygiene and air pollution fields, and also a range of medical devices. For obvious reasons it was decided to set up a completely separate U.E.I. distribution and sales network, although the U.E.I. network included certain Sieger distributors who were considered to have the necessary resources and expertise to handle both ranges in their territories.

Knowing the enormous potential of sales in the United States, an engineer spent some weeks there and MDA Scientific Inc. in Chicago, who were well-known and well respected in the medical electronics field, were appointed as a distributor. A working agreement was drawn up between the two companies, in that MDA would also develop specialist tapes and the information would be passed to the parent company - in return, naturally, all tape information produced at Poole would be sent to Chicago.

In 1973, for administrative reasons, U.E.I. became a Division of J. & S. Sieger Ltd., maintaining its separate identity as far as marketing, sales and overseas distribution were concerned for a time before being completely merged into the main company. Following our experience with the TDI tape, intensive research and development went into the production of tapes for other substances, resulting in a range called the 7000 Series.

The company having been 'born' in Poole, it was natural that it had to play a part in the activities of the town. The Wessex Export Club gave certain prominence to the company and I was asked to attend a meeting held in January 1971 at the Town Hall in Poole to decide arrangements for the 600th Anniversary of the Montacute Charter. This Charter allowed the town to have a Mayor and Sheriff. As Chairman of the Wessex Export Club I was asked to join the Committee and despite the pressure of work of a growing company I accepted the position of Chairman of this Committee. The celebrations were to be held in June, with all guests suitably attired in appropriate costumes. Sylvia and I were appointed Queen and King of the Mediaeval Feast. This event took place at the Poole Technical College and the arrivals were interesting - first of all Sylvia and I, complete with crowns, arrived in the Cadillac, followed by the founder of the Wessex Export Club, Alderman Rowe, who arrived on horseback smoking a Churchill cigar! Mrs Pat Sloman of Southern Television (our local station at that time) arranged the full T/V camera crew and the celebrations were shown on the ITA channel the following evening. A film of the event was made, which I bought and after having the 35 mm. film converted to a 16 mm., presented it to the town.

In addition Sylvia and I held a cocktail party in the Swan Lake pavilion in Poole Park, and as Chairman I spoke to the very large crowd in the suitably decorated Park, for which I had presented £400 to the town to have the trees floodlit. Alderman Rowe presented the town with an ox and a spit had been arranged for a major barbecue, but the following day the heavens opened and it rained without a break so unfortunately that part of the celebrations had to be abandoned.

Meanwhile, on Nuffield Estate, the building of the second storey was completed according to plan and on the 10th May all office personnel moved and the old factory in Stanley Green Road was leased to a local company. Due to lack of any facilities for meals on the Estate, a canteen had been incorporated into the production area and the first canteen operative was employed. Two days after moving a Mini-Conference was held and later that year a full Distributors' Conference took place at the factory.

1971 was a very busy year - from the 9th to the 22nd June we exhibited in Russia at Erevan with one of our Sales Engineers in charge. We were invited by the Royal Aircraft Establishment, Farnborough, to share their stand at the Paris Air Show and two engineers manned the stand for those three days from 27th May to 1st June. To be allowed to share a stand with RAE was a considerable tribute to our reputation.

Much interest was shown by Hungary in our equipment for coal mines and lectures were arranged in the Iron Curtain countries by our Sales Director, Chief Engineer and Head of Research. In July the First Commercial Secretary of the British Embassy in Budapest visited the company, with a representative of the Hungarian Embassy, to look over the factory and report back to the State that we were capable of manufacture and had the facilities to meet their requirements. As a result, in August the Hungarian National Gas Conference was attended by members of the company, which was the start of a long association with

Leaving Stanley Green Road factory 1971.

31 Nuffield Estate, Poole.

Paris Air Show 1971. Shared stand with Royal Aircraft Establishment, Fanborough.

Distributors Conference, No. 31 Nuffield Estate.

Assembly floor in 31 Nuffield Estate 1971.

countries behind the Iron Curtain. An enquiry from Rumania was received for gas detection equipment and a considerable amount of cable for an installation for a petrochemical plant. We quoted for the contract and received an official order but unfortunately there was no cash involved, only a straight barter deal. We, of course, were not in a position to undertake barter but luckily Richard Buchschacher, our Swiss distributor, did the barter and the goods received he successfully sold back to Rumania in a continuation of the barter! In October two engineers attended the XII Wanderversammlung at Keszthely, Hungary.

We did not mind competition, with a proviso that the competitor had to make good reliable equipment, a very important factor because without competition one tends to get in a position of status quo. Our biggest competitor in the U.S.A. was General Monitors Inc. and Dr Linville, the President, and his Marketing Director, Mrs Bernadette Murray, visited us in September and we happily showed them over our factory which duly impressed them. We had a lot in common - Dr Linville was an entrepreneur and produced a very good H^2S sensor which we actually purchased from him as we had not yet devised a really satisfactory unit to compete.

An increase in production staff meant an overall Production Controller and in 1971 we appointed Ted Daley to this position. Ted had been covering Buying and was a thoroughly professional man who had been in the trade all his life and was well respected by the factory employees. Fortunately the three supervisors, Joy Denman, Marion Mitchell and Gwen Maidment were most experienced in their production techniques and they divided the production of the various equipments between themselves so that it was of great assistance to Ted to have these skilled staff under him plus, of course, the assistance received from Reg Stride as Production Foreman. This move left a vacancy for a Chief Buyer and John (Dennis) Wheatley joined us from Wessex Industries to fill this post, a position which he admirably covered.

Following the move to Nuffield Estate an area of the main factory was given over to Suzanne and her assistant where she installed her colour and other processing equipment and was always available to photograph any piece of equipment either in use or on site throughout the UK and in Europe, having an unusual ability to photograph instruments, machines and engineering installations. In 1976, with the great increase in her work, she purchased the building which had been our Machine Shop behind the old factory in Stanley Green Road and in 1984 she bought from me the original factory in Stanley Green Road. Among her customers were British Gas, Plessey, Hamworthy Engineering, Aerograph Devilbiss and Davy McKee. Most of the photographs of Brownsea Island sold by the National Trust are her work and she provided all the photographs for a book entitled 'The Brownsea Islander', published by Poole Historical Trust.

CHAPTER 20

EXPANSION AND NEW RESEARCH VESSEL

Early in 1972 the President of Imbema Regulo, Mr Jan Bloemers, and his Chief Engineer (later a Director of that company) Mr Jacobus Verberne, sent photographs of the 43 seater coach they had purchased and which had been described at our Conference. This coach was converted into a travelling showroom and demonstration unit for all Sieger equipment to tour the Benelux countries. It had a conference section at the rear with facilities for serving light refreshments, and working demonstration units installed. The publicity received was quite outstanding.

Only a year previously we had looked at the 31 Nuffield Estate factory and wondered how we were going to fill it; this we did easily and now needed more space. We viewed a building on the opposite side of the road, No.19, which was an unfinished shell of only four walls, as the people who had started building decided to discontinue business. We planned that Research and Development, Service and the Drawing Office should be removed from the factory proper and No.19 would make an ideal building for that purpose. The owner of the building was found and after a discussion with him, which was rather like a horse dealer buying a horse, the whole freehold was purchased for £20,000. Work then commenced on designing an ideal building absolutely to our needs. Planning permission for the building was received in May, an Industrial Development Certificate (which was necessary in those days) was also received, and work was soon completed by a small highly efficient and enthusiastic building contractor.

A number of company cars had been purchased, including a Ford Transit van, and it was essential for us to do our own service. At the back of No. 19 was a large area and we commenced building three garages, one with a pit; tools and equipment were purchased and a mechanic engaged to service and repair all the company cars, even when the total reached over 40 in 1980.

In October we took a conference room at the Kensington Palace Hotel in London and exhibited all our equipment as a working demonstration. At the end of this year our big competitors in America, England and Germany - Mine Safety Appliances (MSA) - telephoned for a meeting to be held at the Excelsior Hotel, Heathrow Airport. Rosemary and I attended this meeting, where an approach was made by that company to take over J. & S. Sieger Ltd. With all the work and enthusiasm put in by so many people over the past few years and our growing

Imbema Regulo, 43 seater coach.

Interior of coach fitted with Sieger units.

19 Nuffield Estate, Poole.

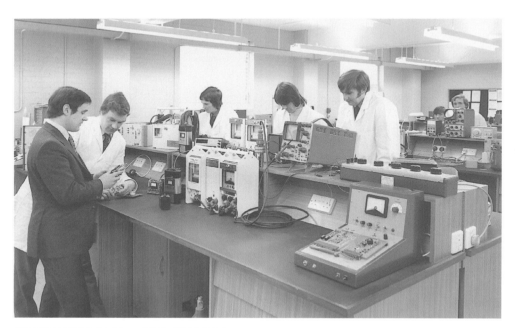

Development laboratory 19 Nuffield Estate.

strength world-wide, it would have been a retrograde move which, although it could have been a lucrative proposition, lost the advantages and incentives for an organisation of people who worked as a team.

An invitation was received from Jan Bloemers for Sylvia and I to be his guests in Haarlem for the 25th Anniversary of his company. The cost of the celebrations, the hotel accommodation and all ancillary expenses were borne entirely by Imbema Regulo, and without doubt it was a Jubilee to be remembered. The first day was fully occupied, starting with an organ recital in the Grote Kerk, Haarlem, by the city organist, a reception by the Municipality of Haarlem following in the mediaeval Gravenzaal at the Town Hall. In the evening a banquet was held at the Frans Hals Museum, a most magnificent building with candelabra holding real candles providing the illumination. On the next day all visitors went on a boat trip through the Amsterdam Canals and the farewell lunch in Haarlem ended a magnificent celebration.

It was very necessary to reward the pioneering employees of the company and Alan Thrower, who had contributed so much to the company, was made Technical Director in this year.

As stated before, one of the most successful distributors was Sciences et Techniques Internationales in Paris, owned wholly by Mrs Kanitz, the wife of the deceased founder, and managed very well by Guy Legrand, a good engineer and salesman, and J. Citroen who controlled the financial side.

Visit to National Coal Board at Barnsley Mine, Yorkshire 1973.

Approximately 20% of our exports went to France and we understood that Mrs Kanitz was quite prepared to sell the company to me, however Guy Legrand would not accept this and demanded at least 51% of the company should be in his name so that he would have control. While discussions were going on Roland Cunnell introduced us to an associate of his who, for seventeen years, had been running the Cambridge Instrument office in Paris, a Mr McAree. We felt that his fluent French and German and his background in instrumentation would enable him to be a good manager and we would then have control of the French company. Negotiations finally broke down with STI so a new company, Sieger SA, was formed in 1972 with Mr McAree as General Manager, his secretary having a single share in the new company in accordance with French law. I borrowed the amount of NF.100,000 from Lloyds Bank in Paris to initiate the company, and an engineer who had been working with Guy Legrand for many years, Mr Van Gyseghem, was employed as Engineer and Service Controller. Over the years sales did not improve and the company showed losses. We realised then that there was a certain amount of difficulty with personality conflict between Mr McAree and his customers. By 1978 he and his secretary, whose agreements had expired, were dismissed from the company and the service operation at St Maur under the direction of Mr Van Gyseghem, took over. Immediately business improved but it was realised that in the attempt to have absolute control of STI we had lost a most valuable contact with many French companies and Guy Legrand became a very active and successful competitor.

In 1973 our work for the National Coal Board was expanding and it was essential for everyone working on that equipment to have first-hand knowledge of mine workings. Early in February a visit was paid to the mine at Barnsley, Yorkshire, by eight of our staff. As a result a development contract was received from the NCB for the manufacture of a methanometer.

Our friendly Bank Manager, Mr Myers, having built up the former Martins Bank Longfleet Branch, was naturally moved to another Branch, presumably bigger and better, and with Barclays Bank taking control a new manager took over. He discovered that the facility arrangement we had with Mr Myers was never confirmed in writing and our limit was £20,000 only. As our considerable export business was faced with settlement payments usually between 90 and 120 days, the facility previously agreed of £100,000 was absolutely essential for us to carry on business. The lower limit was upheld by the Directors at Barclays Regional Office in Southampton, despite a visit by myself with Roland Cunnell and Harry Smith which still produced a negative response. As a result I sent a telex to the Prime Minister, Harold Wilson, asking him if it was the intention of the Government to stop overdraft facilities for export finance on short-term arrangements. The Prime Minister passed this query on to the Department of Trade & Industry who, in turn, contacted Barclays Bank Head Office in London and they immediately reversed the decision of the local Director, who soon afterwards took early retirement.

Equipment had been supplied for ethylene plants in Mexico through Simon Carves and as it was deemed important to visit Mexico, Sylvia and I travelled there in late March/early April. Our Mexican distributors were contacted and considerable time was spent at the petroleum refinery near Mexico City. The

29 Nuffield Estate, Poole.

Mexican distributor spoke good English and it was found that the top people in the refinery also spoke English well, most of their training obviously coming from the United States. We asked what had happened to equipment supplied to Petroleos Mexicanos at Poza Rica so they then got on the telephone with a radio link to this area. The reply they received said that the plant did not have anything called 'Sieger' but they did have an instrument which was still working called 'Syger', as pronounced by them. They said it was the only one that was still operating, they had had American equipment there which was not satisfactory. The reception given by the engineers at the refinery was excellent and our distributor provided them with a considerable amount of literature, particularly the portable, as we found a number of one of our competitor's aspirating portables and it was carefully pointed out to them that our 608 Type 1, as it was finally called, was a more convenient instrument to use.

The German Draeger company was still interested in an arrangement with Sieger. As they appeared to be quite serious it was thought worthwhile to pay a visit to Lubeck and, through a close association with Barclays Merchant Bank in London, Mr Jeremy Seddon of that Bank accompanied Sylvia and I on the visit - he had taken physics at university and was therefore quite au fait with the operation. The Draeger factory, covering their world-wide production, was most impressive, a considerable amount of their work being in the medical field including the chemical tubes for the measurement of very low levels of toxic gases and medical field including the chemical tubes for the measurement of very

Presentation BNEC Award by Sir Peter Allen 1972.

low levels of toxic gases and vapours. Dr Christian Draeger, the President, introduced us to his father Dr Draeger, the founder. The conclusion was the same as before, based on the fact that we already had a world organisation so no real advantage would be gained in being absorbed by Draeger, and this decision remained firm despite further visits by that company to Poole.

Our second application for the BNEC Award for Smaller Manufacturers resulted in our winning, together with four other companies, and I went to the Savoy Hotel in London for the presentation. Sir Peter Allen, Chairman of BNEC, who presented the perspex trophy and certificate, was an old friend of mine during the war years when he was one of the originators of the development of polyethylene. Since that time he had become Chairman of ICI and was an example of how ICI promoted a good chemical engineer to the top position of the company. The Award also consisted of a two week visit, all expenses paid, to East Africa for a nominated employee of the company and companion of his/her choice, excluding management, so we sent our Production Foreman Reg Stride and his wife Joan on the trip, which they very much enjoyed. The Award ceremony in London finished after lunch and in order to let the company and the Press have details as soon as possible a car picked me up at the Savoy Hotel, took me to the Battersea Heliport, and forty-five minutes later I landed on a spare piece of ground in Hatchpond Road, Nuffield Estate, and Press photographs were taken at the factory.

After the sudden death of our Chief Inspector we had an application from a Mr

Showing the BNEC Award to Gerald Moore and Harry Smith

Tom Pope who had been Works Director some time previously of the Brocks Group of Companies but had been made redundant, and he was appointed to the post.

Only three years after moving into the factory we found ourselves again requiring more space. Office accommodation was extremely limited so when the building next door to No. 19, which was No. 21, became available so we took it over on a short lease and moved some departments into it. At the same time we were negotiating with the owner of the scrapyard, No. 29 - Dunstans Car Spares, next to our main factory. Discussions with Mr Hayward, the owner, were finalised; he agreed to make modifications to the building and we had permission to build an extension at the back. The idea was to give up the temporary lease of No. 21 and put our complete Machine Shop, Model Shop and the about-to-be formed Government Contracts Division into this building. It also had a large car park at the side, which was badly needed.

The research vessel 'Laelia' was being used to its utmost but we realised it did not have the full facilities to do the job properly, in that no radar was installed and we needed a vessel with adequate room for testing and much of the equipment working on board which would be encountered on an offshore platform. For example: high powered m/f, h/f and VHF radio, commercial radar, stabilisers, 240V AC generator not less than 20 kW. A complete specification was drawn up of our requirements and the final negotiations were held with the Berthon Boat Co. Ltd. at Lymington, Hants, to build a new research and development vessel to be named 'Environist'. It was to be built of wood (Berthon

Above - Research and Development vessel 'Environist'.

Right - Martin Chase testing on board 'Environist'.

still had specialists in that type of construction), two main diesels would exhaust through two separate funnels and the forward structure would consist of two masts with adequate room to mount sensors, the big radar scanner and other aerials. Fortnightly meetings were held, with all interested parties, either at the factory or at Berthon Boat Co. Ltd., so that the final design was a combination of many practical suggestions and all the trades involved were fully aware of what was going on.

In September of 1973 we had our first major meeting to decide on our Defence Contracts Division to be installed in No. 29. The Defence Contracts Division would have its own Buying and Accounting and was to be headed by Alan Thrower with his deputy, John Stallard as Divisional Manager. John Stallard had remarkable ability as a Design Engineer with a very good commercial brain, and it was he who negotiated so many contracts with the Ministry of Defence. By 1975 the Division had grown to 23 in number and in 1978 employed 60 people. Due to the security implications it was a self-contained unit. The reason for this separation of the business was basically due to the fact that the equipment was founded on the 7000 chemical tape monitor and was to be used in storage systems where Polaris type missiles were situated to detect very small leakages of the propellant fuels. As equipment for the MOD had to be so rugged and pass all the vibration and other special tests it was not possible, in our opinion, to put that type of construction in the same factory with our normal commercial equipment. In addition, the acceptance of some Government Contracts provided a regular and quick return on capital while, in the long-term, benefits of research, development and productive experience should arise and be transferred to the company's commercial well-being. Development and production of MOD equipment brought in £900,000 to the company income between 1974 and 1978 and in 1978 the current orders in January, providing work into the last quarter of 1980, had a value approaching £2 million. On the 1st October all modifications to No. 29 had been made and the various departments moved in.

We were faced with a considerable loss in the sudden death at the end of October of our experienced Production Controller, Ted Daley. There was no time to hire a production man, it had to be somebody already in the company and the only man available was Tom Pope who, as previously stated, already had previous experience as Works Director of the Brocks Company. He was promoted from Inspection to the position of Production Controller and his knowledge of the company, although only brief, was useful in that he had some years of experience.

CHAPTER 21

ROYAL VISIT

In January 1974 it was realised that rewards for hard work and devotion to the company's interests should be further examined and on the 16th January a meeting of the Board was held at our house, to which Rosemary Adams, Gerald Moore and Harry Smith were invited. Rosemary Adams was appointed Personnel Director, Gerald Moore Research and Development Director and Harry Smith Financial Director. In October Suzanne was also made a Director of the company.

Professor Watson, who was head of the Medical Electronics Division of St Bartholomew's Hospital, London, became our consultant through a recommendation by Dr Thomas, the wife of Emlyn Thomas our Scottish representative, as we were thinking seriously of expanding into the medical electronic area. The work done on oxygen cells resulted in Professor Watson stating there was a great demand for a PO^2 catheter for use with premature babies, where too little or too much oxygen could cause considerable harm to the child. We obtained special catheter tubes and inserted two very fine wires leading to the head of the unit where a tiny bead, which was an electro-chemical junction, measured oxygen in the blood. A large number of these catheters were made and given to various consultants but there was always a fear of liability incurred should any of these fail or break down. When it is considered that the catheter had to be inserted into the main artery and pushed along the artery into the heart the dangers were very apparent, however work proceeded for three years then was discontinued in 1976, having cost the company nearly a quarter of a million pounds.

In April of that year we had the first fixed price contract from the National Coal Board, based on development work carried out the previous year. This was the first real entry into the NCB after many years of trying small development contracts.

In June Alan Thrower went to the Poznan Exhibition in Poland, where we were exhibiting, a mission which turned out to be so successful in later years when major contracts were received from Poland.

In August a Mr Dukes from Geneva, Chief Executive of the Raytheon Company in the United States, came to see me and explained that the Raytheon Company, who covered such a wide field, were anxious to get into the safety side of industry and would like to own a company who were known world-wide in gas detection. Dukes was a delightful individual and he brought along, on another visit, a Mr Wilson, Managing Director of A.C. Cossor, the British subsidiary of

Appointment of new Directors 1974. L - R: Gerald Moore, Rosemary Adams and Harry Smith.

Raytheon. Various discussions were held, Sylvia and I visited Switzerland and meetings were held in London. I called on the assistance of two people from Barclays Merchant Bank, Jeremy Seddon who, as mentioned before was a physicist/banker, and Roger Culpin, a lawyer/banker. At one meeting Raytheon introduced the head of their European operation, a Mr John Clare, who was a difficult individual and it did not seem possible for any further negotiations to take place. I received calls from the President of the Raytheon Company in America, Mr Phillips, and the Rt. Hon. Lord Sherfield, who was Chairman of Cossor and Raytheon (Europe), but I had made up my mind that as an association would have to be with the Geneva operation there did not seem to be sufficient friendliness to create a proper working arrangement.

It was realised that despite the very high quality of our production it would be necessary to obtain the 05-21 Approval Certificate from the Ministry of Defence for quality control. Although we realised it meant a lot of additional paperwork, we nevertheless proceeded and a visit by Mr Groves and an Assessment Board to the factory gave an indication that our operation was such there would be no difficulty in obtaining this approval. We had a good Quality Control Engineer who, in his previous company, had obtained approvals, so he produced a document, in conjunction with Alan Thrower and John Stallard, which was submitted to the Ministry and in due course approval was received.

Gerald Moore had been working with Roland Cunnell on the UEI side of the business but there was a certain personality incompatibility so Gerald decided to

Visit by Admiral Scott and Staff, 26th March 1975.

leave and set up as a consultant in the area and a Dr Denney was hired to take over Research. With the inception of the Contracts Division a number of physicists and instrument engineers were hired.

1975 was a red-letter year in the history of the company. Early in February the first sea trials were conducted on 'Environist' and all the hard work put into the design of that vessel began to show. The two independent funnels with phase tuned exhaust systems from the main Gardner 8 cylinder diesel engines showed relative silence when the engines were running at 900 r.p.m., which was equivalent to about 8 1/2 knots, the vessel having been designed for a maximum of 10 1/2 knots. In July a Commissioning Party for the vessel was held at the Shipyard in Lymington and in August the BBC and Southern T/V came aboard the vessel. It was interesting to read the write-up in 'Offshore Oil' which stated that this floating research and demonstration laboratory was the most elegant testbed ever floated out of Lymington Harbour. We had excellent Press coverage throughout that year on 'Environist' and an invitation from the Editor of 'Jane's' for a complete write-up to appear in 'Jane's Ocean Technology'.

With Alan Thrower having become completely involved in the new Defence Contracts Division as Technical Director, it was essential that we found a Chief Engineer who could look after the general operation of the company and after much advertising Mr W.R. Simons was hired, a brilliant engineer from Smiths Industries with enormous experience. He was immediately given the job of supervising the Development Department. Later, in March, Mr Hanbury Brown joined the company as Manager of Research and Development; we had considerable knowledge of him from his association with G.C. Davis in London where he was responsible for some of their major orders for offshore fields. It is interesting to note that I knew his brother, Dr Robert Hanbury Brown, very well as we were associated as Divisional Leaders in the Telecommunications Research Establishment during the war.

One important department, Technical Authors, consisted of four Authors and one Technical Illustrator, producing the technical content for sales leaflets and all the service manuals for standard and special equipment. The Technical Illustrator was also available for any special lettering required.

Previously it has been mentioned that a company holding an important industrial position in Poole automatically becomes involved in extra-curricula activities, which greatly assist the image of the company when hiring personnel. Two things occurred in this connection during the year; the company made a seven-year covenant and a monetary gift to the Western Orchestral Society to build extra facilities in the Poole Arts Centre, which was under construction. I took part in fund-raising and receptions for this as it was felt that the Bournemouth Symphony Orchestra, which was known world-wide, would tend to establish the importance of the Poole/Bournemouth area and, indirectly, assist exports.

The second instance of involvement was when the Strathallan Nursing Home in Bournemouth, owned by the Nuffield Foundation and later called The Nuffield Hospital, was about to be closed and rebuilt as a small private hospital to fulfill a wider range of essential medical activities. Various companies in the area offered to subscribe a sum of money by covenant to have a hospital room named after their company; we had a J. & S. Sieger room.

Going back to the earlier days, I was a member of the British National Export Council (BNEC), formed under the direction of the current Prime Minister, Harold Wilson, and various lunch meetings were held at which I was able to meet Cabinet Ministers. The BNEC, which was entirely made up of industrialists, was primarily to promote export activities and we thought it was unfortunate that when Edward Heath became Prime Minister he disbanded this organisation in 1972 and made it part of the Board of Trade under the title 'British Overseas Trade Board'. After the sponsorship of BOTB, Donald Dick in particular did so much work in tying together the activities of all the Export Clubs in the United Kingdom, of which there were some fifty. We had committee meetings in a little restaurant built into the arches by Ludgate Hill and I was appointed Chairman of all the Export Clubs through Donald Dick's influence. The annual meetings of all the Clubs, held in London, allowed me to personally introduce various Chairmen of BOTB such as Lord Thorneycroft, Sir Frederick Catherwood, Lord Limerick and Earl Jellicoe.

The Minister of State for Trade & Industry suggested to the British Overseas Trade Board that there should be an Advisory Council, made up of the top executives in the United Kingdom, to meet regularly in London and advise the Minister on any problems to do with export. Sir Frederick Catherwood was appointed as Chairman of what was then called the British Overseas Trade Board Advisory Council (BOTAC) with H.R.H. The Duke of Kent as Vice-Chairman. I was appointed to serve on this Council as representative of all the Export Clubs in the

British Overseas Trade Board. Myself, Lord Thorneycroft and Donald Dick.

UK, a position which I held for some six years until the Council was disbanded when the new BOTB Chairman, Lord Limerick, decided the formation of that organisation had served its purpose in that the strong liaison between industry and government had been fully met. The result of that was my receiving in 1981 the honour from the Queen of Commander of the British Empire.

It was fortunate that I had a number of conversations with H.R.H. The Duke of Kent in those years as he was a permanent Deputy Chairman of BOTAC and we met on various occasions. At one time I was waiting for my car to arrive to take me back to Poole and the Duke was also waiting for his driver, so we chatted for almost an hour in the hotel lobby on the necessity of exporters learning languages and being able to speak with reasonable fluency to foreign nationals, so when the company was one of five chosen to present Case Studies on their achievements, he was delighted to learn a visit to the Sieger factory had been planned for him.

This took place on December 10th 1975; a preliminary visit was made a week earlier by the helicopter crew of the Queen's Flight, when the exact timing which is part of a Royal visit was checked. Discussions were held with the crew, the Divisional Commander and Chief Superintendent of Dorset Police and other security officers, whilst communication was held with the Chief Education Officer of Dorset for permission to land in the nearby school playing field about 200 yards from the factory.

It was agreed that the Lord Lieutenant of Dorset, Colonel Sir Joseph Weld,

Duke of Kent's visit 10th December 1975, talking to John Stallard, Lord Lieutenant of Dorset Sir Joseph Weld on right.

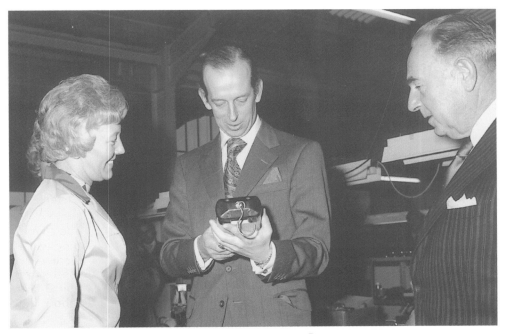

Presentation of portable gas detection to the Duke by Joy Denman.

would meet the Duke with his official car when the helicopter landed and drive with him to the front of the factory where I would be waiting; he would then get out and officially introduce me to the Duke. This was all carefully planned but what actually happened was not quite the same. When the car arrived at the entrance the ceremonial sword worn by Sir Joseph became wedged between the front and back seats of the car and he had great difficulty in getting out, by which time the Duke had stepped out of the car on the other side and, as he already knew me, shook hands, the official introduction following after the meeting!

A very carefully planned itinerary allowed the Duke to see the whole of the operation; he spent some considerable time in the Research Department and his detailed knowledge on technical matters was appreciated by all those to whom he spoke. In the factory Mrs Joy Denman, our Senior Supervisor, presented the Duke with a portable gas detector based on the model we were making for the National Coal Board. Needless to say, despite careful planning and timing, the Duke overstayed his visit by one and a half hours, which delighted the company. One of the most precious possessions we have is a personal handwritten letter and envelope received afterwards from the Duke, thanking me and my company for the very interesting visit and also for the portable gas detector which would be used by him in his garage or boiler house.

Lastly, in May 1972 I had become a Fellow of the Institute of Directors and a few meetings were held locally by Michael Cobham of Flight Refuelling, who was the Chairman of the Hants & Dorset Branch (since re-named Wessex). He called me on one side and said he would like to give up the Chairmanship, would I take it over? I considered it an honour to be asked so soon after becoming a Fellow, and I looked forward to the extra-curricula work that would be involved, so in December I became Chairman of the Branch. Most of the committee meetings were held at the Royal Southampton Yacht Club and the majority of the members appeared to be from that area. One or two of the original committee members of the Branch who were resident in the Southampton area retired, and this gave me the opportunity of expanding the committee to cover members from a wider area. I appointed as Deputy Chairman an industrial banker from Bournemouth, Martin Copp.

I felt it important that as Wessex covered a very large area it would be advisable to have some meetings not only in the Bournemouth/Poole area but Dorchester and Basingstoke in order to attract additional members for the Institute. Martin Copp and I formed separate branches in Basingstoke and Dorchester (called the Casterbridge Centre) with appointed Chairmen. We organised luncheon meetings with speakers more commensurate with the needs of directors of smaller companies who did not have long-term experience in that capacity.

The various meetings of the Institute allowed me to introduce guest speakers such as Earl Mountbatten, the Chairman of the Institute Dennis Randolph, and Director-Generals of the Institute such as Jan Hildreth, Walter Goldsmith and Sir John Hoskins. Also, being Chairman of an IOD Branch, I became a member of the Council of the Institute and was able to meet a number of big company chairmen such as those from Fitch Lovell, Wilkinson Sword etc. I remember asking the Chairman of Fitch Lovell, as a company in a major food industry, how many women he had on his Board and he said there were none. I said "What do men know about food?" and he replied "You've got a point, I'll look into it!".

In 1982 the Council of the Institute discovered that I had reached the age of 75 and the age limit for Council members was 70; I had overstayed my welcome for five years! I therefore handed over the Chairmanship to Martin and it was only right that I should let him run the Branch in his own way, so I gave up my membership of the committee at the same time.

I suppose the early experience of the pre-war years when I gave many lectures to radio societies and at other promotional functions, came out in me when speaking in public, the important thing being that I knew my subject and needed no notes. My external activities covered a large number of years and therefore various notable occasions appear in other parts of this book at about the time they occurred.

CHAPTER 22

VISIT TO LORD MOUNTBATTEN.

Following a suggestion by the Chairman of the British Overseas Trade Board in 1976, a decision was made that there would be an 'Export Year' and companies throughout the country would make special efforts to promote exports, involving everybody in the various companies. The year started on the 1st June and went on until the 1st May 1977.

After I had spoken to the entire staff explaining the Export Year movement and reasons for participation, regular committee meetings were held and various ideas were carried out. Mr Roy Earnshaw, Export Year Advisor and a Director of TBA Industrial Products Ltd., Rochdale, visited and spoke to the factory.

Meanwhile we printed car stickers for company personnel entitled 'Sieger makes it Export Year', packing case and panel labels entitled 'This is another Sieger export' with small stickers for equipment marked 'We support Export Year'. Ten flagpoles were installed outside the main offices and a special Export Year flag was acquired and flown daily, together with the Sieger house flag and the national flags of any overseas visitors, such as the Japanese delegation who visited in June, with small replica national flags on the reception desk.

Export Year noticeboards were installed with information displayed on visitors, exhibitions etc. and this form of information was continued after the special year was over. Paper was printed entitled 'Export News Release' on which bulletins were issued to draw national and local Press attention, and Radio Sieger was launched - an internal radio programme broadcast on the factory intercom. system on current news, interviews, orders achieved and social information, whilst light and informative 'Rainy Day' talks were given by senior management in the canteen at lunchtime about their overseas sales tours. A film was made entitled 'A Year in the Life of the Company' covering daily filming during the year on visitors, orders being manufactured, interviews with staff, exhibition equipments, etc. A computer printout of the Export Year symbol was produced and one of our Senior Assemblers produced various poems on the events. We also showed to the staff a film on the company made previously by the Central Office of Information. An Export Year competition was held, spread over 13 weeks, the first prize being a weekend for two in Paris with all expenses paid, plus prizes for the first three runners-up.

Early in the year Tom Pope was appointed Production Director and Reg Stride Production Manager; later Mr Hanbury Brown was made Research & Development Director.

"Export Year" Joy Denman and Sheila Sinnick assembling equipment.

Winners of "Export Year Competition".

Rosemary Adams organised the typewriters throughout the company and was always concerned that a good impression should be given to our customers and others by the quality of typewritten letters and orders, so all the IBM typewriters were on a 5-year lease which enabled a constant turnover to up-dated equipment. In 1977, following a suggestion by Mrs Jane Short, secretary to Mr Hanbury Brown, and in line with IBM recommendations, a Secretarial Services Department was formed with Mrs Short in charge, centralising the shorthand, audio and typing and gathering all the secretaries together apart from those in Contracts Division and Production. This overcame the problem of unevenness of work distribution. After initial doubts by the secretaries involved it proved to be a happy office which, of course, resulted in a very efficient system.

The need for office mechanisation was growing and after various discussions with IBM in past years, an order was placed for an IBM Type 3 computer and Harry Smith and Richard Frewer, a good Design Engineer, went to IBM for a computer course. Richard Frewer was appointed Data Programme Controller and the computer was installed in an air-conditioned room.

In this year Dr Hucknall from Research presented a paper entitled 'Mechanisms of Promotion of Transition of Metal Oxide Catalysts' at the 5th Ibero American Symposium on Catalysis in Lisbon, Portugal. This paper was printed, with two other papers, in the Journal of the Chemical Society Faraday transactions.

September was a bad month in that the company numbered over 300 and the hard decision had to be taken for redundancies in order to make the company more efficient. These numbered twenty, covering most areas of the company from Research & Development to Goods In, and it was a very sad time for everyone after such a successful progress.

The company, with its rapid growth having been stabilised, received many major orders, the first being for 75 Model 1650 for the Hungarian Post Office Authorities, these portables to be used to safeguard Post Office engineers working in underground tunnels where gas leaks were a constant hazard. An order was received for £40,000 covering more than 130 Model 1400 control modules with Type 770 sensors for No: 6 Olyfines Plant at ICI, Wilton; these were to monitor leakages of ethylene, propylene and butane at concentrations down to 2% of the Lower Explosive Limit. Another order came in from Matthew Hall Engineering via G.C. Davis for £14,000 for a system consisting of 140IB modules and 77 Type 770 sensors for a production and drilling platform in Block 14/20 in the North Sea approximately 140 miles north of Wick in Northern Scotland.

A presentation was made at the Post House Hotel, Heathrow, to a Rumanian mining and petroleum delegation at which methanometers, the portable AFD, the BM.1 and the Model 1400 were shown, and in November a Mini-Conference was held with an informal buffet meal at Matchams House Country Club.

In October a scanning electron microscope was leased on a hire purchase arrangement, complete with its own analyser and computer, and installed in the Research & Development Department in No:19. This enable our physicists to do delicate and complex research on catalytic materials as the microscope was capable of magnifying topographical features by up to180,000 times - surface structures therefore became visible less than a millionth of a centimetre in size.

Most interesting things were going on, widening the gas detector horizon. In the early 1970's a very bright physicist was employed in our Research Department by the name of David Piercy, a practical individual who could turn his ideas into physical equipment very quickly. He designed and made, in a single machine, a mechanical device to produce 16 catalytic filaments simultaneously which applied all the necessary chemicals and ancillary processes including gas testing. With this achievement he went further and a complete microprocessor-controlled testing system was made, testing 100 catalytic filaments over a period of a week with a printout to record precisely the performance of each filament at set times. This was the first step towards mechanised production of that which always had to be done by hand, depending on a certain amount of 'black art'. Early in 1976 David Piercy, having completed this original work, designed and built an infra-red detector called the 'Carousel'. Rather than have the normal chopping disc to compare the gas against the standard, a standard cell was mounted on a disc that rotated and gave a very fast response. This was demonstrated in late 1976 and fully patented in 1977.

At the same time the work on the electro-chemical oxygen sensor was proceeding and a combustion analyser known as the 6020 was made, filling a major demand by power stations and process plants where fuel efficiency was of the utmost importance; some 3,000 of these were manufactured and sold but the manufacture of the cell was extremely difficult and approximately one year of life could be expected before the cell had to be replaced. Pressure of work in other

IBM computer room.

195

Dr Hucknall using the scanning electron microscope.

fields was so demanding that it was decided to discontinue and concentrate on what the market required.

The enormous exploration of offshore platforms, with the need to reduce considerably the size of control equipment, resulted in work being started on a replacement of the 1300 system (which had been selling for some 15 years) and of the 1400 which was the luxury model taking a fair amount of room. A 16-circuit unit using DIN standard sizes throughout was designed. Known as the 5516 the development was completed early in 1978 and after considerable testing was passed to Tom Pope for production early in 1979. It is impossible to cover all the development and research work that was going on in the laboratories and by 1978 nearly 70 people were employed in these two divisions, under the control of Hassall Hanbury Brown.

Towards the end of the year, to our great regret, Harry Smith resigned his Directorship to start his own business as a Financial Management Consultant, acting as company consultant for three months until a replacement could be found. Meanwhile the legislation in employment was becoming a matter for the legal profession and Mrs Mavis Grant was employed to help Rosemary Adams with the paperwork, which was difficult to handle with all the other departments under her control. Mrs Grant later took over as Personnel Manager and Rosemary became Administration Director.

After the departure of Harry Smith we utilised Tyzacks, the well- known London head-hunting organisation to find a suitable replacement. To be quite sure that we would employ somebody really suitable the initial interviewing was carried out by Jeremy Seddon and Roger Culpin of Barclays Merchant Bank, and two applicants were sent down for interview. John Lancashire joined the company at the end of January, having been previously Financial Director of Racal with a very wide commercial experience. The agreement with him was that after one year he would be given a Directorship of the company, and as he proved very satisfactory this was carried out.

An approach by Mr J.P.C. Danny, Chairman and Joint Managing Director of Grovewood Securities Ltd. was made in 1976, and of interest is the fact that they were a wholly owned subsidiary of Eagle Star. Their interest was from a financial point of view only, not a direct takeover but a 35% participation. In the same general period of companies interested in J. & S. Sieger, Mr F.V. Davey, the Group Planning Director of Steel Brothers who owned Becorit GB Ltd., manufacturers of mining equipment and gas detection, showed a particular interest in the work done by Sieger in the mining industry and its good relations with the NCB and Becorit, who had a small proportion only of the gas detection business, seemed like a very good marriage. Steel Brothers owned companies throughout the world

Visit by Mayor and Mayoress of Poole, Mr & Mrs Peter Coles.

Visit to No. 19, Mr Hanbury Brown at back.

and had an excellent record of sound management in all their acquisitions.

The year 1977 started with my 70th birthday dinner, held at the Chewton Glen Hotel, New Milton, a beautiful hotel set in extensive grounds. Although most of my family were there it was almost a Mini-Conference with many of the distributors and their wives attending, as well as the Directors and wives of the company. Four singers were engaged to entertain in the lounge after dinner and it was a very memorable evening listening to the singing and looking out onto snow-covered lawns illuminated by the lights shining from the rooms.

Early in January we had a delegation from the Prague Construction Authority in Czechoslovakia and discussions were held which resulted in orders for equipment in a satellite town which was being constructed, where all the facilities would be installed in tunnels before the main building started. We provided the equipment to detect possible leakages of gas in those tunnels.

An order for £60,000 was received for the Model 7040 for use in Russia for the detection of toxic gases in various plants, followed by a £250,000 order via Schmohl KG, Munich, for gas detection equipment to indicate leakages at the 22 giant compressor stations along a new 1,700 mile natural gas pipeline across Russia. The 'Friendship' pipeline was intended to carry gas from Orenburg, the biggest gasfield in the Russian Urals, to homes and factories throughout the Comecon countries. All six countries joined forces with the USSR to finance and construct the pipeline, the USSR in turn to supply each with agreed amounts of gas. In its 1,700 mile course the 59 in. diameter pipeline crosses the Volga, Don and Dnieper rivers, and swamps, marshes, rocky ground and areas of freezing temperatures.

In January I went on Southern Television (our local station at that time) to talk on a programme 'Our Man in Westminster' and in early February I went to the studios of BBC Solent with a Mr Baker of the T.U.C. and Mr McGregor of the Anglo-German Foundation in a discussion on 'The state of industry'. The British Overseas Trade Board held a dinner at Trinity House in London for members of the Advisory Council (approximately fifty in total) at which Jim Callaghan, the current Prime Minister, was present and I spent some time in an interesting discussion with Sir Derek Ezra, then Chairman of the National Coal Board. These meetings were always very valuable, when a small company in Poole could be well represented in the higher circles of industry and politics.

In February an invitation was received from Lord Mountbatten to go to Broadlands, his ancestral home, for discussion of a venture which he was proposing, so both Sylvia and I attended. The venture concerned the 'CA' class of destroyers (otherwise known as the Caesar class of the 11th Emergency Flotilla built for the Royal Navy in 1943-45) the last destroyer of this class to be built being H.M.S. 'Cavalier' who, when she was paid off in 1972, brought to an end an era which began with H.M.S. 'Havelock' in 1893. The 'Cavalier' was about to be sent to the breaker's yard and Lord Mountbatten was most concerned to form a Trust to preserve the 'Cavalier' to commemorate the role played by the destroyer in two world wars. She was more typical of the British destroyer than any comparable ship in service, for her gun disposition was first tried in 1916 and her machinery and hull design dated from 1936. Furthermore, the modernisation given to her and the class did not alter these basic features; despite the addition of new equipment 'Cavalier' retained many of the standard characteristics of British destroyers. Lord Mountbatten was anxious to obtain money to purchase at breaker's yard price and to fit her out as a museum for future generations to see.

The meeting at Broadlands was interesting, with various Admirals, Rear-Admirals and members of the Royal Air Force. Sufficient money had been collected, although short of about £8,500, to make the purchase possible. A five-year covenant was organised and J. & S. Sieger Ltd. provided that money - as Lord Mountbatten remarked "You now own the forecastle"! He was so delighted that he said "I must go and tell Charles about this" and went off to the 'phone, returning to say "That man is always out, but he will be delighted to hear that we have now got enough money". Whilst the meeting was taking place Lord Mountbatten's dog, a very friendly black labrador, took a fancy to Sylvia and would not leave her side. Later a visit was made to Mayflower Park, Southampton, to see the 'Cavalier' arrive with Lord Mountbatten at her helm, towed by another vessel.

I had received a visit previously from a Mr Long of Translink; this organisation was interested in finding suitable companies to fit in with the needs of their various clients, and as a result of this in April we had a visit by a Dr Bucher, Dr Van Werra and Mr Schaft of Zellweger Uster AG. They showed extreme interest in the company and an invitation was extended by them for a visit to Switzerland to see Zellweger and their other company Polymetron Ltd. In May Sylvia and I, with Roland Cunnell, went to Zurich and saw the operation, which was most interesting, covering a very wide field of engineering in all its aspects.

In June the famous Spithead Review of the Navy was held and it seemed a good opportunity to use 'Environist'; various people were invited on board, including the Chairman of Flight Refuelling, and fortunately, despite the very dull day, we managed to review the Fleet, following in the footsteps of 'Britannia' which had the Queen on board. 'Environist' therefore appeared on a number of aerial shots taken of the Review.

In July we heard that we were one of the fifteen companies featured in a booklet entitled "Fifteen Export Case Studies" published by the British Overseas Trade Board, following the presentations of these Case Studies held in 1975.

In September the President of Zellweger, Mr Walter Hess, visited the factory, together with their Financial Director Dr Kurt Weber, Mr Fred Sutter a Director of Polymetron, and Dr Van Werra. Various discussions were held on a possible takeover. The proposal at that time did not seem to be interesting, in that forty-one other companies had by now approached me and were anxious to get involved but I did not wish to hold a Dutch auction, I wanted to investigate all approaches in some detail.

An old associate of mine, Alex Willis, whom I had known for some twenty years, telephoned from the United States saying he was working with the Bendix Corporation who were particularly interested in the company and would like to discuss details of a possible takeover. He was a good scientist and responsible, in the early days, for quite a bit of work at Mine Safety Appliances (MSA) in Glasgow. He started his own company called Willis Gas Detection and devised a portable for which I made a catalytic filament. Unfortunately Alex, not a sound businessman, was unsuccessful in starting production because he needed the assistance of an instrumentation company so despite an association with Siebe Gorman he decided to emigrate to the United States where he joined Bacarach, who were strong competitors to General Monitors, and devised a number of very interesting sensors. Bendix were interested in taking over Bacarach but in the long-term negotiations they did not succeed and another company stepped in, so they therefore decided to hire Alex Willis to set up a gas detector operation. A number of meetings were held between ourselves and Bendix.

Despite the fact that I made it very apparent to any company who made a takeover approach that my only reason for selling the company was to make sure its future continued should anything happen to me and my family who were the sole owners, these approaches tended to crystallise my mind and the decision was made to sell but retain a certain amount of control and guidance for the future, making sure that those people who had worked so hard and so loyally in building up the company over the years would be rewarded by continued employment. Some of our best customers were those engaged in fire detection and similar services and it was important in our selection to realise that tying up with any of those companies would immediately isolate us from others competing in the fire detection business. It was necessary to very carefully analyse all the companies and select those who would be best for the future. The strong contenders in the final list were Bendix, Flight Refuelling, Grovewood Securities Limited, Steel Brothers & Co. Ltd. and Zellweger Uster AG.

It is interesting to quote part of a letter received from Steel Brothers at that time, who had looked into our accounts and visited the company and who stated "Your excellent results and forecast reflect the wisdom of your philosophy regarding people and long term development programme, and we have read them with considerable interest".

In the main factory, for use by every employee, a 'Suggestions Box' had been instituted as, with 300 employees, it was becoming difficult to talk to everybody in some detail and so many ideas were forthcoming from the employees that the box was welcomed, and cleared by Rosemary weekly. The Directors examined all ideas and those which were put into operation received a monetary reward. At the request of quite a few people it was decided to set up an Employees' Consultative Committee with each department voting for its own representative who would attend regular meetings, together with the Personnel & Financial Directors. Minutes of these meetings were placed on noticeboards in the various buildings so that employees could be kept informed. The meetings were intended to solve any problems brought up by employees, advise of efforts being made to improve conditions, ideas proposed by any the staff, complaints, etc., and the first meeting was held in Autumn 1977.

Following the Safety & Health legislation we provided a First Aid room with equipment and sent for training employees from different departments in the company who volunteered to join the First Aid team. The original First Aider, Mrs Sheila Woodbridge, was promoted in 1978 to Divisional Officer in the Parkstone/Branksome Division of the Brigade.

Don Nichols, the Safety & Training Officer, drew up emergency routines and instituted regular Fire Drills and training of certain people in teams as fire fighters; these attended a course on the use of fire extinguishers organised by Chubb Fire Security Ltd. which included lectures, specialist films and practical fire fighting using a full range of extinguishers, concluding with the presentation of a Fire Fighting Certificate to all those who attended.

The social side was not forgotten and a Social & Sports Club was formed by the employees, fully supported by the management.

During the year Roland Cunnell, who had done an excellent job as Marketing Director, had a number of disagreements with the Board on policy and at the Distributors' Conference, which was held in October, I announced that he would be leaving the company; it was always our method to let the staff and distributors, who were also part of the family, know of Board decisions and this was an opportune time to advise them.

CHAPTER 23

SALE OF COMPANY

Early in 1978 the large factory (No. 35) covering 22,000 sq. ft. at the rear of No. 31 came on the market as a leasehold property. It had been used by a firm called Thomaker Ltd. for the repair and testing of large vehicles, leased from Cummings & Morrish Ltd., property developers. We already had four buildings but it was apparent that by joining the Thomaker building to the main factory we could then dispense with one of the smaller buildings, No. 21 across the road, and gain more space, enabling us to reorganise the whole layout of the factory system, so the lease was acquired.

Meanwhile, in January, the first issue of the 'Sieger News' was published and printed in-house, made up of contributions from the staff to whom it was freely distributed, some copies going to selected customers.

It was realised that the service required for our equipment on the oil rigs in the North Sea could not at that time be covered entirely by the Service Department personnel, so a company in Aberdeen were appointed to carry out this work. In January their engineers visited the factory for two weeks on a training course. The Sieger Field Service Engineers were on call seven days a week throughout the year, and in the past year they had undertaken a total of 600 individual service visits, over half of these on a regular contract basis, ranging from the commissioning of a Model 1100 in a ladies corset factory in Bristol to the servicing of an infra-red system on a liquid gas tanker in New Orleans! Regular visits were made to Czechoslovakia for the routine servicing of 180 circuits of Model 1300's installed in six compressor stations on a natural gas pipeline stretching the full length of the country. Visits were also made to the deepest mine in Europe - the potash mine at Saltby, Cleveland, which is 3,645 feet deep.

350 man/days were spent offshore during the year; in fact the total flying times involved in overseas and offshore visits were 375 hours in fixed wing aircraft and about 150 hours in helicopters with, in the UK, some 70,000 miles by road - equivalent to three times the circumference of the earth. There were occasional incidents which highlighted some of the visits; for instance visiting one of the largest potato processing plants in the UK, a hopper and conveyor belt refused to be switched off and the factory was ankle deep in chips! There was also the time when, in response to a call by an electrical contractor to a school in Gloucester because a newly installed system was not working, it was found that the contractor had failed to run a mains supply! Finally, a visit was made to Scotland to commission a new system for a boiler house and after a long search

35 Nuffield Estate assembly room.

Sieger van meeting service engineer.

the sensors were eventually found mounted underneath the boilers - investigations revealed that this was on instructions from the local Gas Board who were insistent that natural gas was heavier than air!

We negotiated the lease of a small factory with office at Fulwood, Nottinghamshire, very near the National Coal Board mining area, and appointed a Manager and Service Engineer, and this office did very good business.

In February we had a visit again by Zellweger Uster AG of six people including Mr M. Bechtler, a close relative of the owners. Whilst having visits from Zellweger, the Bendix Corporation were pressing very hard and two members of their company came over with Alex Willis to go through the company's records, designs and marketing methods. This was followed in August by a visit from John Spelman, Vice President & General Manager of Bendix, with Alex Willis, to discuss still further methods of co-operation.

The Defence Contracts Division was doing exceedingly well and the chemical tape equipment, which had been specially designed to meet all the difficult performance and structural specifications for the Admiralty, was taken over to Cape Canaveral in Florida for tests of leakages of rocket fuels in the Space Programme. In addition the instrument was used to measure toxic emanations which could come from part of the equipment in the confined areas of the space satellite caused by possible heat from the equipment affecting some of the plastics used, particularly chlorine from the use of PVC. This was one of the many visits undertaken and the tests were highly successful.

In April Alan came to me and said unfortunately he would be leaving the company. The reason was that his daughter, who had emigrated to Zimbabwe with her husband, was having a baby and Joy Thrower wanted to be with her daughter when the grandchild was born and live nearby. This was a great shock to us as Alan had been at that time nearly seventeen years with the company and we lost an old friend and confidant with a wonderful sense of humour.

Fortunately John Stallard could continue the management of the Defence Contracts Division as he had formed excellent relations with the personnel of the Ministry of Defence. John was considerably experienced in production, he was our Chief Designer and certainly one of the most valuable members of the company, always the last to leave and no job ever left unfinished.

In June I was invited to the naming ceremony of one of the roll-on/roll-off Truckline ferries built specially for the Cherbourg-Poole route with a terminal at the New Quay in Poole. This particular ship was named 'Purbeck' and there was also a second vessel named 'Coutances'.

At the beginning of July we were asked by Poole Borough Town Clerk, Mr Ian Andrews, if four Israeli Town Clerks could tour the factory as they were visiting the Poole area to gather information on the Borough, and they were duly brought to the factory. Similarly 35 members of the Dorset section of the Institute of Supervisory Management toured the company; we were pleased to show the factory to any interested parties.

Negotiations with the various companies had been going on for a long time so it was essential to give a deadline of three months to the various applicants, and the three finalists were Bendix, Flight Refuelling and Zellweger. The first offer to come through was from Flight Refuelling but they could not meet the figure which I thought was the real value of the company. Discussions with Walter Hess, President of Zellweger, became more positive and they could meet the figure with the disadvantage, of course, that they were a foreign company. Bendix, who stated they would like still further time for their American people to carry out yet more analysis, were advised that negotiations could not be prolonged beyond the stated time, and after much heart-searching it was decided that Zellweger, being a family concern, should be the lucky company. There were no language difficulties in that all the Swiss spoke very good English, and the fact that they were a family concern meant that there was less chance of their being taken over by a company who could decide to move the whole of the operation to another part of the world or another part of the United Kingdom. We did not think that Bendix would do such a thing but, having lived in America for nearly ten years, I knew the possibility existed with these big public corporations.

Meetings were held with the President of Zellweger and the Financial Director, Dr Kurt Weber, which resulted in agreements being drawn up in draft, based on the memoranda which I produced some time previously.

In August Dr David Hucknall, who was gaining an international reputation as a physicist specialising in catalysis, went to Rio de Janeiro for an International Symposium attended by industrial scientists and academics from Brazil, Venezuela, Mexico, Spain, Russia and major English-speaking countries. The lecture he gave was so well received that this high-level audience applauded him at the end. Dr Hucknall was a very valuable member of the company and his extra-curricula activities plus those of myself and other members of the company tended to build even further the international reputation of Sieger as gas detection specialists.

The electron microscope purchased earlier was an extremely valuable tool, so valuable indeed that pressure from Mr Hanbury Brown and Dr Hucknall to purchase a Scanning Auger resulted in obtaining a Japanese unit ideally suited for our work. The Scanning Auger had the ability to look below the molecular layer and for catalytic analysis was an ideal instrument.

Wormald Brothers, who had been one of the applicants to buy the company, were still not doing good business with gas detection in Australia and we were fortunate in obtaining John Wright, as our distributor, who was President of Group Electronics Pty. Ltd. based in Melbourne, with branches in all state capitals of Australia and New Zealand. He headed an expert team of twelve and his appointment took place during that year; meetings with him previously came to no finality because he maintained he wanted to study gas detection and the market thoroughly. The decision to finally appoint him when he stated he was ready to take up the assignment was a sound one, as our reputation in Australia improved considerably after the doldrums we had been in for some two or three years previously.

Interesting orders were received in this year covering a quarter of a million pounds of toxic gas detection equipment for Hungary, 38 chlorine monitors to be used as general monitors in the working areas of new chloro-fluoromethane plants in Russia, and 250 2-level circuits ordered by Mitsubishi Heavy Industry Ltd., Tokyo, for use at the Shell NGL offshore production platforms near Qatar in the Arabian Gulf. An order for over £30,000 was placed through the London office for 66 Model FS1's with 66 Type 780 sensors for Shell Exploration for St Fergus Natural Gas Terminal which accepts raw gas from the Brent oilfields, treats it, and feeds it into the British gas system. Our distributors in Norway, A/S Garek, won a contract to supply 55 Model 1300 systems with Type 726 sensors at a value of £45,000 to Aker Engineering for two roll-on/roll-off car transporters being bought for Wilhemsen, Wilhemsen SA to operate in the Antipodes. Each ship was to have two deck levels and the monitoring system was for detection of accumulations of petrol vapour in the cargo deck spaces.

The Model 608 portable, the original of which had been going since the early days, was altered to meet the new BASEEFA standards and the approval was received in this year, with a write-up appearing in various publications. It was interesting to note that this portable with the modified sensor head at no time superceded the original Type 1 which is a unit still manufactured today. A report appeared in the publication 'Colliery Guardian' in October regarding one of our Model 1650 portable alarms which was designed to protect personnel and plant against explosive risks. The unit is compact, rugged in construction and convenient to use. This was certainly proved to be the case when one instrument was returned to the factory after having been involved in a fire. A photograph was shown in the publication of two units 'before' and 'after' - even in the 'after' state the instrument still worked, both in normal and alarm conditions.

I had meetings with associates whom I knew in the EEC at Brussels and was informed of the various grants which were available for special research and development purposes. After much negotiation an EEC Grant of £250, 000 for three years was awarded to the company on a project entitled 'Improvements in Gas Detection Systems'.

Our distributor in Spain was Guardian Iberica S.A. in Barcelona, controlled by Mr Antonia Semir; he ran the company very professionally and successfully, not only for us but for his fire alarm and detection side. Unfortunately he died suddenly and a nephew took over, which was not welcomed by the staff so the main people employed in the gas detection side set up independently and we felt, therefore, the time was ripe to form a company in Spain under the name of Sieger Espana S.A. John Lancashire flew to Spain and went through all the formalities to form the company, which was again situated in Barcelona with one of the good engineers from Guardian Iberica as Manager. This company traded for a few years until it was decided to liquidate, close the Barcelona office and sell Sieger equipment through the Polymetron office (associated company with Zellweger) in Madrid.

The signing of the agreement to take over the company by Zellweger Uster AG was carried out in London on the 11th January 1979 and announced formally to the company and the media on the 18th January. I was to be Chairman and Chief Executive for 6-12 months full-time, Chairman and Consultant for 24-30 months part-time, and finally President, Director and Consultant for life. It should now be mentioned here that the employees of the company were aware for some years previously that the possibility of a takeover did exist, and any stranger who came into the factory to visit me was immediately classified as a possible buyer! Various meetings were held in the main factory when I stood up and told everybody that they would be kept fully informed of any action, therefore rumours could be discounted, and that they would all be protected for their future. Full notification of the takeover was given to the Press and BBC South came round to the factory to take a film, which was shown on 'Nationwide' on the evening of the announcement.

On January 15th 1980 a presentation was made to me by the President of Zellweger, Walter Hess, of a large piece of natural grown quartz millions of years old, mounted on a wooden base with the words 'Joshua Sieger OBE - Founder of J. & S. Sieger Ltd., Poole. In grateful appreciation of his great contribution to the successful development of the company. Presented by Zellweger Uster Ltd.'

Walter Hess stated it represented a long-term association between themselves and the founder of the company which he hoped would continue for many years.

The day before the official announcement, on the 17th January, four Directors - Rosemary Adams, Hassell Hanbury Brown, John Lancashire and Tom Pope - who had been invited by Zellweger to see their Swiss operation, left for Heathrow and on the following day flew to Zurich where they visited the main Zellweger factory at Uster before attending a dinner in Zurich that night with the owner of Zellweger, Mr Hans Bechtler and the Directors of the Group. Next day they visited Polymetron at Hombrechtikon and the Zellweger factory at Sargans before driving to Davos where they spent two nights. In February Sylvia and I were similarly entertained but after

Presentation by Mr Walter Hess on my retirement as Managing Director 1st January 1980.

visiting the main factory at Uster we went to St Moritz with Walter Hess and Kurt Weber for six days; although the weather was not good there was plenty of snow! All concerned enjoyed their visits and had the opportunity to meet some of the staff of the various companies in Switzerland.

The plans for No: 35 started in the previous year were put into operation immediately and the 15,000 sq. ft. of floor area was divided into two sections -

approximately 6,000 sq. ft. for the Machine Shop, with a small section for Printing, and the rest for Assembly, Test, Packing/Despatch and Service/Repairs. 31 was joined to 35 by a passageway and because the buildings were on different levels (something like 4 ft. difference) a hydraulic lift was put in one side of the ramp for the movement of heavy equipment. An additional covered section was constructed in 35 to contain the Packing/Despatch, giving adequate access for lorries calling to pick up equipment. The acquisition of No: 35 had the advantage of another office block at the end of the factory.

The first of various departments to move was the Machine Shop, which had never had so much space! A corner of their area was given over to the fully equipped Print Room. Four employees coped with all the work needed and, apart from emergency situations, no printing work was sent outside. When the original survey of the Print Room was made in 1978 and the equipment purchased, total recovery of the equipment price was estimated at 23 months. In 1980, at the request of John Lancashire, a justification of the cost of the Printing Department was produced comparing outside quotations from printers with the actual costing of the work in-house, showing that a saving of 430% was made by carrying out all work in-house rather than everything being sent to outside printers. There was also the non-financial reason that alterations, rush jobs, quick samples etc. could be produced immediately without the difficulty of having to fit into an outside printer's schedule. However it was decided in 1981 by the management at that time to close the Print Room and make three of the staff redundant.

With 200 extensions on our switchboard and 10 lines, telephone bills were becoming very high indeed and it was essential to make an analysis of the departments and their use of the telephone. The obvious choice for a saving was the Buying Department which had now moved into 35, and a telex was provided for their sole use in addition to the two telexes in the main building for incoming and outgoing messages.

An organisation had been formed by a number of gas detection companies in the United Kingdom called The Council of Gas Detector Equipment Manufacturers (COGDEM). Bill Simons joined this organisation and with his duties on the CENELEC Committee which met in Brussels, and his membership of the Council of the British Standards Institute, added to the company's important reputation in organisations responsible for guideline specifications and the standards of international approval boards. This was highlighted by an invitation to me from the Minister of Fuel and Energy, The Rt. Hon. David Howell, to meet the Minister of Fuel for Czechoslovakia at a special dinner party to be held at No. I Carlton Gardens, the official residence of the Foreign Secretary. I was in good company with the Chairmen of the Central Electricity Generating Board, British Gas and the National Coal Board. I had the advantage over most of the fifteen people attending that dinner of having dealt with Czechoslovakia in the provision of equipment and, as I so often found out, I had this personal knowledge against others whose knowledge was obtained indirectly.

Early in the year the increase in our offshore business demanded an office in Aberdeen, the main headquarters of the North Sea oil and gas industry, and the following year an office was also opened in Lowestoft for the southern North Sea area.

The Manager of the Sales Department, obtained a major contract with Davy

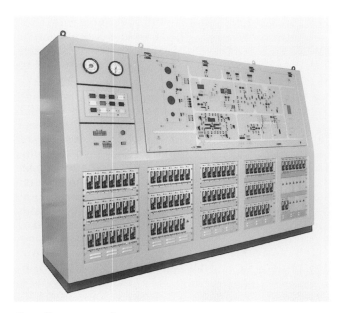

Davy Powergas unit.

Powergas for equipment to be installed in Poland, protecting a very large petro-chemical complex. Display panels showed the location of the various sensors on the site with anemometer equipment to record wind direction and velocity, all in a 12 ft. console. One of the advantages of the Print Room and its facilities showed itself in that large quantities of the service manuals necessary for equipment of this magnitude were able to be printed in-house as in no way could the work be sent out; it did, however, create problems in the quantity of material required and entailed one of the few periods when other work had to be passed to outside printers.

Sieger's received publicity regarding their contribution towards keeping the South Yorkshire coal pits safe. By April the orders received for methane gas detectors for use in a number of pits totalled more than 450 units at a cost in excess of £130,000. A special version of the hand-held Model AFD methane detector was manufactured for the NCB which allowed battery changing in situ without the need to remove the battery from the instrument. This instrument gave a continuous display of methane level as well as a flashing alarm if the concentration exceeded a pre-set value.

We were one of 64 British companies taking part in the first Middle East Oil Show in Bahrain, a five day event, and a picture appeared in the local paper of the new British Ambassador to Bahrain, Mr Harold Walker to a member of the Lowestoft Office during a visit to the company's stand in the BOTB pavilion.

Many discussions were held with Dr Weber and Walter Hess, the President of Zellweger, in order to find a suitable executive to take over after the 6-12 months in which I was to continue being Chairman and Managing Director. Dr Weber was interested in a Swiss engineer who had visited the factory once or twice before but he was obviously quite the wrong type to handle the company. Hess suggested that Bryan Mills, the Managing Director of one of their companies in England, Luwa at Woking, would be suitable as he was an engineer and a successful Managing Director who could quite possibly take over the company, occasionally taking care of the Luwa operation as well. I did not think this would work but they said he was a professional Managing Director and would soon fall into line, and maybe the best arrangement would be to have him adjacent to myself for a period of a year to get to know individuals in the company and the customers, so I finally agreed.

For the first six months of 1980 Bryan Mills paid occasional visits and sat in on various meetings. One of the successful arrangements I had for many years was that Directors, and occasionally senior staff, would come in first thing every morning to the Board Room to discuss and read the morning post and all telexes sent and received, before they took the post away to their various departments. This was successful in that everyone knew the position, good or bad. Bryan Mills did not like this arrangement at all and said he would change that when he took over. However I had found that one of the most important things about running a company successfully was emphasising communication between everybody, nobody was in doubt or concerned about things which were happening as nothing destroys the smooth running of an organisation more than persistent unsubstantiated rumours.

Walter Hess felt that the 6-12 months as Chairman and Managing Director should be shortened to 6 months, so I became Chairman only and Bryan Mills was brought in as Managing Director. Both Rosemary and I moved out of our offices into smaller rooms along the corridor. Correspondence I had with Walter Bechtler said that they did not think Directors should have 'jobs' in the company and be responsible for departments, they should be overall, and he did not think that women on the Board were desirable, I would have to find some way of overcoming the problem.

I think it is important to mention now that it was agreed before the takeover that 'Environist', which was the company research vessel, could be purchased by me at market value, much higher than the book value, but I agreed provided the company would charter the vessel for five days a week for a period of five years, meeting most of the expenses.

At meetings with Walter Hess and Kurt Weber in Switzerland I pointed out that I was very concerned about Bryan Mills as Managing Director of the company. He seldom visited the factory except occasionally on a Friday afternoon for a short time; he made changes by making sure that all people in Sales would have cars, which was a very expensive operation. He then sent a Press Release to our local newspaper with a photograph of himself saying as Managing Director the company would now be concerned with the welfare of the staff and that closer liaison would be had with all employees; this of course was a red herring. He did not like the arrangement of all secretarial work being centralised, in spite of the fact it had proved so satisfactory, so Secretarial Services was disbanded and instead of five secretaries it resulted in many more to cover each department and again caused an uneven workload.

It was fortunate that the Vice-President of Zellweger, Fred Sutter, a very sound engineer and British in his approach to people, was assigned to have the direct liaison with the company. This pleased me and all the staff as he was so understanding. I discussed the matter of Bryan Mills with him and he fully realised the situation; I then had other meetings with Walter Hess and Kurt Weber, explaining to them my concern about the future of the company which was not going into the red, but the nice 'cushion' we had in the bank was slowly disappearing. So finally this made some impression and I had a telephone call to go to London and stay at the Mayfair Hotel for further discussions about removing Bryan Mills and appointing somebody else to take over temporarily. The meeting at the hotel went on most of the day with Hess and Weber deciding on the appointment of Tom Pope as Managing Director. I pointed out that I used to use him as a deputy when I went on my business travels and the reason he was a deputy was that he would never make any major decisions on the company but just took care of the day to day operation, particularly Production which after all was our life-blood, the more we could invoice the better we were.

However they agreed they would try it, against my better judgement, but I had no alternative. There was no doubt that Bryan Mills was having trouble with the Luwa company which seemed to be always losing money and he apparently spent much more time there with various visits to the Midlands which gave him no time to visit my company; a company cannot run without a head.

I was Chairman only and on the appointment of Tom Pope he immediately took over my old office and it was essential, as Chairman, and agreed with Fred Sutter, that we would find premises outside the factory for use as a Chairman's office. Fred and I looked at various buildings and we found an ideal place in Towngate House, Poole which had part of the first floor available.

The space was in three rooms with l, 100 sq. ft. total and the rent was £6 a sq. ft. inclusive, which seemed to be fair. As a result we took the area over on a

Myself and Cadillac outside Towngate House, Poole.

three-year lease and I immediately went to town on equipping a partioned-off section of one of the rooms with a bench and various test equipment I would need for a certain amount of development work I wanted to continue. The boardroom was to be a showpiece so photographs which Suzanne had taken over the years were enlarged and placed round the walls, including photographs from our distributors showing their exhibitions, and the room looked extremely attractive.

Soon after this Walter Hess, a very active President of Zellweger, telephoned me to say that he had decided to resign his position in that company, which was deeply regretted as we had a good understanding between us. This was followed soon after by the untimely death of Dr Maurice Bechtler who had formed a very friendly association with the Sieger company.

It was then decided, after just one year from selling the company, that it would be preferable if I gave up the Chairmanship in favour of the Bechtlers' son-in-law the Earl of Crawford & Balcarres, which would give an imposing title to head the company. Once you have sold a company you don't have any say in its affairs, and that's a fact with all takeovers, but the surprising thing was when Tom Pope and Kurt Weber came to my office and said they would now break the lease and I would have to find other accommodation as they did not want a Chairman's office any more, they would have it at the main factory. This was a great disappointment as I had hoped to still be involved to a certain degree when important customers visiting the company could attend meetings in the boardroom. However I undertook to take over the rest of the lease on my own.

The only visitors we did have before this decision were a Chinese delegation of miners; fortunately two flagpoles were at the entrance of Towngate House and we managed to obtain and fly the Chinese flag and the Union Jack with individual small Chinese flags on the boardroom table, which the Chinese took home with them. I entertained these people at the Mansion House hotel in Poole and Hassall Hanbury Brown also represented the company at dinner, speaking some Chinese. At the dinner each of the visitors was presented with a china dolphin made by Poole Pottery, which is part of the insignia of Poole, and they in turn presented me with a miniature pagoda. Another visit to the boardroom was made by a Japanese delegation from NESL and similar gifts were made to them, and they provided us with many books and papers for Origami.

CHAPTER 24

ANALYSIS OF SUCCESS

These chapters on the Sieger company have been a record of a most successful enterprise which started, quoting financial terms, with gross sales not exceeding £5,000 a year in 1959 to worldwide sales in 1979 of nearly six million pounds. It is therefore time to analyse the reason for success.

All successful operations depend on an outside influence, and in the case of gas detection this influence was an awareness of danger to life through explosion, supported by Governments' legislation. The importance in starting a company is market research - as an entrepreneur if a market is found to exist then the necessary invention can take place; this is basic. However the entrepreneur must have experience of management - management is the understanding of people and any business depends entirely on people, their attitude, their loyalty and their enthusiasm; people must have an incentive.

During various lectures I gave to people who intended to start up in business, I pointed out that management is not a gift, it is based on experience, and experience depends on an individual who has worked for many companies and has been hired and fired or left to seek better employment. This experience is essential because if there has been a dismissal from a company due to something which had not been done correctly or for any other similar reason, the experience of dismissal and why is important to the individual in striving to do better. By joining various companies in different positions, and assuming there is possible improvement in position after each change, an understanding of good and bad management adds to the experience memory bank for future use.

The role of women in business is one of the most important areas of success - their intuition, their attendance to detail irrespective of the subject, gives a valued contribution to successful management. The name of the company was J.& S. Sieger Ltd. and this was a joint operation between Sylvia and I. It was her support that helped to make the company successful and she was actively involved in the entertainment of all our distributors at the various International Conferences that were held. The wives of distributors were nearly always invited to these Conferences and there was a common understanding despite the many different nationalities. Sylvia also helped entertain visitors and their wives from time to time and accompanied me on all visits abroad to various distributors and customers.

The recognition of womens' practical contribution was utilised throughout the company.

The whole of the company was aware that J. & S. Sieger Ltd. pioneered gas detection, the first company in the world to have a sensor remote from a control unit. Despite the competition that grew world-wide the company held its position by investing all profits into research and development. All competitors' equipment was carefully analysed, however small, and despite a very strong patent position on the original inventions no litigation ever took place where these patent rights were violated. The company depended on its sophisticated designs and with the knowledge that all customers and distributors are people - the great benefit of being able to understand this was one of the reasons for success.

In writing this history of my experiences over the last eighty-five years, I have tried to analyse my thinking and the reasons for pursuing my engineering knowledge in the way that I did. The years I spent in the Technical Press designing, making, drawing, photographing and describing various wireless sets at a time when there were very few manufacturers of complete units but many in components, resulted in my joining a company which made components but not complete sets, and it was then I realised the home constructor would be less important in favour of the mass marketing of complete radios. Up to that time the majority of manufacture was carried out by bus drivers and conductors, policemen, postmen, etc., proving the popularity of the technical journals of that day and the very great following amongst the hundreds of thousands of amateurs. After a short time in this area I realised that television would be the future and that is when I joined the Scophony Company who just had patents but no equipment.

Looking back I was one of many pioneers in the field of radio and television which specialised in entertainment in the home; never did I realise how quickly television would progress after the Second World War, when effectively it destroyed the normal habits of people who began to look at television rather than read books or converse with each other.

My work on radar engineering during the war, when all television ceased, allowed me to do more thinking and by accident or design later on I felt my duty would be to use my background knowledge, sometimes called experience, to pioneer an industry which would promote the safety of people against explosions and fire from leaking gas or other flammable liquids. It was the right decision because, as will be seen from reading the section on my gas detection company, the rapid growth of the company from myself to one assistant, then three and so on, continued until I had an organisation which was one of the largest gas detector manufacturers in the world.

Whilst I had enjoyed giving people pleasure by manufacturing radio and television etc., it gave me greater satisfaction to manufacture equipment that saved lives.

Joshua Sieger CBE May 1992

MOVE TO CARMEL COTTAGE

At this point Joe Sieger's illness prevented him from continuing with his book, a source of great regret because he very much wished to see it published.

As a tribute to him and to his remarkable life, his second wife, Rosemary, has endeavoured to recount the last events as they occurred, and these are as follows:

In June 1980 Joe was awarded the CBE, again for Services to Export, and went with Sylvia and his two daughters to Buckingham Palace to receive the award. In 1984 a lunch was held for the entire company to celebrate its twenty-five years, which Joe and Rosemary attended.

Buckingham Palace, June 1980 after CBE presentation.
L - R: Suzanne, myself, Sylvia and Jacqueline.

After remaining in Towngate House until 1985, during which time Joe tried to assist various individuals endeavouring to start their own companies, and was joined in this enterprise by Mr F.A. Harris, a former Managing Director of EIL, he decided it was unnecessary to have three huge rooms and therefore looked around for smaller premises to rent. Meanwhile Rosemary had decided to leave the Sieger company and took up the position of his Personal Assistant.

Whilst still at Towngate House Joe was approached by Mr Paul Barnes to become Chairman of the Southern Science & Technology Forum, based at the University of Southampton. They held meetings usually in the Poole/Bournemouth area to promote the study of science and technology in local

Carmel Cottage, Parkstone.

schools and once a year a Technology Fair was held at one of the larger schools at which Joe was one of the judges. Classes of various ages from a large number of schools competed to build set projects from components provided to make up working models which were then judged. He always enjoyed these Fairs and found it very fascinating to watch the childrens' ingenuity.

Joe was advised by his accountant to buy a small property for an office and found a suitable cottage in Parkstone. Having given up active participation in business, he concentrated on writing this book and studying technical journals, always very interested in any new developments in various fields.

He attended several TRE reunions held at Malvern, and enjoyed meeting people whom he had known at Worth Matravers when working on radar during the war. In 1994 during the D-Day remembrance programme for the area, various exhibitions were held in Swanage covering the history of the work on radar and it was remarked that radar was one of the two most important inventions of the war (the other being the breaking of the ENIGMA code) and that without it we would have lost the war. Details of this work are now held by the Centre for the History of Defence Electronics (CHiDE) at Bournemouth University.

As the five year period of charter fees from the Sieger company for 'Environist' had ceased and mooring fees were high, it was decided to sell her. She was bought by the then Chairman of Rothmans, Sir Robert Crichton-Brown. Joe missed his weekends at sea, which he found very restful.

At this time he exchanged his existing Cadillac Eldorado for another - his sixteenth, a fact which was recognised by the manufacturers, General Motors, who sent him a gold 'Heritage Medal' for the car, a Cadillac history book and plaque of the Eldorado and Seville models engraved on a pewter plate. He knew everything about these cars and could take them to pieces for any adjustment if necessary. As he had lived in an era when ready-made components were not available, he was also capable of repairing any piece of domestic or garden equipment with bits and pieces from his workshop.

In 1986 The Institution of Electrical Engineers held an International Conference at the IEE, Savoy Place, London on 'The History of Television from early days to the present'. This Conference was held over three days 13-15th

T.R.E. reunion, Malvern.

November and Joe was invited to read a paper on the first day in Session 2 on Television Systems, so he enjoyed looking up his old files and gathering illustrations for the paper entitled 'The Scophony Television System'. He found it an interesting opportunity to talk to others reading papers on subjects such as 'The early days of television in HMV and EMI', 'Pioneering independent television transmissions' and 'Personal experiences with early television Chicago and Philadelphia, 1926-1941'.

In 1990, following a series of severe nosebleeds, Joe was diagnosed as having bone marrow cancer - multiple myeloma - and had radiotherapy treatment at Poole Hospital. This seemed to help but he was given a prognosis of three years.

He had remained Chairman of the Wessex Export Club and in 1991 a dinner was held at the Cumberland Hotel, Bournemouth, to celebrate the twenty-first anniversary of the Club, attended by the Lord Lieutenant of Dorset, Lord Digby, together with the Mayor of Poole. In 1992, due to his ill-health, Joe relinquished the Chairmanship to become President, and fulfilled a long-held wish of closer ties with the Dorset Chamber of Commerce and Industry by asking the Chief Executive, Mrs Beryl Kite, to become Chairman, which she accepted and continued to promote the interests of the Club until, in 1994, it became amalgamated into the DCCI.

Wessex Export Club's 21st Anniversary Dinner.
L - R: Joshua Sieger - president, Lord Digby - Lord Lieutenant of the County, Frederick Rowe -
Founder, David Pollington - Chairman and Donald Martin - Vice President.

Joe and Sylvia's elder daughter, Jacqueline, had three children by her first husband and in 1991 married Norman Cowey, whom she met through her business connections of leatherwork, saddlery and dressmaking whilst living in Yorkshire.

In May 1992 Joe and Sylvia arranged a holiday in Baden-Baden, Germany but on the very first night she was taken ill and moved to the Stadts Klinic where she had to have an emergency operation.

Jacqueline and Norman flew out to be with her but she suffered a massive heart attack and, in a coma, was flown back to the Royal Bournemouth Hospital but died on 23rd June 1992.

The stress of all this occasioned the return of Joe's illness, which had been in remission and in August he went into the Nuffield Hospital, Bournemouth whilst Rosemary went away on a pre-arranged holiday abroad. On her return in November Joe was at home, being looked after by a housekeeper, Mrs Rous. Meantime Jacqueline and Norman were urgently looking for a house in the Parkstone area to be near her father. Suzanne had found a flat some time before so was able to visit each day. Joe was also very happy that his youngest sister, Celia and husband Harry had retired to the area and were able to visit him.

It was decided that Joe and Rosemary would be married and she would move into his home to look after him, so a wedding was arranged in Poole Registry Office on 9th December, a very happy occasion. Christmas was enjoyed at the house with Suzanne and three guests but in February Joe was taken ill and returned to the Nuffield Hospital where he died on 1st March 1993.

Both his consultant, Dr Clein, and the staff at the hospital looked after him with great kindness and Joe handled his illness as he did his life, with great courage, researching into all possible ways of curing the myeloma. He has left a great gap in many peoples' lives but has also helped so many in various ways that he will always be remembered, and it is hoped that this book will be a tribute to a very clever and caring man who had gathered such a wide range of knowledge during his life on many subjects and had seen so many advances in the world of technology.

Rosemary Sieger May 2000.

FURTHER READING

THE STORY OF SCOPHONY

Thomas Singleton   Royal Television Society (monograph) 1988

THE GAS ALARM STORY

Joshua Sieger   Sieger Company 1985

INDEX